BURNING DOWN MY MASTERS' HOUSE

BURNING DOWN MY MASTERS' HOUSE

My Life at *The New York Times*

JAYSON BLAIR

New Millennium Press
Beverly Hills

First published in the United States of America in 2004
by New Millennium Entertainment, Inc.
301 N. Canon Drive #214
Beverly Hills, CA 90210

Library of Congress Cataloging-in-Publication Data available upon request.
ISBN: 1-932407-26-X

Interior design by Carolyn Wendt

Printed in the United States of America
www.NewMillenniumPress.com

10 9 8 7 6 5 4 3 2 1

To Zuza Glowacka

*For traveling with me in the light
and not abandoning me in the darkness.*

CONTENTS

Who is the master of one's own house?

In the months following my resignation from *The New York Times,* that is the question that I have asked myself over and over again. The scandal I caused led to the resignations of the top two editors at *The Times,* created an unfairly large black-eye for journalists in general, and was used by those with axes to grind against minorities to justify their opposition to affirmative action. Some might hold me responsible for not foreseeing the results of my actions, but my behavior was first and foremost an act of self-destruction. I am the master of my own house. And I destroyed it.

Most of you pick up this book having already heard of me through news reports, most notably a massive front-page story that appeared on May 11, 2003, in *The New York Times.* That report chronicled acts of plagiarism and fabrications I committed as a promising young national correspondent for the nation's newspaper of record. I would like to take a moment to share a bit about my story, and my rationale for writing it, before you begin turning the pages of this book.

Since my resignation on May 1, 2003, I have appeared on the front page of *The Times,* the cover of *Newsweek* and in many other publications around the globe. This will be the first opportunity that I have had to lend my voice to the millions of words that have been written about me. If I had been in another profession, perhaps I would have chosen another forum to tell my story, but the written word has always been the way I have best expressed myself.

I selected the title *Burning Down My Masters' House* for more reasons than its obvious allusion to slavery. My deceptions have not only let down the employees of *The Times,* but also my family, my friends, my college professors and myself. There are many masters to this house, hence the careful placement of the apostrophe after the "s" in the word "masters." Ultimately, I am the master of my own destiny, and the flames of the fire that I set consumed me.

Although much ink has been devoted to my downfall, very little understanding has been achieved. *Burning Down My Masters' House* is the first time the full story will be told, including many details that have not been reported and with some informed, critical analysis of my own on the actions and events that transpired afterwards. It provides the missing puzzle pieces that put my life in context.

How did a man with so much hope and so much promise end up setting a fire that very nearly consumed everything? The search for an answer led me to write this book. On the journey, I learned a lot about my own strengths and weaknesses, frustrations and insecurities, dreams and delusions. I slowly collected pebbles of information that I believe can help myself and others to heal. At some point, it became strikingly clear to me that to withhold my story would be a disservice. No matter how bad things become, there are valuable lessons to be learned that are universal in nature.

A saying from Twelve Step groups, like Alcoholics Anonymous, comes to mind, "No matter how far down the scale we have gone, we will see how our experiences can benefit others." It goes on to say, "That feeling of uselessness and self-pity will disappear. We will lose interest in selfish things and gain interest in our fellows." I believe that I have been changed in that way.

Many have asked me whether *The New York Times* was responsible for my self-destruction. I say no. I was already on the local train to self-destruction, and *The Times* just helped me transfer to the express train. It was one of many factors, not the least of which was, to borrow a phrase from Martin Luther King Jr., the content of my own character.

I was born into a family with good, strong moral values and at a young age I was taught the difference between right and wrong. I grew up in a world filled with idealistic hopes for racial equality and eyed journalism as a vehicle for social change—an unbiased and objective organ for truth in my mind—that could help better the lives of readers. Somewhere along the way, like so many other people struggling to survive the realities of life, I lost my moorings, something that was surprisingly easy to do in this almost absurd electronic-age of 24/7 news cycles, crazy hours, and budget restraints.

On the Op-Ed page of *The Wall Street Journal,* John McWhorter, a senior fellow at the Manhattan Institute, said he imagined that I would "'spin' the story into a tale of discrimination." The truth of the matter is, that as a black man, it would be impossible to disentangle the role that the color of my skin has played in my life, but this book is about much more than just race.

Throughout my career in journalism I found myself dangling on a precipice—it can be debated how much of it was environmental and how much of it was genetic—above the struggle with addiction and undiagnosed mental illness. My illness, manic-depression, undoubtedly contributed to my success as a journalist, providing me with the energy to write and report non-stop for days and put in countless hours of reporting. It is an illness that I realize, now that I have been diagnosed, that I self-medicated through substance abuse for years. What happened once I put down those substances, though, was a disease spinning out of control, in its worst form taking me from full-blown mania to deep depression in a matter of days, and often leading to suicidal thoughts and psychotic episodes.

The scandal I created was certainly not the first time that a journalist at a prominent American news organization has been caught in similar deceit. In recent years, Janet Cooke, Christopher Newton and Stephen Glass all committed frequent acts of what *The Times* has called journalistic fraud. We all had different reasons. Like Mr. Glass, whose book *The Fabulist* was published by Simon & Schuster in 2003, I want the opportunity to share my story, and I have committed to sharing it in all of its painful and unflattering details in the hope that others who are teetering on the precipice of self-destruction might pull back before it is too late.

In the end, my hope is that you will appreciate this memoir for its candor, and that there is something good that can be gained from its writing. I still believe that journalism has great potential to help people and I still believe that *The New York Times* represents the best that the profession has to offer. I have always believed that everyone deserves another chance. I hope you will extend this generosity to me. At the very least, I hope you will agree with me that everyone should have the chance to apologize, to reflect, and to tell his side of the story, straight-up, in his own words. A friend recently said to me, "Jayson, remember you are now telling your toughest story."

There is no doubt that this is the toughest story I have ever had to write.

JAYSON BLAIR
BROOKLYN, NY
JANUARY 1, 2004

CHAPTER ONE
FIRE

I lied and I lied—and then I lied some more.

I lied about where I had been, I lied about where I had found information, I lied about how I wrote the story. And these were no everyday little white lies—they were complete fantasies, embellished down to the tiniest detail.

I lied about a plane flight I never took, about sleeping in a car I never rented, about a landmark on a highway I had never been on. I lied about a guy who helped me at a gas station that I found on the Internet and about crossing railroad tracks I only knew existed because of aerial photographs in my private collection. I lied about a house I had never been to, about decorations and furniture in a living room I had only seen in photographs in an electronic archive maintained by *Times* photo editors. In the end-justifies-the-means environment I worked in, I had grown accustomed to lying. I told more than my share of lies and became as adept as anyone at getting away with it unquestioned and unscathed.

I suspected that the truth would either set me free or kill me.

I was not yet prepared to go there, however, on this Wednesday morning, at least not in this room full of people. On my side of the conference table were Lena Williams, the chairwoman of *The New York Times* Newspaper Guild, and two other union representatives who were prepared to do battle on my behalf. On the other side of the table were two labor relations lawyers and Bill Schmidt, the associate managing editor at *The New York Times* in charge of news administration.

Lena had warned me about the labor relations lawyers, saying that they tended not to understand the way the newsroom operated and would ask questions, well, like lawyers—designed to catch you in lies, fluster you and leave you off balance. Bill had been among the first people I had met at *The Times,* as he was in charge of recruitment, hiring, staff development and training at the newspaper. Bill had been a foreign correspondent for *Newsweek* in the Middle East and worked for *The Times* in Africa and London, before he was asked to return to New York. He took the job of overseeing the modernization of the management and budget cultures in a newsroom that had remained very backwards as the company, at large, had become more efficient and progressive. Bill's mandate, in many ways, came from Arthur Sulzberger, Jr., the fifty-one-year-old publisher of *The Times* and chairman of the company.

Arthur had set out to make the newsroom more diverse and open to people from all sorts of backgrounds, as well as to push the newspaper into the information revolution. Bill was firmly committed to all of these goals, including Arthur's desire that controls be placed on the budgets and finances of the newsroom.

One of the more unpleasant aspects of Bill's job was handling discipline in a newsroom that previously had been disinclined to fire anyone and that handled most of its problems informally. Bill's overly agreeable personality, it seemed, made him ill-suited for the job, but, in fact, he had used it to his advantage. His kindness actually made people open to what he was saying, and his moves—like hiring a deputy who was in charge of finding and counseling those who were lost in the newsroom—bolstered his solid relationship with the staff and the union.

Under the twenty-month editorship of Howell Raines, though, much of that goodwill was beginning to evaporate. Bill had to break the news to one veteran in Atlanta that he was being ordered back to New York so that a young *Los Angeles Times* writer who had been recommended by one of Howell's friends could replace him. When the correspondent, who was considered among the paper's greatest, protested, saying that he had to stay in Atlanta because of a child custody battle, Bill was the one who had to tell him that Howell was not persuaded. Bill also had the unpleasant job of being ordered to fly to Los Angeles to meet with West Coast correspondents and to break the news to them that Howell was relieving many of them of their duties. The removal of the correspondents, many of whom quit when they began to see the writing on the wall, shook a newsroom where people had historically come to work and stayed for life.

Bill had been instrumental in my hiring and had counseled me through some difficult personal and professional moments. We had laughed about stories he had written about *Monty Python,* and I drank

Scotch with him and other friends in the apartment of his girlfriend, one of New York's most prominent travel agents.

As the meeting began, I felt a strange sympathy for the position Bill was in, charged with having to investigate such a serious matter. Bill smiled empathetically across the table, as if he was saying that he felt for me, that this was a position neither of us wanted to be in. Bill looked down at some papers in front of him and turned in his chair as he shuffled them. He cleared his throat, looked up at me and began speaking.

"Jayson, first I want to say that this is something that none of us want to have to do," I recall him saying. "This is something that we are doing because of the special place that *The New York Times* holds and because of the special priority we place on our journalism. The trust of our readers is based on the principle that what they read on our pages is accurate, reported by the person who it is said to have been reported by, and conforms to our standards of journalism. That trust derives from years of balanced and objective journalism, a trust that we regard highly."

I stared at him as he continued.

"Our readers put trust in our editors, who in turn put trust in our reporters. That trust is very fragile, and it has been damaged in this case. The first purpose of these conversations is to reestablish that trust, the trust between you and your editors, so that before we go forward with any disciplinary action or more reporting, the editors can have faith in you."

He paused for a moment and looked at me. "So, I am going to ask you to be completely honest and provide every detail. We are going to get into the minutiae of your writing and reporting of the story, and may ask you for documentation—including receipts—to back up every element of what you say. This is something that none of us want to do, but I am sure you understand that it is something we must do in order to reestablish the trust between you and your editors. Lena, do you want to say anything before we begin?"

"Yes," Lena said, leaning into the back of her seat, "we are here to protect Jayson's rights as a member of *The New York Times* Guild. I know we all have a good relationship in this room, but in the past, there have been instances where some of the questioning has been irrelevant or confusing. We want to reserve the right, if such a moment comes up, to halt the meeting and go outside to caucus. We are looking forward to resolving this matter as quickly as possible and getting back to business, as we know you are too, and, with that, we're ready."

And, for the next four hours—with the exception of two breaks, the first so one of the union members could berate me for repeatedly admitting that I had made mistakes, and another so Bill and the lawyers could confer—they questioned me and questioned me and questioned me. My lies were elaborate and convincing, particularly my admissions that I had done some things wrong in the reporting and writing of the story ("No, perhaps I should have stayed at the house longer and told my editors that I was not ready to write the story yet," for example.). The story in question concerned the family of a young Marine who was the last American soldier missing in action in Iraq.

A few weeks earlier, Jim Roberts, the national editor, had asked me to figure out a good story about a family that had someone missing in Iraq, and a story about the last soldier missing in action struck a chord with him. Since the war began, the National section had been taking a back seat to the foreign correspondents in Iraq, and it had been virtually impossible for anyone on Jim's staff to get on the front page. I had been the one exception, churning out beautifully-written—if I do say so myself—pieces about a Maryland family watching as their son's colleagues got attacked in Iraq; the prisoner of war Jessica Lynch; a young North Carolina couple separated soon after their marriage by his deployment; and soldiers recovering from their wounds at the National Naval Medical Center in Bethesda.

It was not what I wanted to be doing. I was much more interested in following the trial by star-chamber in Virginia of the young suspect in the Washington-area sniper shootings, Lee Malvo. To me, these other assignments were simply the ends justifying the means. The more prominent, colorful and tear-jerking stories I wrote about the impact of the war in Iraq on the home front, the better display I would get on the stories that mattered. And what mattered to me were the stories I was writing about Malvo. I believed he was guilty, but I also believed he was being unfairly railroaded in the name of justice.

One of the saddest parts of this meeting for me was that even if I managed to reestablish some sense of trust and save my job, I probably would not be allowed to return to covering the Malvo case. I had followed it tirelessly since the day I drove to Myersville, Maryland at two in the morning, to cover the arrests of Malvo and John Allen Muhammad.

After hours of lying, I was not only emotionally exhausted, but also worn with guilt. After all, I was the only one in the room who knew the truth, and it was not as pretty as the picture I was painting. I had told them that the striking similarities between my front-page story and one that had appeared a few days earlier in the *San Antonio Express-News* could be easily explained. The story was about the family of Edward Anguiano, Jr., a twenty-four-year-old Marine who had disappeared in Iraq. I placed the blame for the similarities squarely on the egregious reporting methods I had been using during the assignment.

I told them that before I left for Los Fresnos, Texas, a small dusty town along the Mexican border just north of Brownsville, I had downloaded a set of notes and clippings on Anguiano into a file that I had saved onto my laptop computer. I explained that when I began writing the story, I confused some of the paragraphs in the file with my notes, and had included some of the quotations and details in my piece erroneously and without attribution to the San Antonio paper. I handed over the files, three notebooks, and other material from my assignment that helped explain how it happened.

The only problem, of course, was that it hadn't happened that way at all. I was the only one in the room who knew that I had never flown to San Antonio, had never rented a car at the small rental place across from the airport, and had never slept in it. I had never driven south down U.S. 77 in the blazing heat, had never taken a left onto Texas 100, never turned onto Buena Vista Drive, and never crossed the railroad tracks near the Anguiano household. I had never seen the Martha Stewart furniture on the patio, nor the shrine to Edward in one of the daughter's rooms. I had never missed my exit along the way, nor stopped in Brownsville, nor had I gone to the small town called Port Isabel along an inlet to the Gulf of Mexico. The truth was I had never left my apartment in Park Slope, Brooklyn.

The reasons were beside the point by this time, and I was panicking, trying to stop the bleeding to ensure that they did not find out more. Many would later assume that I had lied in an effort to pull off one last con, to keep my job or my prestigious assignment. It was, in fact, simpler than that.

There were a handful of colleagues at *The Times* who I admired—Bill and Lena included. I did not want to disappoint them with the truth. I was in such a crisis mode, coming up with fake documentation and explanations, that I lost sight of the fact—almost entirely, as if it had evaporated from my mind—that I had done this before. I had taken liberties that some would consider extreme, even by the loose standards of some *Times* correspondents.

"I think we are going to make it through this one okay, something like a short suspension, a reassignment to a section like Sports or City Weekly, where you can be watched over and nurtured as you should have been and wanted to be anyway, and then we will put this one behind us," Lena said as we sat together that evening after the meeting. We were joined by my mentor, Jerry Gray, a former metro desk political editor who was now editor of the desk that writes stories for *The New York Times on the Web*.

"I guess they want to meet again to continue the questions tomorrow afternoon, baby, so I will give you a call in the morning once they call me," Lena continued. "They said eight in the morning, because they want to get this over with and get an editor's note in the paper, but I said 'no way.' So, it looks like it's going to be noon. So, why don't you go home and do something relaxing, and be ready to come to Forty-third Street by about noon. Now, get some rest, baby. We are going to fight for you. That's what the union is here for," she reassured me.

"The one thing I don't understand, Jerry, is why they keep on asking for all this documentation," she continued. "Documentation, documentation, documentation. I'm glad your brother kept all of your receipts and is faxing them up here. We'll get them, hand them over tomorrow, and be done with that; then we can move on to the next thing."

I was barely eating during this conversation, only picking at peanuts and sipping on a cranberry and seltzer, which had become my beverage of choice since giving up alcohol a little more than a year before.

"You have nine lives, and you may very well dodge the bullet on this one, but you have got to . . ." Jerry said. His voice trailed off as we walked back to the Times Building.

My friend Zuza Glowacka was working the late shift on the picture desk, where she was responsible for cropping obituary pictures and managing the department's work flow to the rest of the building.

Two days before, on Monday, we'd had lunch together at an Italian restaurant on Seventh Avenue in Park Slope, Brooklyn. It was the same day I would receive the first call from the National Desk about the Texas story. During our lunch, we had talked about my going to Africa as a foreign correspondent and her coming along. Our idea was to use journalism, human rights work, volunteering and other pursuits to better peoples' lives in small ways and to promote social change.

I called her about my problems while she was reading the final pages of Ralph Ellison's *The Invisible Man*.

"Hey, Jayson, I am just finishing up the last forty pages, so can I call you back when I am done?" she said when I called that night.

"Sure."

I was busy downloading maps, articles and details that would help me sort out the mess I had gotten myself into and smoking cigarettes like there was no tomorrow, letting their ashes land on the floor where they would pile up around my kitchen table. In the latter pages of *The Invisible Man,* Ellison writes about the main character "reporting back to headquarters" and a white woman named Sybil who fantasizes about black men. In the next chapter, the main character realizes how imperfect society is and the real purpose of the Brotherhood and bloodshed as riots break out in Harlem. When I finished collecting what I needed, I called Zuza and got her voice mail. So, I called Alexandra Von Ungern, her roommate, and asked if I could come over.

"Sure, you can tell me what Texas was like. I need a cowboy," she said.

"Okay. I, uh, just need to talk to someone," I replied.

"Honey, are you okay?"

"Yeah, everything is going to be all right. I just have some, uh, work trouble that I need to sort out. But everything will be okay. Everything will be okay."

The "everything will be okay" continued to be my mantra to everyone who expressed concern that night and over the following days. Everything was not okay. On Monday afternoon, after my leisurely lunch in Brooklyn, I had headed back to my apartment to write a story about a hearing in the sniper shootings case. I was busily working when Jim Roberts called my cell phone with a question.

"Hey, Jayson. Howie Kurtz from *The Washington Post* called somebody earlier today, it was either Allan Siegal or Gerald, about the story that you wrote on the Anguiano family, and about some passages that seemed similar. I just saw the San Antonio story, and I've got to tell you that there are some passages that are strikingly similar to your lead."

"Oh, that's strange. I don't even remember seeing a San Antonio story."

"Really?" he asked.

"Yeah. When was it published?"

"Uh, hold on, let me check. April 18. Hey, Jayson, I can barely hear you. Could you get to a landline and give me a call back in about fifteen minutes? I'm going to read the story real quickly."

"Okay. Could you send me a copy?"

"Sure."

The copy never landed. I finished up my sniper story quickly, fumbling over my words. The fleeting thought that this might be the last story I'd ever write for *The Times* crossed my mind. No, so pessimistic of me. Since I did not have a landline in my house, I went down the block, nervously smoking and reading, to a pay phone. As had become my custom in recent months, I dialed "*67" before making my call, in order to block the news clerks answering the telephone at their desks or the editors from seeing what number came up on my caller identification.

"Hey, Jayson. So, are you sure you've never seen the San Antonio story?" Jim asked once we were on the phone again.

"I really don't think so. I don't remember it at all. I am going to have to check my notes."

I was sweating bullets under the scorching sun at a pay phone on Fifth Avenue near the corner of President Street in Brooklyn. I truly, at that moment, did not for the life of me remember the *San Antonio Express-News* story, not that I would have told him the truth if I had. I was beginning to get dizzy, sweating more and more with each question he asked.

"Okay, check your notes and give me a call back later tonight. Here's my cell phone number in case I've already left the office. Gerald is coming down on me to get the details and get back to him as soon as possible."

"Okay. Talk to you later, Jim."

I quickly found the *Express-News* story on the newspaper's website and read every detail, realizing that I had used most of them in my story, in some cases employing very similar phrases. I made a quick, impulsive decision to call the reporter on the story. Macarena Hernandez, oddly enough, had been an intern with me at *The Times* four years earlier. We were both among those selected to return, but she decided against the move after her father died in a car accident. Macarena had toiled from job to job, and had apparently landed at the *Express-News*. I had not noticed earlier that her name was on top of the story until Jim called with his questions.

"Macarena, hey, do you know who this is?" I asked, trying to keep a pleasant tone.

"No," she said sharply.

"It's Jayson Blair," I said.

"Jayson. What do you want?"

"I want to talk to you about this story and just let you know that I never saw it before I wrote my piece," I said.

"Jayson, Jayson. You mean to say that you never saw this before you wrote your story? Jayson, I don't believe you. I can't talk to you about this."

"Okay," I replied. "I just wanted to let you know that I am . . ."

She interrupted me with a sharp "Goodbye."

So much for trying to co-opt the victim.

What I did not know at the time was that Macarena had placed a call to Sheila Rule, the manager of reporter recruiting, earlier in the day, after spending the weekend listening to colleagues point out similarities between the two stories. Sheila had hired both of us as interns in the summer of 1998. Sheila looked at the two stories and brought the matter to the attention of Bill and of Gerald Boyd, the managing editor. Gerald was managing the paper while Howell was on vacation. Later in the day, Sheila, Bill and Gerald sat down with Jim, a middle-aged southerner who liked to wear cowboy boots and plant them on people's desks as he was making a point.

Jim was a demanding boss, but despite all outward appearances, he had a soft underbelly and was much kinder than most to his staff of reporters, which engendered a loyalty that was rare, if not unheard of, in the newsroom. The metro editor and the Washington bureau chief were mainly liked by their charges because they stood up to Howell. The business editor would have been facing mutinies daily if his staff was not being worked so hard that it had no time to put together a revolt. The new arts and entertainment editor was disliked for carrying out Howell's mandate to bring more pop culture to the section. And the foreign editor was viewed as a man without a friend among the reporting ranks. In the meeting, Sheila, Bill and Gerald told Jim that there was clearly a problem, and that he should call me to try to figure out what had happened.

I was on my way to Zuza's that night when the phone rang. It was Jim once again. He said that I should hop on the train from Washington—where he thought I was—and get to New York early in the morning. When Jim told me that he was going to call Adam Liptak, the national legal affairs reporter, and ask him to head down to Washington to cover the rest of the hearings, I knew this was big trouble. Jim told me to get some rest, not to worry about it, and to just come in with all my notes and be as prepared as possible to explain what happened. That night, at Zuza's apartment overlooking Prospect Park from Ocean Avenue, I huddled in her room completing what I told her was a legitimate timeline of events during my "trip" to San Antonio.

"I don't understand what the big deal is," she said to me. "So you copied some paragraphs and quotes from a story by mistake. Why do you have to come up with a timeline and all of that stuff?"

I was not yet prepared to be honest with Zuza, either.

"I dunno. They just want me to have it, and I think it could be big trouble if I don't."

I slept on a black mattress on the floor beside her bed. It was a great improvement over the dirty white couch I had being sleeping on most nights in my ice-cold apartment on President Street. We set the alarm so I could get into the office early Tuesday morning. I was scheduled to meet Jim a little after ten in the morning and I planned to arrive a bit early, but I could not sleep, waking up every few minutes with random thoughts about the Anguiano story and the bind I was in.

When I turned over and noticed that the alarm clock's red digits had gone a little past 6 a.m., I gave up on getting rest, and tapped on Zuza's shoulder to let her know that I was headed into the office.

"Good luck," she said, as I walked out her bedroom door.

After taking the twenty-five-minute ride on the Q train, I popped out of the subway with the light shining on the emptiness of Times Square—its tall buildings, its signs, its flashing lights—at six thirty in the morning. I walked one block north, rounded the corner, and turned right onto West Forty-third Street. I greeted the security guards still working the late shift as I walked through the lobby of the Times Building. My nocturnal nature ensured that I knew all the faces.

I swiped my card above the electronic turnstiles that had been installed after the September 11 attacks and immediately walked into an open elevator door. I pressed the button for the fourth floor, where my desk in the sports section was located. After logging into my computer, I checked the *Washington Post* website. Jim had told me that Kurtz, the *Post*'s media reporter, had promised to hold off for a day, so the paper could do some more research into the story.

"Whew." I felt a slight sense of relief once I discovered nothing about it in *The Post*. I quickly flipped to another screen, typed in a password I had picked up from a photo editor several years before, and logged into the database where the picture desk stores its electronic files. It includes photographs that have been published in the newspaper as well as ones that are being considered for publication.

At first, I had used the database as a resource, to re-imagine details and scenes that I had legitimately witnessed. I found that the camera often captured things that the memory of the human mind does not record, offering different light, different angles. Later, I had begun using it to paint pictures and details that I had not witnessed, a tactic that can be legitimate on some occasions.

In recent months, though, while cooped up in my apartment, I had been using the database to get details about places that I had never been in order to write the kind of colorful details my editors demanded without the traveling it required. It was a simple system of deception—my tools were my laptop, my cell phone, online archives and the photo database, which could be accessed from my kitchen table.

I began looking at the pictures from inside the Anguiano house and recording the details into my notebooks, scrawling some legibly and others messily in order to make the notes seem authentic. I had told Jim the night before that I had in fact seen the *Express-News* story, but had not noticed it was written by Macarena. I also told Jim and anyone else who asked that it appeared to me as if I had mixed the *Express-News* article and some other stories in with my notes.

I fared well in the first day of questioning, and we agreed to meet again the next day to go over more details. Jim was writing an editor's note that his bosses wanted to get into the paper quickly. He told me to give him a call at home or on the cell phone if I remembered any important details that were remaining.

I arrived early in the office the next day, Wednesday, to address some of the issues he raised, picking up the notebooks I had left in his office and adding some more materials to them. On his desk that morning, I noticed color printouts of the pictures from San Antonio, which meant one of two things—he was either trying to check the details about the house I had provided him or trying to determine whether I had pilfered my knowledge from the online database. I suspected it was the former, because few people outside of the photo editors had access to the database.

My phone rang, and my chest seized when I saw the caller's name come across the display on top my phone.

"*Times,* Blair," I said.

"Hi, Jayson. It's Christine Moore. Gerald wants to meet with you. Please come down when you get a chance."

Christine was Gerald's secretary and had risen up through the ranks as his career expanded and he was promoted from assistant managing editor to deputy managing editor for news, and eventually to managing editor, the second-highest position in the newsroom. I had a good rapport with Christine, and I nervously chatted with her as I waited for Gerald outside his office.

"I am sure it's going to be okay, Jayson," she said, and then smiled. "This is not the first time something like this has happened, and I am sure you have made it through worse."

Indeed I had, but she could not have possibly known how bad this really was. I tried to smile back.

Gerald opened his door halfway, his rotund belly sticking out slightly from the blue dress shirt he was wearing, unbuttoned. I was dressed in my Sunday best, a long-sleeve Gap shirt and clean white khakis. As the first black managing editor of the paper, Gerald had always seemed to me to take a special interest in not promoting the careers of minorities over others in the newsroom in order to protect his standing. There was no special treatment once you got in the door. If anything, he was a little brusque. I had watched him devour the careers of more blacks than he saved.

There were, of course, exceptions, like one young protégé he helped get installed as the Miami bureau chief, but, for the most part, his efforts to ensure diversity in the newsroom were focused on the outside, recruiting talented minorities. I always wondered what the purpose of recruiting them was if he was going to leave them to be eaten up once they arrived, but I also understood that behaving otherwise was not politically expedient in an environment where many would claim that he was protecting blacks. Gerald, at times, seemed to me like the black schoolteacher who was harder on his black students because he knew they would have to work three times harder to get the same respect and success.

"Where should we sit?" I asked.

Gerald pointed to the brown wooden conference table between his desk and the door, not once bringing his eyes up to make contact with mine. A bad sign. Jim had agreed to meet with me before I talked with Gerald, warning me that he would likely attempt to knock me off balance. I was prepared to answer any of his questions, to ask for forgiveness and a chance for redemption, and to take full responsibility—well, at least for what they knew about.

"I have always been an advocate of your career," he started in.

Under other circumstances, I would have had to try to fight the urge to laugh, but not at this moment.

"I have always been an advocate of yours," he repeated. "And I just want to say that this is a very serious matter. I don't want to go over the details of the story. I know you have been talking to Jim and Bill Schmidt, and others are going to meet with you today to look into that. I just want to say that whatever has happened, *whatever* has happened, you should be completely and totally honest. That's it."

"Thanks, Gerald," I said, surprised that there was not a forthcoming barrage of questions. "Can I say something?"

"Sure," he said.

"I know you have always been an advocate of my career. I want to say, first, that I am sorry. I have made mistakes, and I recognize the seriousness of them. I know that I have had some problems in the past, but if, in the end, once all the facts are out, you decide it is worth it to give me another chance, I would like an opportunity for redemption. And I just want to say again that I am sorry."

I knew I was going to get knocked off the sniper case, but I was vying not to get sent back to the metro desk, where I was uniformly disliked by the senior editing team, or some other place where I would have been lost, writing about fashion or real estate. Gerald looked up and glanced into my eyes. There was sadness, clearly, in his face.

"Okay," he said, and then slowly began to stand up.

"Thanks for your time and support, Gerald," I said, as I walked out of his doorway.

He did not say a word. He just nodded as he walked toward the doorway.

I had not had a drink or any drugs in well over a year at that point, but I was beginning to worry that my stress level might cause me to relapse. I went to the elevators and took one up to the eleventh floor. As most of the crowds headed toward the cafeteria, I went in the opposite direction, down a hallway that few in the Times Building seem to know about, and took the first right into an even more desolate corridor. There was a brown door with no window on it. Its nameplate read "Employee Assistance Program."

"Hey, Joyce," I said to the woman behind the desk.

"Hi, Jayson. How are you?"

"Oh, I am good. I am just wondering if Pat is around by any chance."

"She is in with someone. Do you want to set up an appointment?"

"Sure. What's a good time?"

"How about three p.m.?"

"Okay, three p.m. it is."

I had gone to Pat Drew before, and I really needed her now. The newsroom was full of hard-charging investigative personalities, which made it difficult to try to open up to any of them. It was about as smart as having a conversation with a prosecutor right before you knew you were going to be charged with a crime. Pat was not like that.

Some people found her stiff, but I found her to be one of the most calming and soothing people I had encountered at *The Times*. I had opened up to her about problems before, and she had held my hand as I had attempted to find balance in my life.

Pat was among the few at the newspaper that seemed to recognize the importance of balance, and, in many ways, I credited her with being one of the key impetuses to my personal reformation. My first priority was to talk with her about making sure I stayed sober, but I also thought she might be a good escape hatch, someone I could trust, someone to confide in about all my lies and someone who, if asked, could pass it all along to management. You see, it was not so much that I wanted to keep my job. The problem was that I could not face the truth. I could not look into the eyes of Jim Roberts and tell him what I had done.

"Jayson!" Fern, the sports department secretary, yelled across the newsroom floor, minutes after I made it to my desk. "Jayson! It's Lena. She's on the phone for you. What's your extension?"

"7717," I said. "Send her over."

"Baby, hi," Lena said rapidly into the phone. "I just heard about this mess that you are in. I was in guild negotiations for the new contract today when I got a call on my cell phone from labor relations saying that they wanted to sit down and meet with us today. I want to go over all the details with you when I get into the office, but first I want to ask you a couple of things."

I sat across from Lena in the sports department, and we had bonded. She was the only black woman working in the sports section and had been at the newspaper long enough to know where all the bodies were buried. When we weren't gossiping about the way things worked in the newsroom, we talked about being black or just life in general. Lena had received her share of beatings from *The Times* and was fond of saying "I was not born Lena Williams of *The New York Times*, and I am not going to die Lena Williams of *The New York Times*. As soon as I hit retirement age, I am outta here. I am going to get me a house around Washington, a nice porch, get me a nice drink and sit there."

None of the beatings struck me as quite so cruel as the blistering review *The Times* Book Review gave Lena's book, *It's the Little Things: Everyday Interactions That Anger, Annoy, and Divide the Races*. The book was based on a 1997 article Lena had written for the paper that examined the subject of everyday misunderstandings between blacks and whites. Lena made the mistake, though, of perhaps writing too much about the perspectives of blacks for the Book Review's tastes.

"Nobody could disagree with her conclusion that 'what the races need more than anything else is to lighten up, to cut one another some slack, think before they act on questionable presumptions about other people and memorize a few hitherto unsuspected offenses to be avoided,'" Judith Martin, the author of the Miss Manners column, wrote in the review. "Yet by the time she gets there, her readers may feel that there is no use trying. Missing between the anecdotes and the truisms is a serious examination of the social forces at play in any given incident, with workable suggestions for preventing further friction."

"I guess you can't write a book that talks about the foul odor of white people when they are wet and expect a good review in *The Times*," I used to say to Lena. Still, she had done well for herself, keeping the hardcover of the book in print for three years and getting a trade paperback edition released later. Lena continued to promote the book and had hit the lecture circuit when she was not busy negotiating policies and contracts, writing for the sports section, and defending people like me. Lena had taken the time to advise me on the book I had proposed writing about the life of Lee Malvo and my career in recent months. She had also become concerned in recent weeks about my appearance and the sadness on my face, so much so that she and Charlotte Evans, the manager of copy editors, had stopped one day to have a long chat about the perils of covering death without seeking some counseling.

"It'll be okay," I had told them.

Little did they know how much I was not okay.

The *Post* story landed Wednesday on their website, and immediately colleagues began calling and writing e-mails of support, offering examples of similar situations where they had inadvertently plagiarized something.

No one was more supportive than David Carr, a friend and media reporter who had covered magazines, but I could not break the truth even to him, despite our close relationship. I guess it was because, in part, everyone was asking about the Texas story, and to answer truthfully would mean delving into my own mind and past much deeper than I was willing to go. The *Washington City Paper* had also called Carr, telling him that they planned to write a story saying that other reporters covering the sniper trials believed that I had not been attending the court hearings and instead had been writing them off the wires.

It had happened on occasion, although most of the time I used stringers and telephone interviews. While the datelines that ran above those stories were not correct, I knew it was not the first time a *Times* reporter had done that on a running story. Perhaps, though, the lengths I went to were a bit excessive. I suppose that is an understatement. Carr had attempted to fight the *City Paper* editor off, asking him to wait until more facts were known. What Carr did not know, though, was that I was not being honest and that the bucket of water he was carrying for me was filled with lies.

"This is pretty bad, but it could have been worse," Carr said when he read the *City Paper* story.

I could tell he was moving from "save Jayson's job" mode to "don't kill yourself" mode when we were smoking a cigarette outside of the building with John Schwartz, a talented technology writer and class-A prankster, and Lynette Holloway, another media reporter and one of my closest friends in the newsroom.

"Just be honest, man, no matter how bad it is," he said.

"I know. I know. I will be."

"Has anyone asked you, if you, well—are there any questions about whether you actually went to San Antonio?"

"No," I said. "I mean, they have asked me for documentation."

"And you've got it, right?" Lynette asked.

"Yeah," I said.

As we walked together into the building, David stopped me, turned around, and started telling me about a conversation he'd had with his wife Jill the night before.

"I was explaining to Jill that you were born to do this, that you are nothing but a journalist and that it's in your blood. She just could not understand what the big deal was and why you couldn't do something else. I told her that 'if Jayson is ruined in journalism, that's it. That's what he does. That's what he is. It's in his blood,' and she finally understood. But if it does come out worst-case scenario, and I don't think it will, you always have the 'Rise and Fall of the Young Black Man' story to sell."

The *City Paper* story became crucial to the equation because it mentioned something that *The Post* had missed. I had pointed it out to Jim, who had missed the fact that another quote, one he did not know about, had been plagiarized from an Associated Press story. This sent the normally calm Roberts into a rage. Before that point, Jim had been focused mainly on the basic details of my reporting, whether I was tired on the assignment, whether they had asked too much of me over the last few months, and ways of coming up with an end-game that did not destroy me.

"Jayson, I am tired of this bullshit!"

"What do you mean, Jim? I am not bullshitting you. The Associated Press story is in the computer files I gave you, and I think that and other stuff has been mixed up. Listen, do you not believe me?"

"I am not saying that. I want you to answer me honestly—were you in Los Fresnos?"

"Listen, Jim, I was there. I remember the beads that hang in the archway between the kitchen and a room where a shrine is. I remember the pictures in one of the daughter's rooms. I remember the back door of the kitchen leading to the patio. I remember the furniture. I remember that there was a satellite dish on the front lawn, an American flag and I think a POW or MIA flag also. I remember a tree on the left side of the house. I remember a truck being parked in the driveway. I remember the plants on the front of the house. I remember a ton of details."

"Okay, okay," he said.

That conversation ended when I told Jim that I needed to get upstairs for the meeting with the union, Bill, and the labor relations lawyer. In fact, I was late to meet with Pat Drew, the employee assistance counselor. When I arrived in her office, Pat was standing by Joyce's desk.

"Hi, Jayson," she said. "I thought I was supposed to see you at three?"

"Yeah. I just got caught up in a meeting. Do you have time now?"

"I am actually meeting with someone right now. Do you want to reschedule for tomorrow? Let's see, I am all booked up in the morning."

"Actually," I said. "It's okay."

"Well, how are you doing?" she asked.

"Oh, I am all right. Just wanted to talk to you about life. I am trying to let the Twelve Steps guide me and just wanted to talk about that a bit."

"Okay. Well, call Joyce and we'll figure out something."

She walked into her office. My last escape door, I felt, had closed.

* * *

After leaving Lena and Jerry Wednesday night following the first round of questioning by Bill and the lawyers, I could not get my mind off of what she had said about the documentation. Bill had demanded the receipts from my trip and I had lied, telling him that they were in a bag at my brother's house in Virginia, and that I had asked him to fax them to me. I had falsified my notes and other documents, but for reasons beyond me at this point, I did not have the mental energy to create a whole fake set of receipts—even though it would have only taken a scanner, a printer and some creative thinking about how to make them look as if they were faxed from Virginia. I would also have to prevent Bill and the lawyers from calling to authenticate them.

As I was waiting for Zuza, Jim called from his cell phone.

"Hey, Jayson. How are you doing?" he said with a tinge of compassion in his voice.

I could tell he was worried. It was nearing eleven. I was in the empty sports department on the fourth floor, pacing from my desk to the windows.

"I am fine. I am just trying to get ready for more questioning tomorrow."

"How was it?" he asked.

"Pretty rough."

"Well, I am headed out of town for a couple of days and I had considered staying in town to take care of this, but then finally made the decision to go ahead and make this trip. Frankly, one of my worries was leaving you alone in this. You know, you have been pretty stoic through all this, and I just wanted to let you know that if you want to talk about anything, on or off the record, you can."

"Thanks, Jim. I am okay."

"Are you sure?"

"Yeah. I am a little numb, I guess. A little in shock."

"Well, let me make the point again, if there is anything you want to talk about—how you are feeling, where your head is—even if it does not involve the stories, call me anytime, night or day, on the cell phone."

"Thanks, Jim."

"Are you going to be with someone tonight?"

"Yeah, I am going to be with some friends, some good friends. I am going to stay at their place tonight, get some rest and get ready for the questions tomorrow morning."

"Okay, take care of yourself, and call me if you want to talk."

"All right, Jim. Thanks a lot and, I am, uh, sorry about this. I just wanted to say that I am sorry about doing this to you, doing it to Nick. We have done some good work together." Nick was the national assignment editor.

"Look," he said, "you don't have to say that. Nick and I know. Look, just get some rest and answer all their questions. I might need you tomorrow to finish up the editor's note, so call me in the afternoon in the Washington bureau. All right?"

"Sounds good. Okay."

"Are you sure you are okay, Jayson?"

"Yeah. I am fine."

Zuza met me at my desk and we agreed to get out of the building. I told her about the prosecutorial nature of the questioning and the fact that I was convinced, by its nature, that this was going to result in a serious suspension at the least, and perhaps termination. This made no sense to her since, of course, she did not have all the facts. We decided to head downtown to grab a table at Café Mona Lisa on Bleecker Street in Greenwich Village.

We would often go to cafés like this one to sit down, drink coffee, eat pastries, write and discuss the world, our plans, and our dreams. As I explained to her the same cover story I had been telling everyone else, my phone began ringing. Among the calls that came in were ones from the *City Paper,* Kurtz at *The Washington Post,* and the student newspaper where I had once been editor at the University of Maryland. There were calls from colleagues and others offering support as well.

"I still don't understand why this is such a big deal," she said.

As the calls continued to pour in, I became increasingly irritated, knowing clearly that the more reporters who were following the story, the more likely *The Times* would figure out that I had never been to Texas. My irritation, by this point, was turning into distress, and it was obviously on my face.

"Are you okay?"

Was it my facial expression, I wondered. Or was it that I—the coffee addict—had barely touched my cappuccino?

Zuza had been there the night before when my parents, who had been called by two friends from the University of Maryland College of Journalism, phoned to find out what was going on and to make sure that I was all right. She could probably see that I was deteriorating into numbness.

"Oh, I am fine."

I was staring somewhere, off into the distance.

"I am fine, I am fine. I just think it's over. I just need to go to the bathroom."

I placed my cell phone, which I had been clutching, on the table. I slowly pushed my chair back and laid my napkin beside the cell phone.

"I'll be right back," I said.

"Okay."

"Dead man walking," I mumbled softly as I made my way to the bathroom.

I walked in, shut the door to the bathroom, and stared into the mirror. I cannot remember what I saw; I was just thinking that I was tired, so tired, but not in the way one gets tired when they are annoyed or frustrated or physically exhausted. I was tired in the way one gets when they are done, when there is no more fight in them, when the numbness gives way to a feeling of total loss, to nothing but blackness.

I remember seeing darkness. I remember it enveloping me, and I remember giving in wholly, finding comfort in its lack of questions for me, its lack of disappointment, its lack of emotions. In a quick flash, I saw an image of myself hanging from the door hinge, the life gone out of me, the pain dissipated. There was no pleasure or joy in this image, but simply relief.

I began slowly, carefully, pulling the black belt looped through my khakis. I turned again, looking in the mirror, hoping to see my face. I turned back around and slowly unbuckled the single latch to the belt, slowly and carefully pulling both ends apart, letting them hang in my hands. I dropped one end and pulled from the right side, the one with the buckle on it, until the full belt had gone through the loops and was cradled in both of my hands in front of me. I looked up at the strong metal hinge in the bathroom and saw nothing but relief. I wrapped the leather around my neck. It felt cold and slightly sticky, but I did not jerk from it. I felt out of my body. Then a ray of light appeared, almost as if it had found its way through a crack in the door and into the bathroom, but it was in my mind.

No matter how bad it has been, I thought to myself, *life has gotten better over the last year. You are still sober, you have not picked up, and you are happy. You have found love and your best friend and partner in many good things. No matter how bad this gets, your life, regardless of what any outsider may think, is better. Think of the woman outside that door, think of all the things you can do together. Think about her face when she finds you, think about your life. Think most, though, about how much better you are.*

I quickly ripped the belt from my neck, with such force that I accidentally whipped myself with it. My heart was now pounding. I ran over to the sink, washed my hands and face, and quickly made my way for the doorway, picking up a paper towel along the way. I sat back down at our table and began crying, tears slowly making their way down my face.

"Are you ready to go?" Zuza asked, alarmed by the tears.

"I am," I replied, not betraying a hint of what had just occurred, or hardly any emotion for that matter, other than the blinding, deafening, muting numbness.

"I am tired of fighting for a job that I don't really want," I told her. "I'm just tired."

"Okay, let's go home."

We paid the bill and walked out onto Bleecker Street and then onto Seventh Avenue, where an antique yellow Checker cab was parked. We walked into the street, Zuza with her arms around me, as we hailed a cab and made our way back to her apartment in Brooklyn. That night, I decided it was time to resign. No matter what happened, I was not going to keep fighting for a job that I didn't really want, for a position covering something that mattered even less than the meaningless stories I had been writing about lately. I wasn't going to fight for a job at a newspaper that had disappointed my idealism, for a newspaper that I had allowed to take something very precious from me. I didn't tell Zuza what had happened in the bathroom, but I did tell her that I planned to resign from the paper. We fell asleep on her soft yellow sheets. It was the first night of good sleep I had in months.

When I woke up Thursday morning, I called my parents to inform them of what had happened in the bathroom, and told them that I planned to resign. I called Daryl Khan, a freelance reporter for *The Times* and friend from college, to say that I was planning on leaving. He attempted, unsuccessfully, to dissuade me.

Outside the apartment building, I called Catherine Mathis, the *Times*'s vice president of corporate communications, to let her know that I planned to resign and that she should expect calls from the news media. Catherine had been a friend, not just a colleague, and I understood that Howell kept her far out of the loop in the newsroom, even though her deft advice could have saved him a million headaches. The call was my way of hinting that there was more to come, though I gave no details.

"Catherine, I just wanted to let you know that I am going to resign today."

"Jayson," she said from her cell phone on a trip to Boston. "I don't know any of the details, but I would encourage you to reconsider and think about that before you make any decisions."

"I will," I said. "I will give you a heads-up if there is anything more."

The first place I went that morning once I arrived in Times Square was, oddly enough, a bar. Robert Emmett's Bar and Restaurant, run by two Irish business partners, is located around the corner from *The Times* at the intersection of West Forty-fourth Street and Eighth Avenue. I had spent many a drunken night there, but in recent times, the daytime bartender, Maria, had been a great source of strength and support. She talked to me about love, life, and everything else when I came by for lunch and the soup of the day. The blue cheese and broccoli soup was my favorite. Maria would pour a cup of coffee and a cranberry seltzer as soon as I sat down. Whenever I got ready to leave, she would pour another cup of coffee. Maria was a saint and the one person that I wanted to say goodbye to more than anyone else.

I waited outside that morning, on a crate across the street from the bar's door, beside a Broadway theatre and a hotel. I stared into the windows of the bar and thought of the many good times and the many bad ones I'd had there. I remembered the night we stood by its windows watching the New Year ushered in when we were supposed to be working and then proceeded to the bathroom to snort some cocaine; the Saturday drunken lunches with Stephanie Flanders, a brilliant Harvard graduate and correspondent brought in to cover world poverty, who was perhaps the only person less suited for *The Times* than me; the time young *Times* staffers and workers from *The New York Times on the Web* gave me a pair of inflatable breasts for my birthday; the day that the bar's owner told me to stop doing drugs as I teased him by dancing the night away with his teenage daughter; my first visit back after getting clean and sober with Sabine Heller, a public relations executive who was my friend, and her client and friend, Gary Coleman; and of course the many lunches with Maria.

When Maria finally arrived to open the bar, I walked across the street and knocked on the locked glass doors and she let me in. She could tell something was wrong, and I began to explain to her the details of the Texas story.

"Let's just say it's complicated and that I have disappointed a lot of people. So, that's why I have decided to resign. I am just not going to fight for a job I don't want anymore," I said, repeating my mantra. "And Maria . . ."

"Yes honey."

"There is much, much more."

I started crying. She came from around the bar and comforted me.

"It's going to be okay," she said. "Oh, honey, it's going to be okay."

At some point, Lena called and told me to meet her in the union office on the ninth floor of the building. As I walked out the door of Emmett's for the last time, Maria called out my name.

"Jayson, good luck, take care of yourself and be in touch, okay, honey?"

"Okay. I am ... I am ... I will."

I wanted to say that I was going to miss her, because I would. I would indeed.

In the union office, Lena laid out the game plan and gave me an update: we were supposed to meet with *The Times* labor relations lawyers and Bill in thirty minutes, but that meeting had been rescheduled because they wanted to review some things. She asked me some questions, one about whether I was definitely in Los Fresnos. I said yes, for some reason, still holding out some hope that what I was about to say would end it all, the questions would stop, nothing more would be found out, nothing more needed to be found out.

"Lena," I said. "I have to tell you something."

"What, baby?"

I looked in her eyes, tears welling up in my own.

"What, baby?"

Her facial features were drooping, a sense of alarm spreading over her face.

"Lena, I can't take it anymore. I want to resign."

"No, we are going to fight this ..."

"Lena, I can't take it anymore. Can I tell you something?"

"Sure, of course."

"Last night, I almost killed myself. I wrapped my belt around my neck and was going to do it. I can't fight anymore. I can't fight for a job that I don't want anymore. I just can't take the questions. I can't do it."

"No, no, no, baby, no. Don't do that to yourself. No, no, no. You can't do that. No."

Lena was crying, bawling, tears rushing down her face.

"No, no, no, no, baby." She kept on repeating it.

"Okay, here's what we are going to do," she said when we wiped our tears. "We are going to go down to that meeting and tell them that you plan to resign today, that you will help them with any questions that they have, but that you are not prepared to do it now, because you are not in an emotional state where you can discuss it. We are going to tell them that you will provide them with all the documentation, and we'll ask for unemployment and a confidentiality clause. That's what we are going to do. I am not going to have somebody die over this place. No sir. Okay. Here's what we are going to do, I am going to call Doc up and we are going to have ourselves a little prayer. We are going to have ourselves a little prayer, and then we are going to do this. Okay?"

Doc was an old-timer, a black man who worked as a clerk on the sports desk. As she dialed Doc's number on her phone, I wondered whether I should tell her more about what was going on. I resisted, hoping that it would not come to that, that I would not have to think about this for some time, that I would be able to just go home to Brooklyn, perhaps to Prospect Park to walk around and put this all behind me, and begin, somehow, rebuilding my life in another field.

When Doc arrived, Lena told him that "Brother Jayson is going through some trials and tribulations, and we just need to say a prayer."

Doc commenced as we held hands in prayer, and after a lot of *Lord, we ask thees* and *Yes Lord Jesuses,* we broke up. Just then, the two other union members arrived and Lena informed them of the plan. When one suggested that we continue to fight, Lena sharply said that it was not in the cards. They went downstairs to labor relations to inform Bill and the lawyers of my decision to resign. When they came back up a half-hour later, Lena looked flustered.

"They asked if they could have about thirty minutes to review their options. They want you to come downstairs and answer some questions. We told them that you are going to resign, but they still want you to come downstairs and answer some questions."

"I don't want to, Lena."

"You don't have to," the other female union member said. "Once you resign, you owe them nothing. They are likely consulting with legal right now to see if they can refuse your resignation."

"They say they have evidence that you never went to Los Fresnos and they want to ask you about it. We told them that you are not in a position to answer any questions and just left it at a stalemate. Now, we are going to go back down there in a couple of minutes and see what they have to say. We need to have that resignation letter in hand and ready to bring it down to them to show that you are prepared to resign immediately," Lena said.

"Okay, let's do it now," I replied. I pulled out my wallet and handed Lena my *Times* identification card. Lena quickly typed my brief resignation letter into her computer, we printed out the appropriate number of copies, and the group went back down to the labor relations office, leaving me alone in the guild office.

There was a knock on the door a few minutes later. It was Lynette, who was staring at me like a drooping puppy dog.

"I am going to resign," I said.

"Shut the fuck up."

"Yup, I am going to do it."

"Why?"

"I don't belong here. They are going to fire me anyway."

"Are you fucking serious?"

"Yup." I showed her my resignation letter.

"Can I have a copy of this?" she asked, laughing out loud, a big smile on her face. Lynette had seen some shit in her life and could take about any old crisis and turn it into a joke.

"Let's grab a smoke," I said.

"Where?"

"The stairwell."

"Are you crazy? I don't need to get caught and end up here with you."

"Come on," I said.

She followed me into the stairwell, and then onto a landing between floors. I knew this would be our last smoke. When she found out the truth, I knew she would be disappointed. We laughed and joked and made fun of most everything that had happened to us over my four years at *The Times*. We raced back up the stairs, though, when we heard footsteps from below, both of us discarding our lit cigarettes as we made a last mad dash, our final minor act of rebellion together. Back inside the guild office, I was handing Lynette the letter as Lena walked back in with the troops.

"What are you doing here?" she asked, looking at Lynette. "Goodbye, Miss Holloway," she said pointedly, not waiting for an answer.

"Okay." Lynette said goodbye for the last time and left.

"Okay, so here's the deal. They can't refuse your resignation, but they would like to ask you some questions. We said, 'No. Not now. Later.' Now, after that happened, Bill pulled me aside and asked if he could come up and talk with you off the record. He just wants to talk to you and find out how you are doing, not about the details of the story. I can tell he is just really worried about you. I mean, they are all worried about you. There are some people in this building, Jayson, as fucked up as this place is, who care about you. Even the lawyers like you, and are worried about you, and want to make sure you are okay."

"Lena," I said, my voice cracking. "I love Bill. He's great. I just can't talk to him right now. I will call him. I just can't talk to him right now."

"Okay, I will let him know."

Lena called the labor relations office and informed them that we were leaving, and then called Jerry Gray. Jerry had stopped by the office earlier in the day to inquire about my well-being.

"We are going to meet Jerry outside," Lena said. "Here is what is going to happen. We are going to walk you to the elevators and walk you out the front door, and if we run into anyone from management, we are going to protect you."

They were like guardian angels.

I walked, flanked by my three union reps, Lena remarking on how crazy all of this had been, how we needed to get a drink, and how she needed one of my cigarettes.

"What have you got?"

"Camel Lights."

"That'll do."

We made it to the elevators and began taking them down to the first floor. The elevator stopped on the third floor, the main space of the newsroom. In stepped Glenn Collins, a talented writer who had been one of my cubicle mates since my early days as an intern at the paper.

"Hey, Jaysona," he said, using the nickname he called me. "How's it going?"

"All right," I said.

Lena smirked at me.

"Great stuff out of Maryland and Virginia. You've been all over the place."

"Thanks, Glenn."

When the elevator doors opened on the first level, Lena and I could hardly hold back our laughs.

"No, seriously, Jayson," Lena said. "That is what everyone has been saying about your work, and this does not take that away."

Little did she know. Lena, Jerry and I decided to go to the eighth-floor bar at the Marriott Marquis. I nibbled on a small sandwich at their behest and drank a cranberry and seltzer, as Lena ordered a gin and tonic and Jerry had a Grand Marnier. We sat there together as the telephone calls came in.

Kurtz from *The Washington Post*: "*. . . heard you resigned, was wondering if you would be willing to comment.*"

Wemple from the *City Paper*: "*Please call me back Jayson.*"

Jim Roberts: "*I am still trying to finish the editor's note . . .*" He had no idea.

Jennifer Preston, Bill's deputy: "*Jayson, it's Jennifer. Sweetheart, I heard you resigned and that just breaks my heart. Please call me . . .*"

Sheila Rule: "*Hi, Jayson, it's Sheila . . .*"

Jacques Steinberg, the media reporter who covered newspapers: "*Jayson, it's Jacques, I am working on a story about . . .*"

I only picked up the phone when Zuza called.

"Are you okay?"

"Yeah. I am at the Marriott Marquis with Jerry and Lena."

"The strangest thing just happened. Gerald Boyd called me and told me to leave work."

"What?" I asked.

"He told me to leave work and go find you, to be with you, that you would need me. And then he came up to my desk and asked me to go find you."

"Okay, that's the weirdest thing I have ever heard," I said, perhaps not entirely grasping what I was hearing.

I then received a call from Carr, who had also received a call from Gerald, who had brought him into the office. After Lena and Jerry went on their way, offering to drive me to my parents' house in Virginia the next day or over the weekend, I walked with Zuza down Eighth Avenue to meet Carr at West Forty-third Street. We could see him across the street, standing alone, his black bag over his shoulder, black sunglasses on. He was nervously rocking back and forth.

"Carr!" I yelled.

David made his way across the street and I introduced him to Zuza.

"Oh, God, I am so glad you are here," he said, giving her a big hug. "I am so glad you are here."

David embraced me. He was crying, tears pouring down his face under his sunglasses.

"You're not going to go west, are you?" he plaintively and emotionally wailed.

West was toward where the drugs were, my spots.

"I don't want to man, I don't want to."

I too was crying.

"Don't go, don't go. I don't want you to die, man. I don't want you to die. Listen, I don't know what happened, but I know that you were not honest with me, and a time will come when we will sort that all out, but I just don't want you to do something stupid. I just don't want you to go west, I don't want you to pick up, I don't want you to kill yourself, and you know that picking up is just killing yourself slowly. Whatever shit you have going on that you think it will make better, it's just going to make it ten times worse. Ten times worse, and you are just going to kill yourself. This time it might not be all that slow. Don't do it. Just don't do it."

"I'll try. I'll try. I'll try."

We left each other on that corner. I informed him that we were going to walk for awhile and would probably go to Prospect Park. I reassured him that Zuza and I would stick together.

At Eighth Avenue and West Thirty-fourth Street, near Madison Square Garden, my dying cell phone rang.

"Hi, Jayson. It's Pat Drew. I heard that you resigned today and remembered that you had come by earlier in the week and connected the dots. I guess this is what you wanted to talk about. How are you feeling right now?"

"I am okay."

"Well, I talked to Lena and she suggested that I get in touch with you. She mentioned that you had been having some suicidal thoughts."

"Not right now, really, I just feel numb. I just want to go home and sleep. I am most worried about a relapse, really."

"Well, Jayson, she mentioned something about a belt."

"Yeah," I said.

"What happened with the belt?" she prodded.

"I put it around my neck last night at a café, but ..." my voice trailed off.

"Jayson, I think you really need to see someone. I have called the Realization Center. Marilyn is there right now, and she has agreed to see you. Would you be willing to go there and talk with her?"

"Of course. I think that's a great idea, Pat."

"Okay, I will call her and tell her that you are headed there. What time do you think you will be there?"

"We are not far at all, we could probably walk and be there in fifteen minutes."

"Okay. That's great. Please call me when you get there, okay?"

"Okay."

Pat had come through again. The Realization Center is where I had gone to rehab. Marilyn White was its founder and director, and she had been my therapist in the outpatient program. Once I arrived, I was quickly taken into Marilyn's office, where we talked a bit about the events of the last few days.

"I think you need to go to the hospital, Jayson. You have to be under constant watch, and I don't think we can put all of that responsibility on a twenty-three-year-old girl. She seems very strong, but it's just too much to ask. You need to rest, and you need to be in a safe place. Will you agree to go to the hospital?"

I would have agreed to anything at this point.

"Yes," I said.

"I am going to try to get you into a good one, like Silver Hill, but you would have to find a way to get up there. Otherwise, if we have to call 911, they will take you to any old hospital and you could end up in Bellevue or some place like that, and we don't want that."

"Okay."

We worked out the details with Pat at *The Times,* who promised to address the insurance issues. My parents, who had been alerted to come up by Lena, called to say that they were on their way. Marilyn called Zuza into her office to explain the situation and ask that she witness an agreement that she and I were about to sign.

Pat was still on the speakerphone as Marilyn read aloud the suicide contract—the one where I promised not to kill myself, at least until I was in Silver Hill. I signed it and Zuza witnessed it. She rolled the paper up into her back pocket and we made our way out of the Center's office to grab dinner at a Polish restaurant in the East Village.

I argued over the phone with my friend Daryl, who felt like I was not being honest about what a deep hole I had been in; I cried on the phone with my brother. There was not much time, but as we ate Polish cuisine, I cried and Zuza comforted me.

The truth was about to come out, and I knew it would not set me free.

CHAPTER TWO
SILVER HILL

I winced at the sound of the doors closing behind me, the electronic locks latching into place.

A large but gentle hand landed on the royal blue hooded sweatshirt that was covering my shoulder. It guided me through the atrium, past the glass-enclosed nurses' station, a pay phone and down a long hallway. Everything felt as if it were in slow motion. I was taking in every detail of the modern building but processing nothing. The hand attached ever so gently to my shoulder belonged to a big man who introduced himself as Kevin. He explained that he was a psychiatric technician at the hospital, and that he would be completing the rest of my intake. I had spent the last thirty minutes answering questions that included, among other topics, whether I had ever had suicidal impulses, been on any medications and what my sexual orientation was.

"Do you have a religious affiliation?" a nurse asked.

"Agnostic," I replied.

"Practicing?" she asked.

"Yes. Practicing agnostic."

"Practicing agnostic," elicited laughs from nurses eavesdropping on our conversation. It was reassuring. I hoped that some of the hospital employees had senses of humor, otherwise I knew that if I had not lost my mind already, I would be certifiably crazy by the end of my stay.

Kevin explained in a voice surprisingly squeaky and polite for a man of his size and shape that this would be my room for at least the first few days of my stay, and chances were good that I would not be given a roommate. I was obviously staring beyond his eyes and the curly black mustache on his face because Kevin positioned himself squarely in front of me for the rest of his statement. He made sure I responded with head nods as he explained the hospital's rules about searching through the bags that I brought with me, the clothes I was wearing and my body.

Kevin asked for my belt, and I handed it to him and he examined it and then took similar glances at my shoes and my laces. "You are not going to be able to keep these—not even the shoes," Kevin said, explaining that the laces that ran through the side of my shoes were considered dangerous "for a patient of your classification."

"Okay," I responded, not even flinching at the fact that as a twenty-seven-year-old man, I was having my belt and laces taken away from me.

By this time, a second large man entered the room and introduced himself, although I do not recall his name. The man politely asked if he could begin looking through my belongings. I agreed with a nod, as he took hold of my black shoulder bag and the navy blue plastic bag filled with shirts and socks that we had picked up at the mall in Stamford, Connecticut earlier in the day. Kevin promised a pair of hospital socks, with special traction pads on the bottom, if my feet got too cold.

After Kevin performed the cavity search, I turned my attention to the other man who asked about some of the items he had found in my bag, including several pens with slivers of metal on the caps, a razor, my cellular telephone and several condoms that had long passed their do-not-sell date.

"You won't be needing those here," he joked as he threw them away.

Kevin collected the eighty dollars in cash and change I had brought with me and suggested that I send half of it home, along with my cellular phone and credit cards, with the people who were waiting on the other side of the locked glass doors in the lobby. As soon as I agreed, the other man asked if I had eaten dinner and when I said "no," he told me he would try to find something for me. He opened the deck so I could have at least one cigarette break before heading off to bed.

Then Kevin put his hand back on my shoulder, smiled and said I might want to have one last goodbye with the people in the lobby before it got too late. I agreed with a nod and then followed him back out the doorway and down the long hallway to the atrium.

I could see my mother, my father and Zuza standing on the other side of the glass. Zuza's arms were crossed high above her waist, her long wavy blonde hair dropping in front of her chest and face, her deep almond eyes staring at me through the door. Her nervousness was as palpable as numbness was to my face. My mother, Frances Blair, a full seven inches shorter than Zuza's five-foot-seven frame, stood beside her, arms also crossed. Her foot was tapping on the ground, as if that were all she could do to keep her nervousness contained. My father, Thomas Blair, stood to the left of them, mustering that reassuring smile he could display in any crisis situation.

Kevin signaled to the nurses who pressed a button that unlatched the locks of the glass doors. Zuza was the first to stop in, rushing toward me, followed by my mother and my father. Zuza had never been much of a fan of institutions, having volunteered while she was a college student to work in an upstate New York prison. She learned to deplore the conditions of locking human beings behind gates, and was hardly comfortable with the voluntary nature of my stay.

My mother and father had arrived at Zuza's Brooklyn apartment earlier that morning and slept in her room, as she and I took our places on a pullout couch belonging to one of her roommates. My parents were hardly prepared for the call they had received the evening before, recommending that I be taken immediately to a psychiatric hospital.

It seemed my dad's reassuring smile was directed toward my mother and Zuza as much as it was to me. After all, I suppose it is not easy to lock up your son or your best friend in a mental institution.

The three listened carefully as Kevin explained that visitations were allowed for one hour in the evening each day and that patients had unlimited access to a pay phone in the hallway, except during group therapy sessions and after the ten o'clock nightly curfew. They listened as Kevin assured them of the high-quality care, the hospital's drug and alcohol recovery programs, and its psychiatric services. My eyes were going back and forth between Zuza and my mother when Kevin explained it might be a good idea to bring me a couple of packs of cigarettes on their first visitation.

"No!" Zuza and my mother shouted in unison.

I tried to explain that it was better that I smoke now, despite recent health concerns, than that I lose my mind as seemed to be happening over the past few days, but Zuza and my mother kept on going with some poorly choreographed combination chorus of "You're going to kill yourself!" "You're going to die!" and "No way Jayson!" that drowned out my explanation.

"How old are you?" Kevin asked me, interrupting the screaming.

"Twenty-seven," I said.

"Yeah, well, how old are your lungs, Jayson?" Zuza fired back. "How old did the doctor say your lungs were?" she continued. "You have the lungs of a sixty-year-old, right?"

My mother stopped and looked at Zuza. I could almost swear she seemed pleased that the blonde Polish woman she had just met less than twenty-four hours earlier was launching such an impassioned attack on me in the name of my health. I don't think my mother had ever seen one of my friends stand up to me so ferociously. I know she had never seen me cower like this.

It was a standstill.

"At Silver Hill," Kevin said slowly, as if he had given this speech more than once before to other nervous and worried loved ones, "we encourage our patients to take it one step at a time, and while cigarettes are dangerous, they are much less dangerous than what can happen when a patient gets too stressed out."

My father interceded just before the yelling was about to begin again, asking what brand I preferred. "Camel Lights," I said, staring down at my feet, as if I were trying to escape the shame.

That settled, Zuza pulled me off to the side of the atrium, away from my parents, Kevin, and the nurses' station. The whites of her almond eyes took on that fiery appearance that I had come to notice right before she started crying. She rattled off a long list of reasons why she didn't "like this place," including the story of a patient who had started crying at the glass doors while I was in my room, when the nurses would not allow his parents in to see him.

"This is like prison," she said softly enough so that my parents and Kevin could not hear our conversation.

I nodded, and said, "Yes, Zuza, I need to be in a safe place."

"Jaysonku," she continued, using the Polish diminutive form of my name. "Are you sure this is a good idea? Are you sure this is the best place? I just don't understand what part of you can allow yourself to be locked up in this type of place." I didn't have a ready explanation.

I grasped her arm softly, stopping for a moment to take in the contrast between my brown hand and her off-white skin.

"I need this," I said. "I need a safe place."

"Okay, just call me, please," she said. "Let me know how you are doing."

"I will, baby, but I will see you soon, you are going to come visit, right?" I asked.

"Yes," she said, putting her strong, long arms around my shoulders in a tender embrace.

"Thank you, Zuza," I said as we held each other for a few moments. "Thank you."

She let go. For a moment, the numbness receded, and without her in my arms, I felt empty. I watched Zuza and my mother and father walk slowly through the atrium back toward the glass doors, where Kevin led them outside to where my parents' dark green sedan was waiting. I knew that in a moment my mother would be worrying, Zuza would be crying and my father would be attempting to console both of them, but the numbness had returned by then, just in time to block out the things I had not wanted to think about lately.

Kevin put his arm on my shoulder as I watched them leave. "Don't worry," he said. "You are now in a safe place."

Not long after the three of them had made their way out the building's front door, a female nurse came by and introduced herself. The woman asked me to follow her to the side of the atrium opposite the hallway leading to my room. There, she walked in through a doorway, and then opened its top half where she placed a plastic cup and poured water into it. In another plastic cup, the woman placed a pink pill, a yellow capsule and then two orangish-brown tablets.

I looked at her, dumbfounded, and then explained that I did not need any medication.

"Well, Jayson," the nurse said in an all-too-chipper voice, "the psychiatrist who talked with you during intake has prescribed an anti-depressant and a mood stabilizer, and these are two vitamin supplements. If they cause any major problems, you should alert the nurse on duty immediately. Otherwise, you should wait to talk to the doctor on Monday."

I was not a fan of pills, but I was not going to argue with anyone on this gloomy Friday.

I nodded. "Sounds good," I said.

"Now, do you have any questions about the medications?"

"Yeah, um, what are they?" I asked.

"This," she said pointing to the pink pill, "is Paxil, an anti-depressant that should help you with any negative thoughts. The yellow one is Neurontin, a mood stabilizer that should calm you down a bit and make it easier for you to relax."

She fumbled through the charts on a shelf behind her and scanned a piece of paper.

"You take 25 milligrams of Paxil and 300 milligrams of Neurontin at night," she added. "In the morning you take another 300 milligrams of Neurontin."

Just then I heard the sound of the door latch clicking on the other side of the atrium. I felt, for an instant, the slight desire to make a run for the doors, where I would get outside and then run like hell until I found the nearest pay phone. I would call Zuza on her cell phone, and even though my parents were staying at her apartment, she would secretly arrange for me to be picked up and taken somewhere no one would find me. She would visit me there, and hold me, comforting me as she had done over the past few days in a way I felt no hospital or medications could.

We would live happily ever after, traveling to places like Africa and Southeast Asia, writing, painting and doing volunteer work. Then we would have two children together—one a boy and one a girl—and we would give them exotic names, and raise them using the best of the parenting tools from both of our families—my mom and dad's love and tenderness combined with the independence and intellectual strength she gained from her parents. We would grow old together, having accomplished many important things that would change the world, and we would have done it in the most exciting of ways; our actions and our partnership being an inspiration to millions.

The doors slammed shut, jolting me from my daydream.

"Jayson, Jayson, do you understand what I am saying?" the nurse asked.

"Uh, yeah, I do," I replied. "Sorry."

With that, I nodded, took the pills one by one, each chased by a gulp of water. For the first time, I entered the world of prescribed psychiatric medication. I noticed out the corner of my eye, between the Neurontin and one of the vitamin supplements, that Kevin was escorting a skinny twenty-something woman with stringy brown hair and sad eyes down the nearest hallway.

Back in my room after dinner and a cigarette break, I immediately went for the copy of Bram Stoker's *Dracula* that I had picked up at the Stamford Mall early in the day on the notion that I needed to be engrossed in someone else's horrible fantasy. It was already early morning when I flipped open to the first chapter, which begins with Jonathan Harker's journal entries on his trip from London to Transylvania that begin on May 3, which was coincidentally today's date. I chuckled, hoping I would not meet a similar fate.

I did not make it past Harker's entry on May 5, where he describes awakening to the courtyard and castle of Count Dracula, before my eyes began shuttering rapidly and I began to see flashing lights, which seemed like visual hallucinations. I was asleep within seconds, the medications having taken their effect. I couldn't stay awake. It was the best night of sleep I had in at least eight months, maybe even a decade.

When I woke the next morning, I felt surprisingly rested. One of the first things I noticed was the precision design of my room. There were no metal objects attached to the chairs, desk or drawers that could be broken off and turned into weapons; there were no hinges or door springs that could be used for a good hanging, and there was no curtain bar above the shower. The glass in the bathroom was not glass at all, but some form of plastic. The main rule that I had recalled from the previous night was that here in lock-down—as it was called—they checked in on us every fifteen minutes.

On my first night, I was so sound asleep I didn't even notice. The other rules I remembered were about the limited visiting hours and how we were only allowed out on the deck for cigarette breaks every couple of hours. I was craving one badly. I had tried to quit smoking several weeks before, but in the days before being brought to Silver Hill I had picked it up again, inhaling more than a pack a day. As I waited for the first morning cigarette break, I got to know some of the other patients in this locked ward that was known as the acute care unit.

One girl I met that morning had made an unsuccessful attempt to stab her sexually abusive grandfather in the chest a few years before. She had developed serious physical and psychiatric disorders in the weeks and months that followed, including deafness and multiple personality disorder. It was as if she did not want to hear the sound of her own screaming voice each time her grandfather crawled into the bed she was sleeping in, as if she had killed off a piece of herself with the knife that missed his chest that evening years ago. The woman suffered from a rare disease known as conversion disorder where a psychological problem—usually a major trauma like sexual abuse or witnessing violence such as war—converted into a physical symptom such as blindness or deafness.

The woman—Sarah or Michelle, depending on which of her two personalities were engaged—had a sign language interpreter with her most of the day, and the doctors were convinced that they could at least tackle some of the psychological elements of her disorders. At one meal on the second day, Sarah and I sat across from each other. She read my lips and I deciphered her English. Even though her real name was Michelle, I was talking to Sarah and wondering whether I really needed to be in this place—among the suicidal, the hallucinatory, the deranged.

Karen, who was sitting next to us, suffered from alcoholism, seizures and an addiction to the prescription pill Xanax, which is used to treat patients with panic disorder and is often abused for its cocaine-like qualities.

Then there was Maryelyn, a young anorexic woman from South Africa with long black hair. She did not like to talk, but loved to pull the staples out of magazines and cut herself so much that the nursing staff had to strap her arms to her bed at night. There was also Rachel, who was as sure that she did not have any psychiatric disorders, as she was that strange men in black uniforms were breaking into her house and changing the locks to her doors.

Among my favorites was Janet, a short skinny woman with dark hair, who shook constantly because of her anxiety disorder and the medication they had her on. Janet was the one who would always pull me out of my books or wake me from sleep to let me know that another cigarette break was about to begin. One of the most touching moments was when Janet told me that in her heyday, she loved black guys, and that if she had been about twenty years younger she would have definitely gone after me. In my college days, I would have said that age was just a number and encouraged her all the way.

Gwen was a gossipy schizophrenic who had once been a lawyer before her disease left her homebound—in a total paranoid state about talking to anyone or going anywhere—for the last eleven months before she'd arrived at Silver Hill. I wondered whether this was where I really belonged—after all, I was just a former drug addict who needed a good rest after some drama at work. That's what I thought, until Sarah and I started talking. After complaining to me that she did not understand why everyone was calling her Michelle, Sarah began talking to me about the things she missed from the days of hearing.

"I miss hearing the birds chirp," Sarah/Michelle said, striking a chord that was dear to my heart. Since getting off cocaine and booze a year before, I had relished waking up to the birds chirping, instead of them jangling me as they had when I was drinking and using drugs.

"I miss being able to watch television without closed captions," she said, pointing into the television in the room where we were eating. "I miss being able to listen to conversations with people."

I felt overwhelmed with guilt for the things that were upsetting me, remembering all the things I took for granted and more, when Sarah/Michelle paused and added one line.

"I love to dream," she said. "I can still hear the birds chirp in my dreams."

Hearing this, I had to excuse myself from the table, and went to my room to cry. It was sad to think that Sarah/Michelle could not just close her eyes to find beauty, but that she had to actually dream. I was touched by the beauty she found in her dreams. I had not dreamed in a long time. I wondered why.

It was Michael, not my doctor, who gave me as good an answer as any to that question. I met Michael a couple of days later when I moved into the Main House, a less secure unit where patients were actually allowed to light their own cigarettes. I had gotten my belt, shoes and laces back by then, and had moved into a room in the old mansion with Steve, my roommate.

When I first arrived in the Main House, I was handed a pink sheet, which I knew meant that I was considered a psych patient, as opposed to being put in the dual diagnosis group, which was made up of those with both psychiatric issues and substance abuse problems. I seemed to relate more to the patients like Michael, who were considered dual diagnoses.

The bottom two floors of the house included dozens of rooms for patients, a lounge, television room, living room, dining room and offices for the nursing and psych tech staff. In the basement there was a beauty shop and a room with a ping-pong table where we met to hear speakers who were "a part of the program," as we called Alcoholic Anonymous members.

My favorite feature, though, was the back porch where patients gathered between meals and group therapy sessions to talk. It was a much less restrictive environment than the first unit I was in. I was sitting with Michael on the porch one evening. Michael was a dreamer, with an idealistic and creative mind matched only by his ideas to change the world that he constantly, and persuasively, talked about. Michael had been diagnosed with manic-depression less than a month before, after a bizarre episode in college.

Michael was one of those people I could relate to, someone who would spend his entire day on a giant attention deficit disorder trip, bouncing from one miscellaneous curiosity to another. Michael was the type of student who was bright and gifted, but one who teachers wished was on Ritalin.

Michael rarely went to class—there were too many other things to be explored—but scored high on tests because of his sharp mind and ability to stay up until five each morning, then turn around and be bouncing off the walls by 8 a.m. He had little control over his impulses, no filter that would tell a normal person not to walk on the ledge of that tall building. Michael also dabbled a bit in drugs and alcohol in college, in what he would later find out was a bit of self-medication.

Michael, a freshman at a southern college, had been up late one night talking with two friends about his philosophical views, droning on excitedly for hours and hours. This was nothing new for Michael. Nights without much sleep were the norm. But this time, Michael continued to talk until he, by his own account, lost his grip on reality.

By his best recollection, Michael spent the next two days talking to himself, with his thoughts spinning and swirling in his head at a rate of speed that would be hard for someone to imagine. After two days of talking and thinking about his ideas, he marched into a dean's office and attempted to explain his amazing ideas, including how they were all linked to his newfound belief in God. The dean, alarmed by Michael's high rate of speech, disheveled appearance and seemingly wild ideas, called the campus police, who took him to a hospital. Soon, Michael would be diagnosed with manic-depression and it would become clear that he had had a psychotic break from reality.

Michael explained that his psychotic break began as the normal hyperactivity he had been accustomed to and had harnessed throughout his life. Somewhere along the way, though, his rapid thinking became uncontrollable and he found himself pacing around in circles and eventually lost in his head, not being able to verbally translate all the things that were swirling in there. Michael said he became completely dysfunctional, and that in addition to his obvious delusions, he also began to hallucinate. It was amazing, I thought, the power of a couple of chemicals in the brain.

"It explains so much," Michael said out on the smoking deck.

I asked him what he meant.

"Well, my feelings about issues, the things I cared about were very real. I never understood why they caused my head to spin so much, why I was in so much angst. I thought they were just my normal feelings; I didn't realize that drugs and alcohol just made it all worse, that I was self-medicating. I mean, I was spinning out of control, always on the verge of having psychotic breakdowns, and all I could think about was doing coke to keep my euphoric feelings going or having a drink or smoking a joint to just bring myself down when I was going crazy."

I thought about how lucky Michael was. It would have been easy for the doctors to conclude that his strange behavior was due to drugs he was using. They could have diagnosed him as just having an alcohol and drug addiction without even realizing that he was a manic-depressive. Then he would have left rehab feeling so much better, ready to conquer the world. He would have "worked the program" and applied the steps of Alcoholics Anonymous and taken comfort in seeing how his life had changed for the better.

What he wouldn't know was that he had a ticking time bomb called manic-depression waiting to go off in his head, and now that he was clean and sober he would be left in a world in which he would be suffering from his terribly painful disease—without his primary mechanisms, drugs and alcohol—to cope with a mind spinning out of control. Then he would have had another psychotic break in six months, or a year, or maybe even later, and everyone would have been confused. No one would believe that he had not picked up drugs or alcohol again. Finally, someone would figure it out, probably after he had been institutionalized again.

"God, you're lucky," I said.

"Yeah, I really am."

Something about what Michael said stuck in my head like a splinter that slides under your skin, nagging at you until you pull it out. Maybe it was the bit about self-medication.

I wonder if that was what I had been doing in college when I would start my mornings with a glass of Scotch from the bottle of Johnnie Walker Black I kept above my refrigerator, and end my day with a glass by my side, sitting in bed, still drinking. Is that what I had been doing during my summer internship in New York when I used to keep a liter of gin beside my bed? Is that what was happening during my first few years of work when I used to knock off a bottle of red or blush wine to get to sleep at night?

I was an oddball at Silver Hill. Most of the patients at the hospital had either come into a treatment program for the first time or because of a relapse after some period of sobriety. The patients came after experiencing some type of psychotic episode or after long periods of destructive behavior. My circumstances were a bit unusual, given that I was a recovering drug addict and alcoholic who had checked himself voluntarily into the hospital without having picked back up. That made me wonder.

Had I gone stark raving mad? Did that explain some of the things I had done that just made no sense after a seemingly wonderful year of recovery? Was I in denial about something? I felt good. Could I even tell if I had gone crazy? After all, I was on powerful medications and I was behind locked doors, in a safe place.

Several months before, maybe in December, I had gone to the Brooklyn Public Library in Grand Army Plaza and pulled a couple books on manic-depression off the shelf. I told myself I was concerned about a friend's health. Since we had met, I had noticed that every couple of months my friend swung from deep depressions that I had a hard time coping with, to manic phases that I enjoyed. In reality, it was a bit of projection. After all, I too had suffered from depressions, although not as deep, and manic phases that people could hardly keep up with. It somehow made it easier to read through the books if I was doing it out of concern for someone else.

In college, I can remember waking up from my sleep with my head spinning in full motion, ideas swirling around inside so rapidly that I would have to jump onto my laptop to keep them in order.

People would also remark about the 5:50 a.m. e-mails they would receive from me. Often I would be up all night, writing and thinking, and spinning myself in circles. At college, and later in work life, this was sometimes a plus—with so many parties to get to and people to see—to come up with a great solution to all the problems in media consolidation at two o'clock in the morning, and to have the energy to write it all out by seven. I remembered too many nights, like Michael, where I had to have a stiff drink to knock myself out and to go sleep, to stop my head from racing at night. Little did I know how much the source of this energy could spin out of control.

I had long known that I was beholden to my moods, hyperactive as a child, mercurial as a young adult, first severely depressed as a college student and caught, I would later discover, in the unrelenting cycles of manic-depression by the time I began my professional life.

My depression came in cycles that were generally followed by much more productive and happy times, which I used to counterbalance my lack of enthusiasm during the low points. I did not translate it as illness, or something that needed to be treated, but just the way my moods were. The depression at times helped me feel sympathy for people who were subjects of my stories, and I used the mania to work and write during all hours of the day. These cycles were not yet out of control, and I saw my mercurial moods as something that gave me great advantages. A view which was, in part, true.

Nowhere in the books I had read at the library did I come across a mention that mania could actually turn into full-blown psychosis, delusions and hallucinations. I thought that such distinctions were reserved for schizophrenics, and at first I wanted to reevaluate my self-diagnosis. Michael's experience, particularly the psychotic break, put manic-depression in a new light for me, one much less becoming.

The more I heard Michael talk, though, the more I saw how we were alike. We were both seen as overachievers, the come-in-early-stay-late types. We were both known for our lack of sleep. We were both known for our high energy and hyperactivity. We were both known for our ubiquitous natures. We both used drugs and alcohol to self-medicate our problems. We both knew how to isolate and hide when the depression set in. I was not, though, ready to share with anyone the similarities I saw between Michael and myself.

Dr. Scott D. Marder, the young psychiatrist who was my doctor at Silver Hill, was at a bit of a disadvantage in making a diagnosis, because during my stay at the hospital I was feeling all right. By Monday, when we first met, I was, some might say, high on life.

"I am just here for a detox on life," I told him, explaining that recent troubles at work had made me decide to seek help.

Later, I told him the truth. That on April 30 I had considered committing suicide, going as far as to wrap my belt around my neck and hoisting it above the door hinge in a Greenwich Village café. It was true, but since that moment, I had not had any suicidal thoughts. In fact, I was looking forward to getting back to Brooklyn and starting my new life. I wanted to stay in the hospital for at least a few more days, I explained, because I was worried about the media and the outside world in general.

I did not explain the details, but his nod seemed to suggest to me that he already had heard it from the nurses who had been fielding reporters' calls. The mood stabilizer and anti-depressant were working fine. I was getting some of the best sleep that I'd had in years. There was, of course, no mention of my fears about manic-depression. I didn't want to believe that I had any mental illness. Besides, I told myself, this is not about my past, but about how I feel now.

"I am just concerned with resting and getting a little bit better before I head out into the real world," I explained.

Dr. Marder told me he wanted to monitor my progress over the next few days. I sounded good, but he expressed concern that I was recovering from a traumatic situation that might be masking any other problems that existed. We agreed to meet again the next day.

* * *

"My name is Michael and I am an alcoholic and an addict," says Michael.

"Hi, Michael," chants the circle.

"I'm exactly where I need to be," says Michael.

"I am having a bad day, and I really don't know what to do," he adds.

Michael looks across the room at a member of the circle, briefly, before looking away.

"I know I have manic-depression and I know it has the potential to drive me crazy. I just don't like what my medications are doing to me. They slow me down. I just need to surrender to my illness, and admit that I am powerless to stop it, as well as drugs and alcohol. That's all."

"Thanks for sharing, Michael," the addicts say in one voice.

A brief, small forced smile passes over Michael's face as he scans the members of the group.

As was explained by a counselor earlier in the day, rehab is not seen as the end of the journey, but the beginning, where you get better and then are handed off to Alcoholics Anonymous and outpatient therapy programs to facilitate recovery in an outside world, one that made Silver Hill look like the Magic Kingdom. Each night the addicts met in the basement, near the beauty parlor, to hear a speaker who had some time in recovery.

The speaker that night did not show up, so Chad, a restaurant owner and self-appointed mayor of Silver Hill ran the meeting, sharing his story of almost sinking his marriage and business into the ground because of drug use and drinking. A counselor who was sitting in a chair by the ping-pong table passively monitored us.

Zuza had called that night and I had talked with her on the pay phone.

I said, "I am beginning to feel comfortable in the 'looney bin.'"

Zuza had programmed "Looney Bin 1" and "Looney Bin 2" into her cell phone so she could speed-dial the Silver Hill pay phones.

"Comfortable," she shot back. "Comfortable. Jayson, if you don't come home soon, *I am going to lose it.*"

Lena had called Zuza earlier in the day demanding a *Times* laptop that was in my possession. The clear implication was that if Zuza did not comply, her job at the paper would be in jeopardy. This pissed me off because I wanted to make copies of my computer files. I also didn't want to put the twenty-three-year-old woman, who I happened to love, in a horrible situation. Getting the laptop into her hands meant interrupting my treatment at the hospital, something Lena had promised not to do. I did not know what was going on in the outside world, but this told me that, at the very least, Lena was under a lot of pressure. I focused on getting Zuza out of the jam.

At a house meeting the night before, I asked group members not to take messages for me on the pay phones because crafty reporters had been calling the hospital trying to figure out whether I was staying there. The next day, though, there was a message on the board in all-caps letters that read "JAYSON, PLEASE CALL ZUZA, IT'S AN EMERGENCY!!!!!"

My heart started beating at about three times its normal pace. I felt like I had done a gram of cocaine with a codeine chaser. Zuza explained that Lena had called. "She told me that I need to find your laptop, that they need it and that they will pay to have a messenger come over and get it."

"Why do they need it?" I asked.

"She wouldn't say. Jayson, this is ridiculous, she promised she would not put me in the middle of this. Jayson, what I am I supposed to do? What do you want me to do? She said I have to get it to them today. "

"Today, my ass. Don't call her back. Give me her phone number and let me take care of this."

I dialed Lena.

"Hey, it's Jayson. I am calling about the laptop. You called Zuza and I am just a little concerned because we all agreed that we are not going to put her in the middle of this. Can't they wait until I get out of the hospital?"

"Baby, baby, baby, listen, they are on my ass, and they want that computer now, and they mean now, they don't care about anything. They just want it, and they want it in the hands of a company employee. Now, listen, baby, everybody's concerned first and foremost about your health and well-being. Bill just came over to ask me if I had heard anything. He's concerned, Gerald's concerned, Jerry's concerned, everyone's concerned about you, baby."

I explained to Lena that, in case she had not noticed, I was in the mental institution that she helped me get into, and that she had been the one to promise not to get Zuza involved in the mess. We agreed that I would get the laptop to her, somehow, by the next day. Zuza and I arranged to have one of our mutual friends pick it up from the location where I had hidden it to take it to the office.

After recounting the absurdity of the conversation in my head, I turned my attention back to Michael, even though somebody else was speaking.

Michael had been having just as bad a day. His meds were driving him a little batty, he said, and he had not been able to concentrate, focus or think rapidly. He knew that the meds would help keep himself together, but Michael said they were making him stupid. I felt sorry for Michael, because I knew that if I ever had a mental illness that had to be treated by something that dulled my mind, I would go a-whole-sort-of-different-kind-of-crazy. I reminded myself again of what Dr. Marder had said earlier in the day about how I was fine and would be out of Silver Hill in a couple of days.

Jessica, a twenty-something from a Manhattan television company, was across the table, at the corner getting red-faced. I watched her as her face contorted and gathered red splotches as she forced down the snack that all the patients with eating disorders had to consume each night after dinner. I thought it was all about the difficult and painful process of attempting to consume food while struggling with a disease like that. Then, after the meeting, I realized it was more than that.

Jonathan had come down to the acute care unit with Kara, the person I became closest to in the locked unit. Kara arrived at the Main House early Tuesday evening with Jonathan, an older man with a drinking problem, who was condescending toward almost all the patients at the hospital other than Kara and me.

Kara and I really fell for each other one afternoon on the acute care unit's deck, which we were allowed out onto for fifteen-minute breaks. The deck was surrounded by an eighteen-foot fence, and on that particular afternoon, I had taken a spot on a bench beside it. I was reading Ralph Ellison's *Invisible Man* when Kara approached me in a sort of walking squat as if she were a cat hunting a mouse, staring at the cover of the book. She squinted her eyes, and then jumped to her knees, her stringy brown hair flopping up into the sky.

"I love that book," she said, still on her knees, her hands clasped as if she were praying before the statue of Ralph Ellison that had just been erected in Harlem.

"It's one of my favorites," she continued.

Kara was twenty-four, had grown up in New York City, graduated from a college in the Midwest and returned to Manhattan, where she worked for her family's company. We chatted like junior high prep school children about discovering T.S. Eliot, Ralph Waldo Emerson and Fyodor Dostoyevsky. It was clear that we had some similarities. Kara had been brought to the hospital the same night I arrived and we had both suffered sexual abuse at the hands of people who were close to us when we were children. In a meeting with everyone in the unit during one of the early nights when I used my standard "detox from life" line, Kara told the other patients that the goal of her stay was "pharmacological," essentially to make sure that she was on the proper medications, and she was looking forward to seeing the doctor on Monday.

* * *

Six days after arriving at Silver Hill, my doctors declared me fit for release. As I was waiting for them to finish up the paperwork for my release into the real world, and whatever was waiting for me out there, Kara and I sat on a bench on the front steps of the house discussing the sexual abuse that we experienced as children. She confessed to me that she was at Silver Hill for more than "pharmacological" issues.

"I never told you why I really came here, Jayson."

I sat on the green bench outside the Main House, giving her a smile.

Kara rolled up her sleeve and showed me the underside of her right arm. On the upper end of her forearm there were pink marks, slashes and scars, located too high to be a serious suicide attempt.

"I had been on medication and started getting depressed and started cutting myself. My sister got worried and called my parents who brought me here."

Kara's sister was her roommate, and they shared a family apartment in Manhattan. I had met her sister once on a visit to the hospital where the family had gathered to discuss Kara and her health. Her sister did not know that Kara, who did not use drugs, planned to bring up her sister's drug problem, and I had coached her on how to reply.

"So, I now know that I needed some help and I am going to get it. You have been so important to me. You have really helped me, and I hope you stay close when we get out of here."

We stared at each other for a moment, smiling.

"I hope we do too."

"Jayson, you've never told me how you ended up here. I mean, if you don't want to share, that is perfectly understandable. I am just curious."

I waited a moment and then began telling a story about a group therapy session that occurred several days earlier.

In one group session with psychiatric patients, we were asked to write about—and then share—a moment in our lives that had been traumatic. I chose to write about watching the World Trade Center collapse from across the Manhattan Bridge in Brooklyn, and later traipsing through the dust and finding what seemed to be pieces of a head. I told the story of how my drinking and cocaine use increased after that incident, spiraling into a freefall that took me to what I thought was rock bottom, and landing me in rehab.

I thought about it a little more than a year later, sitting on the Manhattan Bridge with Zuza, staring back at the former site of the Trade Center and thinking to myself that it's okay, there's no dust, it's finally okay that those buildings were not there. I talked about how in the last year I had learned to appreciate things like the smell of dew, the changing of the colors of leaves, the sounds of birds chirping.

When I finished, the group broke out into applause, and more than one person suggested that I should pick a career where I could write for a living. I could not help but laugh to myself. I told Kara my story.

"Four years ago, a year or so before I was supposed to finish college, I was hired as a reporter for *The New York Times*. I enjoyed the job at first but began to have some problems. The place is just not what everyone thinks it is," I said. "On top of that, I had long had a problem with drugs and alcohol. Cocaine was my drug of choice. Anyway, I went into rehab on January 7, 2002 and have not picked up a drink or used coke since."

"Last week," I told her, as I stared off at the white birches that surrounded the house, "I was caught plagiarizing some details in a front-page story from Texas about this soldier who was missing in action in Iraq, and I resigned. I had put everything into journalism, you know, hoping that I would be able to help people. But I just lost it. I don't know why, maybe I was tired. At first, I fought to keep my job, and lied to my editors about actually traveling." I paused.

"I began planning a suicide one night and then decided against it. No matter how bad things had gotten over the past few weeks, I still had my sobriety, and nothing could change how the last year of my life had gotten better in sobriety."

Kara's face was filled with sympathy. She stared into my eyes on the moments that I took them off the trees and glanced back at her.

I added that part of what kept me from killing myself was my friend Zuza, who was outside the bathroom where I was planning my death. It was too much to think about the reaction she would have to finding me, it was too much to think about giving up on all the dreams we had. I found a lot of comfort in her, and even though I had made these "mistakes" and continued to lie, I could stop it now, stop the lying.

"It sounds like you made the right choice, Jayson," she said, reaching out as if she were about to pat me on the shoulder.

Kara slowed her speech and adopted a measured tone. "Even if you can't work at a newspaper for a while, I am sure you are going to be able to somehow write and help people," Kara said sweetly.

I turned and looked at her, tears welling up in my eyes. I had yet to really consider much beyond my lies about the one story from Texas that I had been caught plagiarizing. Most of my time at Silver Hill, so far, had been dedicated to getting some rest, regaining my footing, and reminding myself of how I needed to be on guard against the bottle and white lines of cocaine that were awaiting me out in the real world.

"Soon, though," I said, acknowledging it to myself for the first time. "They will discover, much, much more."

Kara nodded her head, acknowledging that there was more to the story. We commenced what we dubbed a virtual hug, an embrace meant to show signs of affection without actually touching.

I was frightened that the doors would be unlocking in a matter of days, and just as this place was beginning to truly feel comfortable and safe, I needed to be out there in the real world to get on with my own life and also to support Zuza, who had been holding up the fort without me.

"Jayson, if you are wondering whether you are a good person, there is no doubt in my mind. Look what you have done for me," she said, noting our conversations about how to resolve struggles she was having with her relatives and the help I provided in fending off a male patient who had been bothering her. "No matter what happens, I know what's in your heart, and it's a heart of gold."

I did not share my fears, though, about the similarities between Michael and me. Instead, I changed the topic to what I had heard about *The Times* story about my misdeeds. It was in the works and was slated to run on the front page on Sunday.

"I don't care what they say," Kara said. "I am going to rip it out of the paper."

At this point, it became clear that Chad, the patient who was the self-appointed mayor of the Main House, had been listening to part of our conversation.

"They are going to write about you in *The Times*?" Chad asked with a puzzled tone in his voice.

"Yes," I said. "It's going to be on the front page, and I am not looking forward to it."

"Will it have your picture?" he asked.

I said yes.

"Cool," he said.

Not cool, I thought.

"What's your last name?" he asked as he continued to walk down the stairs toward the lawn.

"Jayson," I said. "Jayson Blair."

CHAPTER THREE
MOTHER'S DAY MASSACRE

I was sitting in a restaurant in Union Square that was one in a long row of buildings due east of the park, just above Fourteenth Street. Its neighbors included a Starbucks, a McDonald's, a New York University dorm, a deli, several high-end restaurants, various offices, and a Staples. Summer was just around the corner, and the park's open-air café facing the Barnes & Noble bookstore just north of the park appeared ready to begin serving guests.

It was a restaurant that I had eaten in many times before when I was one of the virtually thousands of unknown people who passed through this particular Manhattan block each day. There was something different about today, though. Perhaps it was that I was sipping coffee at a time of the morning when I would normally have been working, or perhaps it was the company I was keeping, or perhaps I sensed an intangible "something" that had forever changed in my life. While I had been in Silver Hill Hospital, Zuza and one of her roommates, Chris, had helped my parents move my belongings out of my old apartment in Park Slope and into one in Zuza's Brooklyn building. The two of them were keeping a constant watch on me. Zuza was so worried about my fragile state of mind that she would not allow me out of her eyesight, even at night, and I slept curled up in the fetal position on the edge of her bed.

Across from me in the booth at the twenty-three-hour-a-day restaurant called the Coffee Shop were Zuza and a former boyfriend of hers named Chandler. We had decided to go into the city for breakfast after Chandler showed up at the front door of the apartment unexpectedly that morning. I had awakened to the voice of one of Zuza's roommates, Alexandra. I rolled over and saw Alexandra's body peeking through the half-opened door of the bedroom. I was still in the fetal position but no longer facing the wall when the door opened. Alexandra was smiling.

"Chandler is here," she said. "Yeah, he showed up this morning . . ."

"What?!" Zuza said. "You've got to be kidding."

". . . and was at the front door when I walked out this morning. I don't know why, but he took a train from Minnesota or something, and just came by to visit."

"What?"

'Yeah, he is sitting out in the living room right now."

"Tell me you are kidding," Zuza said.

Alexandra smiled and then shut the door. I could tell she was taking some pleasure in the absurdity of the situation.

"God, this is going to be fun to explain," I said.

"What? What happened to your job, or why you are in my bed? He shows up at . . ."

She paused to look at the white alarm clock on her dresser.

". . . at eight o'clock in the morning, he doesn't get any explanations. I am going out to check to see if he is really there."

Zuza crawled out of bed, looked back at me with an expression of bewilderment, then made her way out of the bedroom. Indeed, Chandler was in her living room, and he decided to join us for my first trip into Manhattan since *The Times* had run a 14,000-word, four-page story about my deceptions on Mother's Day 2003.

A friend at *The Times* had tried to convince me to stay in the hospital at least until the May 11 story was published. The friend had also asked me, during a conversation over the Silver Hill pay phone, whether I had considered helping the team of *Times* reporters on the story sort out some of the more murky details.

"I think you should consider it, Jayson. I mean, otherwise, the ramp-up from you being a troubled guy who made some mistakes to Journalistic Antichrist is about to jump from zero to fifty come Sunday."

"Do you think they would be willing to wait for me to get out of the hospital?" I asked. "I really have to put my health first, and they are not ready to release me."

"I totally understand that, but as a gesture of professional courtesy to your colleagues who have been asked to dig into the life of someone they sat by for several years, you might want to consider helping them. At least make sure they have covered all the problem stories," he said.

"I don't know, I have not even thought about it yet," I replied. "I have sort of blocked out the details of everything apart from the Texas story. I am just trying to stabilize. Do you think that they would be willing to wait until I get out of the hospital?"

"No way. I don't know if you want to know the details, but they are getting hit over the head every day with new revelations, and they have put hardly anything into the paper. They were smacked over the head with stuff about the Jessica Lynch stories today, there were other things yesterday."

Shit, I thought. They had figured out the problems with the Lynch stories that I had totally blocked out. I was still in denial and knew I couldn't help them.

"Howell was on them to get something into tomorrow's paper, and they stood up and said it wasn't ready. They can't let you dictate the timing of the story, and I think that's right. Howell wants to get this over with—a big Sunday piece—they just want to carpet-bomb the whole damn thing, answer all the questions and make it go away."

"I know I shouldn't say this, but I have spent the last four years doing things on the *Times*'s schedule . . ."

"Look, man, they shouldn't let you dictate the timing of the story . . ."

"My health has to come first," I interrupted. "There is a lot more wrong than I realized, and I am just trying to get my head around that. If they can't wait, they are going to have to do it without me. I don't understand, though, how they can cover everything when I can't even remember everything. It's just going to make it a bigger story."

"I totally understand, Jayson, and you might be right about it becoming a bigger story, but you should think about one thing."

"What?"

"Don't leave the hospital until after the story runs."

I was exasperated.

"I am leaving whenever the doctors tell me to."

We ended the conversation with the atypical "I love yous" that men do not normally share among themselves, and agreed to disagree. As it turned out, I was right in that the story, which ran on Mother's Day, would backfire, raising more questions than it answered, but my friend had been right about one thing. I probably should not have left the hospital until the dust had settled.

The night the story appeared in *The Times* was the first time I dared to venture out of Zuza's apartment. I went with Alexandra and Zuza to Mike's International, a Caribbean restaurant not too far from their building, for a dinner of barbeque chicken sandwiches with sweet plantains on the side. On a cigarette break outside, I walked over to a nearby deli and looked at the front page of the Sunday *Times*. In the position of the second most important story of the day, an enormous headline read, "*Times* Reporter Who Resigned Leaves Long Trail of Deception."

I looked at the top of the story and noticed the names on the byline: Dan Barry, the former City Hall bureau chief and one of the best reporters and writers at *The Times*; David Barstow, a reporter from the investigative unit who was one of two key reporters on the Florida presidential election recount; Jonathan Glater, a smart young black reporter in the business section who had a law degree; Adam Liptak, a former *Times* Company corporate counsel who was now the chief national legal affairs reporter; and Jacques Steinberg, a former education reporter who had acknowledged me in his book *The Gatekeepers*. I did not have to look past the bylines to know that very few stones had been left unturned, but I took a breath and started reading the story.

"A staff reporter for *The New York Times* committed frequent acts of journalistic fraud while covering significant news events in recent months, an investigation by *Times* journalists has found. The widespread fabrication and plagiarism represent a profound betrayal of trust and a low point in the 152-year history of the newspaper."

I was grabbed by the first few words. I thought about other disgraced *Times* editors and correspondents like Walter Duranty. The statement put me in the same category as Duranty, whose dispatches for *The New York Times* denied the existence of a government-induced famine that starved millions of Ukrainian peasants. By some estimates more than 25,000 people a day had died, with children left to die of starvation after their parents were hauled from their homes and executed for the crime of owning property. (Months after my resignation from *The Times*, the Pulitzer Board examined Duranty's work, and while concluding it "falls seriously short," decided not to revoke the prize). An asterisk beside Duranty's name on *The Times*'s list of Pulitzer Prizes in their headquarters in Manhattan is followed by the words, "Other writers in *The Times* and elsewhere have discredited this coverage." Many Ukrainians have said that Duranty's reports kept the West from intervening.

The front-page story about me was in the same category as the *Times*'s coverage that led to espionage charges against Wen Ho Lee. *The Times* later apologized after a federal court judge threw out the charges against Lee, saying that the paper "fell short of our standards in our coverage of this story." I was now in the same category as Herbert Matthews, the reporter who described Fidel Castro in the *Times*'s pages as an "agrarian reformer" who supported democracy while ignoring evidence that he was torturing and murdering his own people.

I wondered where that put me in comparison to the *Times* coverage of the Holocaust, which was covered primarily on the back pages; an omission described in a November 14, 2001 article as "the staggering, staining failure of *The New York Times* to depict Hitler's methodical extermination of the Jews of Europe as a horror beyond all other horrors in World War II—a Nazi war within the war crying out of illumination." It took a lot of time for the meaning of those words to sink in.

By May 12, the day after the Mother's Day Massacre story, it had become clear that the *Times*'s efforts to "carpet-bomb" the story had failed. They had raised more questions than they answered about race, hiring at the newspaper, and affirmative action. There were quotes in the story like this one from a former editor: "I told him that he needed to find a different way to nourish himself than drinking Scotch, smoking cigarettes and buying Cheez Doodles from the vending machines."

We left the apartment that morning with Zuza's other roommate, Chris, who was headed to class at Hunter College, and jumped on the subway near Prospect Park. As the Q train came from underground and we began to cross the East River on the Manhattan Bridge, I noticed a large headline in bold letters blazed across an entire page of a copy of the *New York Post* that a man on the row of seats to the left of me was reading. "*Times* Trickster Falls Ill," the headline read above an enormous picture of me.

Zuza noticed the picture at the same time, and she just stared at me. I could feel butterflies scurrying through my stomach. Out of the corner of my eye, I could see Chris, his tall lanky body swinging from pole to pole, coming fast toward me.

"I just saw your picture in some Russian and Chinese newspapers," he said.

I pointed him toward the man with the *Post*.

"God," he said.

Chris walked over and took a read as the man stared at another page of the paper. "It says something about drug use and alcohol, something about rumors of you being in a mental institution," he said.

The butterflies turned to a heavy ball. I did not have to read the *Post* story speculating about the fact that I was staying in a mental institution to know that it focused on alcohol and drug addiction. I knew that the story would get picked up on television stations and the details would be reprinted across the country. My cell phone, which Zuza had been checking, had filled with messages over the last few days from friends, reporters, and reporters who had once been friends but now were focused on the story. The ones from journalists went something like this:

"Hey, Jayson, I hope you are doing well and I just wanted to call to check to see how you were doing," went a typical message. "This must be a really rough time, and I hope you, and your family, and Zuza are okay. I just want to send you my best. I was also wondering whether you would be willing to give an interview to . . ."

I got a text message from a Web producer at *The Times,* one of my closest colleagues at the newspaper. I saw her number and expected to see the words, "Are you okay?" Instead, it read, "Tell me why?" Management officials at *The Times* had said the paper would put my health first, and I interpreted that as a promise that while they would certainly correct the facts of my stories, they would not drag the details of my personal life into the pages of the newspaper.

After being retold some of the personal details that illustrated their piece, I could not help but believe it was meant to drive me over the edge. At the very least I felt it had been written and edited with no regard to the harm it might cause the one person who had the most to lose in the situation. I wanted to be in the weekend Page One meeting where the editor of the story presented it to the senior editors of the paper. A similar question, of course, could and would be asked of me: *What were you possibly thinking, not showing up for your job, damaging the reputation of* The Times, *harming your family, friends and others who care about you?*

Still, at the same moment, I wanted to hear them talking about the details, like my Scotch drinking and penchant for fast food, and make the case for why it was really relevant, something the readers needed to know about me in order to correct the record. They wrote about my medical leaves of absence and my seeking help from an employee assistance counselor, as if writing about my struggle with alcohol and drugs somehow corrected the record.

Though I knew my anger was irrational, I felt a white-hot rage come over me for the first time. I could not control my anger; my eyes closed, shuttering. I wanted to know how they could do this to someone they said they cared about. I also knew that they wondered how I could do what I did to them. I knew they must have been just as angry.

My actions had tarnished the one thing that mattered to so many of them: the pride and respect they got for having their name on a *Times* business card and being able to mention at parties that they worked at the glorious *New York Times*. Even as the angry thoughts flashed through my mind, I knew the feelings ran much deeper for them. It was about the trust they had put in me, and the trust that readers had put in the institution.

By the time I got to the restaurant, I had calmed down enough to nibble on my spinach-and-feta-cheese omelet. Zuza handed me a magazine, and as I thumbed through it, I noticed an article about Stephen Glass, a writer who had been caught several years before fabricating stories for *The New Republic*.

* * *

Over the next several days, I went to therapy, met with psychiatrists and attended the Alcoholics Anonymous meetings I had gotten out of the habit of visiting.

Almost every step of the way Zuza was by my side, watching over me, comforting me and serving as a sort of walking suicide-prevention. *The Times* said they had given her two weeks off from work to assist me, and also because they were concerned that many people in the newsroom would be hostile toward her when she returned because of her close relationship with me. She had every intention of returning to work.

That was until Tuesday morning. We had been up late the night before moving my belongings from her apartment to mine and working on a letter in response to a query from a literary agent. Zuza was awakened by her ringing cell phone.

"Hey, Chris," she said. "I am still asleep . . . What? You're kidding!?"

As she talked I checked my messages and listened to one from a mutual friend at *The Times*. "I hope you and Zuza are okay. I had called this number earlier and thought it was disconnected. I am just glad you have not gone underground, and I just love you guys. I hope you are okay."

Zuza hung up the telephone and turned and looked at me. One of Zuza's roommates whispered in my ear what she was told over the phone.

"There is something about you in the *Daily News*," I said.

I jumped out of bed.

"Let me go check it," I said.

I grabbed her cell phone, put on my white slacks that were balled up in the corner of the room, and ran down the stairs and out of the apartment building. I jogged down the tree-lined street to the deli that was on the corner. I picked up the *Daily News* and the *Post*, fumbling for change in my pockets as I flipped through the pages of each paper. After I paid, I headed onto the street, still flipping. Nothing. Nothing. Nothing. I went through the *News* again. This time the headline on the second page jumped out at me.

"BAD NEWS BLAIR SAGA AT TIMES," the headline screamed.

The article was about a meeting planned for that day where Arthur Sulzberger Jr., the *Times*'s publisher, and Howell Raines, the executive editor, were going to address angry staff members at the Loews Theater in Manhattan. I scanned the story for a mention of Zuza's name, not wanting to absorb and internalize any of the bad things that were written about me. I couldn't help but notice a reference to a memorandum that had been written in April 2003 by Jonathan Landman, the metro editor at *The Times* and my one-time supervisor.

I had long suspected that Landman had opposed me being hired and had been forced to accept it by others who were above him in the chain of command. This suspicion had long clouded our relationship and probably contributed to his unwillingness to help me transfer after I had begun recovering from some personal troubles. I believed that Landman, who smiled in my face, was working overtime to undermine me in the background.

Landman had—unbeknownst to me—sent a message to two newsroom administrators in April 2002 that said, "We have to stop Jayson from writing for *The Times* right now." I never knew about the message, but did remember receiving a tersely-worded letter around that same time from Nancy Sharkey, the assistant to the managing editor for staff development, who was one of my biggest advocates and constructive critics. I remember thinking that the letter must have been written by someone else, and that Nancy's name had been put on it so I would take it better.

They left me to guess, when they could have been more open. The letter admonished me for the one correction I had picked up in the last few months and for not showing up at a personal lunch appointment with Daryl Alexander, an assistant metro editor. I suspected it was another attempt by Landman to take a swipe at Gerald Boyd, the senior black editor at the paper, who he assumed incorrectly was my protector.

I read a quote that followed from Sulzberger, who was asked whether Howell and his top deputy, Boyd, should resign because of what had now been dubbed the Jayson Blair Scandal. "The person who did this is Jayson Blair," he said in a series of comments in which he demanded that people not demonize the company's executives.

It's a little more complicated than that, Arthur, I thought to myself. I felt dejected, hurt, and then seething with anger. Still, more pressing matters were at hand. The article continued.

> Meanwhile, staffers buzzed about whether Blair's relationship with a woman who is a friend of Raines' wife helped win him favored treatment. Sources said the woman, Zuza Glowacka, has worked in *The Times*' photo department. *The Times* reported Sunday that Blair, when confronted with a charge of plagiarizing a story about a Texas family, was able to describe their house in detail, possibly because he had seen the paper's computerized photo archives. Glowacka, 23, a Polish emigre who could not be reached yesterday, is said to be a friend of Raines' Polish-born wife, Krystyna Stachowiak, whom the editor married in March. Stachowiak, a former journalist who later worked in public relations, and Glowacka's mother . . . were among three people who set up "Poland on the Front Page, 1979-1989," a media exhibit in Warsaw last fall. Raines said through a spokeswoman last night that he never socialized with Blair.

As I walked down the long yellowing hallway to Zuza's apartment door, her telephone began ringing. I picked up the line and it was her mother, who had treated me with care and kindness, like an away-from-home mother. Zuza's mom had left for Poland just before the scandal had erupted, and we had not heard from her in the weeks immediately afterward. This morning she was in no mood for pleasantries. She was in a panic.

"Hello," I said.

"Where's Zuza?"

"Uh, I am just outside her door, I borrowed her phone. Let me get her for you."

We both went silent.

While Zuza was on the telephone for the next thirty minutes, I started checking some of my messages. There was one from Lena.

"Hi, baby, it's Lena. Now listen to me. You are going to need to get a lawyer. In a couple of hours you are going to get a call from Ben Weiser, who is writing a story about how the United States Attorney is considering pressing charges against you. Now, baby, I understand this is not an easy time for you. Just remember, God don't make junk. Okay? Call me if you need anything. Don't freak out. You just need a good lawyer who can handle everything. Okay? Call me if you need anything. All right?"

The next message was from Weiser, the federal courts reporter for *The Times,* and a man I was very fond of. "Hi, Jayson. It's Ben Weiser. I hope you are doing well, and I am sorry to call you about this, but the federal prosecutors are examining whether to press fraud charges against you and I have been asked to write . . ."

How could this day get worse? I thought to myself.

As Zuza continued to talk with her mother, I huddled up at the desk in Chris's room and began making a list of people who could help me find an attorney, a group that was dwindling by the day. I called everyone from a family friend to Johnnie Cochran, and asked Lena to pass the message on to Ben that I would not be able to comment until I had legal counsel. By the end of the night, though, I became concerned by persistent rumors that the *News* was doing other stories on Zuza.

I called the *Daily News* switchboard and asked for the newsroom.

"Hey, do you know that guy from *The Times,* Jayson Blair?" I said to the night editor who picked up the phone a little before midnight.

"Yeah," the editor said.

"I am him."

"Really, can we ask you a couple of questions?"

"No," I said. "But I might have a statement. Does your story for tomorrow mention Zuza Glowacka?"

"I don't know, let me switch you to rewrite."

The editor transferred me to the rewrite man, a news reporter who I had worked with in the field on other stories in the past. I knew it was standard practice not to read passages from stories to subjects prior to publication, but I also knew that the fundamental rule of journalism—above fairness, objectivity, truth-telling and all the evangelistic-sounding stuff— was that all the rules could be bent for a scoop. I was the scoop, and I had them. The rewrite man read me the passages in the article about Zuza, and my heart sank when I heard the quote from Catherine Mathis, the vice president for corporate communications at *The Times.*

"She is currently not working at *The Times,*" Catherine said.

I was furious. I knew the way the public relations game was played.

I called back the *Daily News* and began reading a statement I had scrawled onto the back of a piece of computer paper in the event that she was mentioned in the *Daily News* article. It was the first remark I had made on the incident, other than a private letter of apology that I had sent to Howell and Gerald hours before checking into Silver Hill.

"I remain truly sorry for my lapses in journalistic integrity," I said. "I continue to struggle with recurring issues that have caused me great pain. I want to make clear that no *Times* employee assisted me in my deceptions."

The next morning, I woke up at about five in the morning in a full panic. I jumped out of bed and headed out of the building to the corner deli. I found the article in the *Daily News* that quoted Catherine saying that Zuza no longer worked at *The Times* and my statement that no one had helped me in my deceptions.

I knew my lawyer, whoever he or she might be, would not be pleased with me admitting to the deceptions in print, but I thought it was the only way to get Zuza off the hook. I thought that because I had not said anything so far, after all the negative things that had been said about me, the papers would take seriously my exoneration of Zuza and other *Times* colleagues. It was a risk I was willing to take, even if it meant that it would help prosecutors.

The *Post* story, which focused on the Loews Theater meeting, read, "Sources said no one at the meeting mentioned the fate of photo desk staffer Zuza Glowacka, who had not been seen at the paper since Blair was fired. She is Blair's gal pal and her mother is a friend of Raines' wife."

"I was Molested as a Kid, Scoundrel Scribe Wrote," another headline read. It was a reference to an article I had written about sexual abuse in college.

I could not believe the *Post* was dragging the fact that I had been sexually abused as a child out into the open and then using it to beat me over the head. It was like being raped in public. Below the article was another one on the potential fraud charges being considered by the United States Attorney.

By Friday, Zuza had decided to resign from *The Times,* and the union had agreed to release a statement saying that she was on an indefinite leave of absence. Lena had come up with the idea to counter suggestions that would be made that Zuza had resigned under pressure. She also received assurances from the paper's management that despite Catherine's suggestions, Zuza had never been and was not under any type of investigation. Lena also called Polish newspapers and others with this information on Zuza's behalf and bent over backwards to help her.

"She doesn't want to go back to that newsroom," Lena said. "I mean, I have been here for more than twenty years, and as a black woman and all, I can't tell you how hard this has been. I can only imagine how hard it would be for a twenty-three-year-old girl. Baby, I know God's on your side because you have a great woman standing by you right now. Hell, I would have left your ass a long before this ever happened."

Lena started laughing.

In the Loews meeting, Howell said that as a white southerner from Alabama he had been guilted into giving me too many chances. Several days before, Howell had written a memo that suggested that he was unaware of my problems with corrections. This told me that he was beginning to cave under the pressure of those who viewed me purely by the tone of my skin, as a straight-out affirmative action hire.

"For the past week, I have been reviewing information from our files on Jayson Blair's career, and I have absorbed most of that information, along with an awareness that much of it remained in our records rather than in the foreground of our editing process."

I wondered how could Howell be both unaware that I had problems with drugs, alcohol and corrections, and at the same time have given me too many chances? They were mutually exclusive propositions.

The next morning, Zuza and I were sitting in the living room when her cell phone began ringing. The Caller ID showed that the call was coming from Ed Keating, a former *Times* photographer who had been forced to resign in January after being accused of staging a photograph. Ed was among the most talented photographers at *The Times*, but he was troubled, having been suspended twice for infractions that had nothing to do with his work. I had been there for Ed during the latest controversy over the Lackawanna pictures, where competing photographers accused him of staging a photograph of a young boy pointing a toy gun toward a sign in Arabic.

Ed left a message, begging and pleading that we call him back.

"Zuza. I don't know if you know where Jayson is or what's going on, but I have tried your cell phone and his cell phone dozens of times. You guys helped me out when I needed you, and I just need to know if you guys are okay. I just want to make sure everything is fine, and I think we should get together. I just want to look you guys in the face and make sure you're okay. Come on. Call me back. Come on. Come on . . ."

"Jayson, I think we should call him back," Zuza said after listening to his message. "Only if you are up for it," she added.

I thought about it for a moment. Ed had helped me before, when I was coming off cocaine and booze.

"Okay, I will call him back."

She handed me the telephone. I looked up his number on speed dial. Within minutes, after discussing getting together at some point to attend an A.A. meeting, we agreed to meet at the Kinko's on Court Street in downtown Brooklyn, where Zuza was going to type up and fax in her resignation letter. Lena had also suggested that she write a personal letter to Howell thanking him for the chance to work at *The Times*.

We took a cab over to the Kinko's, even though we were both running low on money, and began working on the letters. Ed may have been there to provide moral support, but it quickly became clear that he had been asked by *Newsweek* to obtain pictures of us for its upcoming cover story. In the fog, we agreed to have our pictures taken, neither of us thinking out the consequences of our decision.

I checked my e-mail and found some messages from friends, former colleagues and reporters. One message was from Seth Mnookin, a *Newsweek* media reporter I had met through David Carr. Seth had written a long piece for Salon.com about a heroin addiction he kicked and its impact on his relationship with his mother. David had shown me the piece when he and I first met. As a new person to sobriety, I found what Seth had to say helpful. Though the media storm was raging around me, I was comforted that some old friends were reaching out to me and were concerned about my welfare. They had good reason to worry.

CHAPTER FOUR
TOXIC WASTE

When you spend a week reading newspaper articles that describe in detail how your former college classmates do not believe that you were sexually abused as a child; play up false allegations that your best friend and romantic interest is assisting you in lying; say that federal prosecutors are trying to drum up a fraud case against you to win points with your former employer; report that the man who most contributed to your meltdown—outside of yourself—has come up with a crafty way to blame his bosses, who really had nothing to do with it one way or the other; use your life as lesson number one for why whites pay the price for being too compassionate to minorities; note that your college has taken your name off their website; print that people believe you have been drinking and using drugs, even though you have been clean and sober for more than a year, and generally paint you as the poster child for affirmative action gone wrong, it tends to piss a man off.

When reporters are camped outside your parents' house hundreds of miles away; when your best friend's relatives are getting harassed by television camera crews; when the hunter becomes the hunted, it's easy to lose your bearings. When your former employer is attempting to deflect any responsibility for your downfall by pointing out that you were enrolled in a confidential company employee assistance program, and implies in a 14,000-word story that your problems stemmed from drug and alcohol abuse without acknowledging that you emerged clean and sober, guilt for your actions can give way to a tidal wave of anger.

I know, from experience.

Eighteen days after resigning and eleven days after getting out of the mental hospital, I foolishly gave an interview to *The New York Observer*, a weekly newspaper that caters to the city's elite. After giving the interview, I received a call from Marilyn White, the counselor who had begun seeing me when I got clean in 2002 and had sheltered me in the days after my resignation and recommended Silver Hill. I always had a warm spot in my heart for Marilyn. She was a fighter, and an example of someone who had turned a negative in her life around and into something very positive. She was proof that F. Scott Fitzgerald was wrong when he said that there are no second acts in American life. When she was drinking, Marilyn slept in Union Square Park, and now she had an office overlooking it.

I was thankful that Pat had put me in Marilyn's hands. Marilyn believed that proper care of a recovering addict involved the mental, spiritual and the physical. Her organization, the Realization Center, also prided itself on being open to all sorts of people, and everyone from Wall Street executives and gay fashion designers to mailmen and subway track workers could be found in group meetings. There we all were. It did not matter whether we worked at *The New York Times,* Salomon Smith Barney, or the Department of Sanitation—we were all addicts, on an equal plane, trying to get ahold of ourselves, trying to fight our addictions.

Above all else, I respected Marilyn. Marilyn took pains to understand the perspective that her patients were coming from and to give them the straight truth, regardless of their potential reaction to it. I did not know it, but I was due a dose of the straight truth, whether I liked it or not.

When I arrived at the Realization Center Marilyn ushered me into her office with a wave of her hand and said that she wanted to have another counselor join us for the meeting. Planted on her big brown leather couch, I clung to the soft gray teddy bear she kept located there.

"Jayson, we are a little concerned about your behavior," Marilyn started in a soft and sympathetic tone.

The other counselor, Beverly, sat silently next to her, nodding.

"We feel that you are still very angry and were frankly alarmed by some of the comments that you made in this interview," Marilyn said, holding up a salmon-colored copy of *The New York Observer.*

She turned to Beverly.

"Did I show you this?"

"Uh-huh," Beverly said, nodding at me.

"I know, I know," I said, looking out the window. "It was like I was having a therapy session in public."

"Yes," Marilyn said. "You need to worry about healing now and getting better, and you can save whatever it is you want to say for later. Save it for your book. What you are doing right now is continuing to self-destruct, and you are going to take other people with you. For example, you know

Zuza is probably going to distance herself from you now, right? If not for herself, for her family."

"I sort of realized that," I said. "She's writing a piece that does just that for *Newsweek*."

"I brought Beverly in because she might be able to address some of the issues of race."

After fifteen minutes of discussing some of my anger and resentments and feelings of abandonment, Marilyn surprised me with what followed. "We want you to go back to the hospital for at least thirty days. You need to be under doctor's supervision for at least a month."

At first I agreed to return to the hospital, and then I reversed myself, primarily because of the costs of hospitalization, deciding to stay in the city and find some counseling. I had an appointment the following week with the Realization Center's psychiatrist, Dr. Alexander Kolevzon, a laid-back practitioner who worked part-time at the Realization Center and full-time at Mount Sinai Medical Center's Upper West Side campus.

To me, the pressures of the job explained most of it. After all, I was not the first to lose his or her mind at *The New York Times*. Almost every department had its story.

News researchers would regale the curious with the story of Carol Threllfall, a wide-eyed, red-headed, freckled twenty-seven-year-old research librarian, who killed herself after a year of working at *The Times* in 1969, on the same day that her boss couriered a letter of reprimand to her house. Foreign correspondents would tell you about Jim Markham, the forty-six-year-old Paris bureau chief, who put a gun to his head and pulled the trigger after being ordered back to New York to become a deputy foreign editor. Old metro desk hands told the story of the black woman reporter who committed suicide soon after quitting the paper and, before my departure, the deaths of three colleagues could be attributed, at least in part, to the pressures they faced at *The Times*.

Monte Williams, a forty-year-old black reporter, died while on a medical leave in 2002 as she struggled with mental illness that I believe was made worse by callous treatment she received from some metro desk editors. Agis Salpukas, a sixty-year-old business reporter whose career had been sidelined and who suffered from depression, was found floating in the Hudson River in 2000 after jumping off the George Washington Bridge. Allen Myerson, a forty-seven-year-old business editor whose career had also been knocked off track and who faced marital and other family problems, scribbled out a note at his desk early one morning in 2002, walked to the roof of the Times Building and plunged to his death on top of the garage next door.

Although I am alive by the skin of my teeth, I am destined to become another one of them, a promising young reporter who came to *The Times* with energy and talent, who somehow lost it, and lost everything.

I had not planned to talk with reporters after resigning, but got caught up in the machine anyway. I was smart enough to know that nothing good would come out of it, that my words would get twisted just as I had twisted so many other people's words for years as a *Times* reporter.

To me, the pressures of the job, the loss, the quick severing of friendships and the strange media coverage explained most of it. The rumors were persistent and rampant. People I had met only briefly were profiting off of my demise by selling pictures and writing stories about me for magazines and websites. As the rumors about why I had supposedly been protected began to show cracks in their foundations, others replaced them quickly. The latest, from a website called *Media Review,* claimed that Howell had protected me because I was gay.

In the *Observer* interview, I had unfairly attacked just about every member of *The New York Times* masthead, made disparaging comments about Howell and Gerald in a foolish attempt to distance them from me while their jobs were in jeopardy, and even laughed at some of the fabrications I had made in several articles about Jessica Lynch, the young blonde prisoner of war who had become a military war hero and America's sweetheart. Only reading the words in print showed me how much I had set myself up to be hated. In reality, I was far from the person who was reflected on the pages of *The Observer*.

They had illustrated the article with a drawing that was a clear allusion to Ralph Ellison's *Invisible Man*. In many respects, it was not off the mark, at least when it came to media perception. In the eyes of the media, I had become a modern-day version of the angry, nameless protagonist in the novel; Howell had become a symbol for the well-meaning white headmaster; and Gerald had become the black teacher who had cut his pupil loose once it began to cost him. There was truth in some of the descriptions, though they were exaggerated.

To say that I wish I could alter what I said in the *Observer* interview is a bit of an understatement. If I had it to do again, I would never have conducted it. My comments were ruthless and unfair, my tone callous and flippant. I had walked into the interview calmly and somewhat deadened;

prepared, I felt, to answer the questions that the reporter in the room with me asked with as much candor as possible. The disastrous interview was an example of me overestimating myself and my ability to heal. I had not even acknowledged how much I was wounded.

The hurt, the anger, and the frustration all came pouring out in the interview, and the words that took me off the carefully prepared script were all about affirmative action. One quote among the mounds of unintended rang true. It was a quote about Stephen Glass, the former *New Republic* writer, whose book *The Fabulist* had just been published.

"I don't understand why I am a bumbling affirmative-action hire when Stephen Glass is this brilliant whiz kid, when from my perspective—and I know I shouldn't be saying this—I fooled some of the most brilliant people in journalism," I said when the *Observer* reporter asked me about affirmative action. "He is *soooo* brilliant, and yet somehow I'm an affirmative-action hire."

A broken clock is right at least twice a day, and this was about the only thing I was on the mark with in my interview with *The Observer*.

Soon after the comments, a black colleague wrote a short e-mail that summed up the feelings of some of those caught in the middle.

"I don't have any real resentment towards you, actually, though some would just say I'm unusually forgiving," the colleague wrote. "I suppose we could be angry at you for not knowing better, for not anticipating that this whole affair would turn into one grand opportunity for the right (and the middle, and some of the left as well) to happily skewer affirmative action. And to some degree that's all true.

"But it is also true that we have all been equally surprised at how much the debate has devolved on the issue of race," the colleague continued. "We have all asked ourselves the same question that came out in your *Observer* interview, 'Why is this suddenly about affirmative action when Stephen Glass was not?'"

Affirmative action had been a central element in each of the three black journalistic pariahs, myself included, that had come up over the past two decades. Glass received a book contract with a major New York publishing house. Mike Barnicle, a white columnist who plagiarized and fabricated at *The Boston Globe*, started writing a column for the New York *Daily News*, and Ruth Shalit, who plagiarized at the *New Republic*, moved to the world of advertising. Shalit and Glass were viewed as wayward young reporters who had lost their moorings in the race to stardom, and Barnicle was given somewhat of a pass for whatever reasons.

Patricia Smith, a black *Globe* columnist, was caught fabricating characters just before Barnicle was forced out at the paper. She left journalism altogether. Journalists at the time claimed that she was a victim of the pressure of being a black woman in the business and protected for years, even though the *Globe* knew she had problems, because of the color of her skin. Janet Cooke, the black reporter at *The Washington Post* who fabricated an eight-year-old heroin addict for a story that won the Pulitzer Prize, was also labeled a victim of the pressure associated with being a black woman in journalism. She left the business and spent fifteen years in silence.

It was hard to know the truth of these varied situations that I was not involved in, but it was hard, as a black man living in white America, not to make comparisons. If I had a point, though, it was clearly being obscured by my hate-filled, misdirected comments.

My days after the *Observer* interview were filled with dark images, and wanderings into an expansive field of impulsive behaviors that could not be explained by anything bordering on rational thought.

* * *

In my mind, the only reason I had an appointment at the Realization Center late that evening was because Dr. Marder at Silver Hill had prescribed Paxil as an anti-depressant and Neurontin as a mood stabilizer to be taken for several months after my resignation.

I had viewed the sadness and the sense of loss that I was going through as circumstantial, something driven by the events that had been unfolding since my resignation. I was supposed to stay on the pills for a few months until the media coverage subsided and I had stabilized. I knew, though, that to some extent, the doctors were not operating with all the information that was necessary to make the most accurate diagnosis. I knew that they were unaware of my suspicions about manic depression, the similarities I saw between myself and the patients at Silver Hill during my week-long stay. They did not know about my behavior in the months before my resignation.

I don't know why so much came out at that particular moment, but when I told Dr. Kolevzon about the grueling side effects of the medications, how badly I was feeling, and several restless nights spent up at the local copy center and friends' homes, the young psychiatrist who normally practiced at Mount Sinai Medical Center started asking me a seemingly routine set of questions.

Have you been getting too few hours of sleep? Have you been more talkative than usual? Have you been talking faster than usual? Has anyone told you to slow down or that they couldn't make sense of what you are saying? Have you felt a pressure to talk constantly? Have you been more energetic than usual? Were other people saying that they were having difficulty keeping up with you? Do you find that you work better at nights? Have you been involved in more activities than usual, or undertaken more projects? Have your thoughts been going so quickly that you have difficulty keeping track of them? Have you been more physically restless than usual? More sexually active? Have you been spending more money than you had? Acting impulsively? Have you felt more irritable or angry than usual? Have you felt as though you had special talents or powers? Have you had any visions or heard sounds or voices that other people probably hadn't seen or heard? Have you experienced any strange sensations in your body? Have you ever had any of those symptoms earlier in your life?

I said yes to nearly every one of the above, and yes again to another series of questions about depression. "We need to have you screened for Bipolar II," he said, reassuring me that many people with this illness, also known as manic-depression, have above-average functional lives with the appropriate awareness and treatment.

Diagnostic and Statistical Manual of Mental Disorders, the Bible of psychology and psychiatry, groups mental disorders into four distinct groups: major categories; personality disorders and mental retardation; medical conditions; and psychosocial and environmental problems.

Manic depression, or bipolar disorder, is considered a major mental illness and is classified with other clinical disorders, including schizophrenia, depression and disassociative identity disorder. The basic way a psychiatrist diagnoses the disorder is first determining that a patient has experienced "a distinct period of abnormally and persistently elevated, expansive or irritable mood, lasting at least one week."

I scored one out of one on that first screen.

Next, the psychiatrist must find that during the period of mood disturbance, at least three of the following have persisted: inflated self-esteem or grandiosity; decreased need for sleep; more talkative than usual; flight of ideas and thoughts that are racing; attention too easily drawn to unimportant or irrelevant external stimuli; increase in agitation or sexual, school or work goal-directed activity; and excessive involvement in pleasurable activities that have a high potential for painful consequences like buying sprees, sexual indiscretions or foolish business investments.

I scored a perfect ten on that screen; I had never done so well on a test in my life.

CHAPTER FIVE
REBUILDING

*L*uza was finally able to escape New York in the beginning of June, only days after my new diagnosis and before I had a chance to get to understand or explain it.

I thought about the broadsides that had been made against her as I walked down the hallway of her apartment to the kitchen where I opened the refrigerator, pulled a glass out of the cabinet, and poured myself some cranberry juice. My daily regimen of pills began with a mood stabilizer and an anti-depressant. I walked over to the computer on the glass desk I had turned into an office and tapped the space bar.

A long set of new messages was at the top of the screen. I clicked the first one open. It was a message from a producer at CNN who had been among the dozens of members of the media who had been writing me since my resignation. I swallowed my first pill, and then the second, chasing them with the juice.

> Jayson,
> Assume you heard the news by now about Raines and Boyd.
> Any chance you'd consider coming on our show sooner given this breaking news, even tonight?

I flipped to my web browser and opened the CNN site.
"Oh, my God," I whispered as I stared at the headline.
"Top *New York Times* editors quit."
I stared at the pictures of Howell and Gerald in shock. I had never thought it would come to their resignations. At newspapers across the country, editors are routinely forced out of their positions, but it was a rarity at *The New York Times* to see a mid-level manager pushed aside, much less the top two editors cast out. All of a sudden, the two men who had pushed

The Times to grab onto every scandal with sharp teeth—Enron, WorldCom, the intelligence failures before the September 11 attacks—were being consumed themselves by a scandal that others in the media would not let die.

Not for a minute did anyone believe that Howell and Gerald stepped down voluntarily from their positions. Howell idolized Coach Bear Bryant of the University of Alabama football team, a man who did not quit. Gerald had worked too hard, for too many years, against too many forces to simply walk away. What had begun a month before as an interrogation in a conference room inside the Times Building had exploded into something much bigger, something that eventually consumed the leadership of the most powerful newspaper in the country.

From the moment I resigned, there were persistent rumors that *The Times* was examining the work of other correspondents and when their Mother's Day story ran, they listed an e-mail address where people could send comments about previous stories of mine that they thought might be fraudulent. One tip sent to the e-mail address led to the resignation of Rick Bragg, a Pulitzer-winning correspondent who was friends with Howell.

In the poisonous atmosphere that had become *The Times* after my resignation, Rick had been accused of using a freelance writer to do almost all of the firsthand reporting on a 2002 story about Florida oystermen. The complaint prompted an editor's note that said credit should have been shared with the freelance writer. The only problem was that Rick said what many correspondents did not want to be known by the public: that *The Times* often used freelance writers to do the bulk of the reporting for stories, from Beijing to Brooklyn, without giving them credit. They are the hidden army behind most *Times* stories.

Part of the reason that they remained hidden was a desire among management, made clear in memorandums, that they wanted readers to be left with the impression that *Times* reporters were omnipresent. The lack of credit given writers sometimes made stories seem absurd, with firsthand observations from a potpourri of cities appearing under one byline and dateline. What made Rick's situation different, they said, was that he had written about a situation where he could have made the trip on his own and did not require a freelance writer's assistance because of time considerations.

Howell's decision to suspend Rick set off a series of complaints from freelance writers across the globe who had not received credit in similar situations with other reporters. Howell's failure to defend correspondents in the wake of those allegations led to even more uproar and loud calls for some immediate and decisive action to be taken. *The Wall Street Journal* also began its own examination of *The Times* and its journalistic practices under Howell, and that only increased the drumbeats of change.

I sat at my computer for what felt like an eternity, staring at the pictures of Howell and Gerald. Regardless of how I felt about them, I knew that they were hardly responsible for my actions. I realized that the scandal had become much bigger than me. To paraphrase the words of a former colleague, I was no more responsible for their resignations than Gavrilo Princip, the man who killed Archduke Franz Ferdinand in Sarajevo, was responsible for starting World War I. I knew the groundwork for their resignations had been set long before I began fabricating stories, but it was hard, as the catalyst, not to take responsibility for the entire situation.

The phone rang. It was Daryl Khan on the other line.

"Jayson, hey, how are you doing?"

"I am fine. I just . . ." I couldn't finish my sentence.

"I want to come over. I want to check on you and see how you are doing."

I got up and started pacing. "I'm okay, I'm okay. I . . . I just need to sit down. I just need to digest this. This is crazy, I can't believe it. Why?"

Daryl tried to convince me to tell my side, that I was not as angry and hateful as I came across in the *New York Observer* interview. By the end of the day, I had done interviews offering apologies to Howell and Gerald on WCBS-TV and in *Newsday*.

"I owe them one million apologies," I told Daryl as we ate in an organic food café on Spring Street in SoHo.

Indeed, I do.

Howell's abrupt announcement of his resignation, in front of a small group gathered in the newsroom, lasting only a few minutes, sent my body overflowing with sorrow.

> As I'm standing here before you for the last time, I want to thank you for the honor and privilege of being a member of the best journalistic community in the world. It's been a tumultuous 20 months, but we have produced some memorable newspapers. I will always be grateful to Arthur for giving me this opportunity and to you for contributing your hearts and talents to this effort.

I am proud of what we accomplished so far and I'm confident you will achieve the goals mapped out by the publisher. *The Times* is about continuity. In that spirit, the publisher has asked that Joe Lelyveld come back on an interim basis. I set out many years ago to live a life devoted to literature and the arts, and I return to that calling with a wider set of interests in writing, the study of history, in painting and photography.

After 25 years at *The Times,* I look forward to a different kind of adventure. I am blessed to be embarking on this journey with a beloved partner. Krystyna and I wish for you the same blessing that we share today: that you find lives you love and get to live them with the love of your life. And remember, when a big story breaks out, go like hell.

For me, the resignations of Howell and Gerald marked the beginning of a sorrowful and deep examination of my own actions, an attempt to put them in a broader context that would provide, at the very least, my own enlightenment, and perhaps a chance to have something good come out of what seemed to be an entirely horrible situation. I had always been a bundle of seemingly paradoxical contradictions—one moment giving twenty dollars to a homeless man and the next day not being there for a friend. I was a vegetarian who smoked a pack of Camel Lights a day and had a cocaine addiction. During my last few months at *The Times,* I was full of anger, pain and self-destructive forces at a moment when almost everything seemed perfect.

And, so began a quest of looking back—my search for answers.

CHAPTER SIX
YOUNG AND HAUNTED

Columbia, Maryland bore little resemblance to the real world. It was founded in 1967 by James W. Rouse, a Maryland developer, who wanted to take 14,000 acres of farmland midway between Baltimore and Washington and turn it into a utopia. Rouse's image seemed to be inspired, in part, by Martin Luther King's "I Have a Dream" speech.

In his speech, King said, "One day this nation will rise up and live out the true meaning of its creed: 'We hold these truths to be self-evident; that all men are created equal.' I have a dream that one day on the red hills of Georgia the sons of former slaves and the sons of former slave-owners will be able to sit down together at a table of brotherhood. I have a dream that one day even the state of Mississippi, a desert state sweltering with the heat of injustice and oppression, will be transformed into an oasis of freedom and justice."

It wasn't in the red hills of Georgia or the state of Alabama, but Rouse did his best to re-create that dream in central Maryland. The streets and man-made lakes were named after the Indians and the trees they replaced. The most defining characteristic of Rouse's "New Town" was its socio-economic mixture of race, religion and class. Instead of using suburbs as a way to separate people by their race and economic status, Rouse viewed them as a way to bring people together.

In addition to opening the community to people of all races, Rouse built some of the most expensive homes in locations that forced their residents to interact with others in Columbia's village centers. Some of the lowest-income housing was built next to expansive fields, forests, lakes and, in one case, along a golf course. There were interfaith centers located in the village centers, where synagogues and churches shared worship space and resources.

In 1967, the year the first home was sold, his idea was by no means popular within the surrounding rural community. Those of us who were children of Columbia were isolated from the realities of the world around us. Growing up in a town like this sharply altered the way I believed the world should be and what I thought was possible. Many black men have been accused of idealizing white women because they are trophies, that they are what we are programmed to find beautiful. For me, the white people who were in my life as close friends and lovers were always a symbol of the beauty that James Rouse taught me could be found in anyone.

Columbia was a social experiment. It was a place that I felt proud of every time I walked into the local McDonald's full of children of all races, not segregated at separate ends of the restaurant, but all mingling together refreshingly unaware of any difference in skin color or economic status. I would smile each time I noticed a child or teenager whose race could not be determined, who was clearly some mix that was the product of integration. I just hoped that people would read about places like Columbia and know what was possible. In many respects, growing up in Columbia shaped me and my idealistic dreams, and provided a startling contrast when I left its safe harbor and headed out into the rest of America.

When I was a little more than six years old, our family moved to Clear Lake, Texas, a suburb of Houston. In many ways, it was culture shock in comparison to Columbia. We lived in a neighborhood that included Guy Bluford, the first black astronaut in space, Sally Ride, the first woman astronaut, and others my father worked with at the National Aeronautics Space Administration. Soon after our family left Texas for Marietta, Georgia, a suburb of Atlanta, I began having my first serious conversations about race with my parents.

They warned me that life was not fair and that sometimes, because of the color of my skin, I would have to work twice as hard to get the same credit, and, in some cases, would never be accepted by certain people. By the time I came of age, in junior high school, when my first dating relationship ended because of the objections a white father raised to me dating his daughter, my dreams of flying to the moon were replaced by nightmares of the Ku Klux Klan burning crosses in our family's front lawn. The word "nigger" would be scrawled, anonymously, a number of times in my yearbook alongside the more casual notations of junior high school years.

The idealism that so fueled me in my youth often gave way to the harsh reality of race relations in America. The combination of these two competing forces, in many respects, led to my choice of profession. I had always been curious, full of energy and enjoyed writing, but journalism became a passion in high school when I saw how it could help people. Our family had moved by then from Georgia to Fairfax County, Virginia, a suburb of Washington. The move came just as I was entering high school. While doing volunteer work to help raise money for a friend who was suffering from anorexia (and whose family needed help paying her medical bills), I watched the dollars flow in after Courtland Milloy, a columnist at *The Washington Post*, wrote about our efforts. Soon I joined the student newspaper at Centreville High School and found myself increasingly attracted to journalism's pursuit of balance, fairness and objectivity. Those principles, I felt, if upheld, were the ultimate equalizers. They did not see the color of one's skin, one's gender, sexual orientation or anything that was not of merit in a given situation.

Before I graduated high school, I began writing for a local weekly newspaper in Centreville and set up an internship with them for the summer. Within months, I was at the University of Maryland, writing for the campus newspaper, *The Diamondback,* and working my way into the good graces of many of the college administrators there. I was able to obtain my internship at *The Washington Post* through submitted clippings of stories I had written for *The Diamondback* and a college-run news service. The first shadow of doubt about journalism's practical power to be a great equalizer came in 1996 while spending a semester working in the Howard County, Maryland bureau of *The Washington Post,* sitting in a desk only a few miles away from the place where my idealism was first stoked, the city where I was born.

* * *

Peter Maass is a tall and lanky man with big hands and big eyes who would look like a character out of a fifteen-year Ivy League reunion if it weren't for the fact that the collars on his white shirts were never, ever, buttoned.

Peter was sitting in a chair behind my desk one afternoon, unplugging the telephone cord that ran into the fax machine, putting it into his laptop so he could download his personal e-mail. Compared to Anna Borgman, the other reporter in the office, and myself, Peter was the oddball of *The Washington Post* news bureau in Howard County, Maryland.

Anna had worked as a reporter at *The Post* for several years in a trainee program, working her way up from writing for one of the paper's suburban weekly sections to writing for the daily newspaper (albeit in the sticks of Howard County, the northernmost suburb in the circulation area). I was a sophomore at the University of Maryland, where I had worked at the student newspaper and Capital News Service, a journalism college wire service with offices in Annapolis and Washington. What made Peter most different from us was that his route to Howard County was much longer and much more complicated than either of ours had been.

After graduating from the University of California at Berkeley in the early 1980s, Peter went to Belgium as a copy editor for the European edition of *The Wall Street Journal,* a posh job by newspaper standards. Eventually Peter gave up the good life in Brussels for a much less glamorous assignment in places like Korea and the Balkans, where he traded in French coffee, croissants for breakfast, and weekend jaunts to Amsterdam—not to mention a steady paycheck—for the life of a freelance reporter for *The New York Times, The International Herald Tribune* and *The Washington Post.*

In Bosnia, Peter saw enough death and destruction for *The Post* that he eventually wrote an award-winning account of his experiences there. His book, *Love Thy Neighbor,* chronicled life, death and the strange realms in between that frequently converge during times of strife. The Maryland suburbs were a far cry to the excitement of Bosnia. Trading in listening to crickets chirping instead of bullets flying was a bit of a letdown for Peter, but the *Post* editors who wanted to bring him on as a staff member thought he needed a little seasoning in the suburbs before carrying the distinction of being a member of the *Washington Post* foreign service, where he would get a chance to sit in an equally cushy office as the one he had in Brussels. It came as little surprise to me that Peter was not exactly excited about Howard County.

I shared Peter's interest in Yugoslavia. One of my closest friends from high school was a foreign exchange student from Montenegro named Katrina Zizic. Montenegro was one of several republics that made up Yugoslavia, a region of the world that was undergoing its longest period of peace and prosperity after centuries of ethnic violence. Yugoslavia had the unique distinction during World War II of being occupied at the same time by the Nazis, Italians, Bulgarians and Albanians.

In Bosnia, that ethnic violence was directed primarily toward Muslims, who in large part were descendants of the Ottoman Turks who had ruled over the Balkans for centuries.

"I can't figure it out for the life of me," Peter said, staring at the front page of *The Post*.

I thought for sure that he was referring to the latest dispatch from the Yugoslavian battlefield.

"It just does not make any sense," he continued.

I stopped and thought for a moment, trying to remember what story about Yugoslavia had been on the front page.

"What doesn't make sense?" I asked, glancing toward the paper.

"This," he said, pointing to an article stripped across the top of the front page. Peter had many talents, but guessing what would appear on the front page was not one of them. Anna was better suited for that. If he had a nose for news, she had a nose for what editors wanted.

Peter was surprised by the accuracy of Anna's ability to guess where editors would place the story. "She did it again," Peter said, glancing towards Anna, as he sat in the chair behind my desk. "Look at this," he continued, not waiting for me to respond.

"Scottish Gunman Kills 16 Children In Primary School"
By FRED BARBASH
Washington Post Foreign Service
DUNBLANE, Scotland, March 13
A man carrying four handguns invaded the primary school in this small Scottish town this morning and killed 16 children—5- and 6-year-old kindergartners—and their teacher in the school gym before killing himself. Another 12 children and three adults were wounded in modern Britain's deadliest mass assault.

I read the first few paragraphs and looked at Peter with a questioning expression.

"It's not every day that sixteen schoolchildren get killed in England," I said. He shook his head.

"You are missing the point," Peter responded.

"I don't get it," I said.

"I covered massacres in Bosnia that put this one to shame, and Lord knows that in Rwanda many more people than that were getting killed every day," he continued. "But it was damn near impossible to get a word of it on the front page unless hundreds and hundreds of people were getting killed. Sure, sixteen schoolchildren in England don't get killed every day, but somewhere in the world in some war-torn country equal that number or even more are getting killed on a regular basis and are not even making the back pages of American papers. What are we saying about the value of an English life compared to a Bosnian life or an African life, when we hardly cover massacres of thousands of one group, and put stories about sixteen children getting killed from another group on the front page?"

"Anna just knows how they think," the bureau manager said as she passed by.

I was mentally debating Peter's point. We had been taught in journalism school that there is a simple formula for determining how newsworthy an event was. Timeliness. When did the event occur? Prominence. How well-known are the characters in the story? Proximity. How close was the news either psychologically or physically to the reader? Uniqueness. How odd, when taking in all factors, was the event? It had occurred to me before that there was an inherent value problem to this system. First, it presumed—and probably correctly—that a newspaper's readers cared primarily about news that was occurring in their own backyard. The second problem was that the formula put a lot of emphasis on celebrity and the third problem was that the uniqueness provision seemed to be a blanket excuse to ignore certain stories: a shooting in a predominantly upper middle class neighborhood was news because it was *rare*, when a similar shooting, or half-a-dozen in a lower-class neighborhood might be written as briefs.

This rationale allowed the news media to run stories about four hundred and fifty Somalis being killed in cross-fire or about a refugee camp in Yemen on the back pages, while running stories about the new horticulture techniques being used on cherry blossoms in Washington on the front page. The cherry blossoms were closer to us in proximity, and they were certainly more unique than a couple of hundred people getting killed in the Middle East. Under that value system, a New Yorker has more psychological proximity to an Israeli killed by a suicide bomber than a dead Muslim in Bosnia or a couple of million dead Tutsi in Rwanda. And, by the logic, most Americans would have more psychological proximity to sixteen children getting killed in Scotland than they would to sixteen hundred being killed in Bosnia or Rwanda. It was a nice, dressed-up way of saying that readers did not care about those people.

"Anna argues that it's about proximity," Peter continued, "that Americans are more like the British than we are like other Europeans, and that we relate more to Western Europeans than we do Slavs and other Europeans, who we value about as much, or perhaps a tiny bit more, than we do Middle Easterners and Africans."

"Isn't that a nice way to say we are xenophobic?" I asked.

Peter looked up at me and smiled. He nodded his head again.

"Yes," he said.

Anna had argued that the story would end up on the front page simply because it was white Western Europeans who were being killed. The logic was that if someone walked into an American school and killed a handful of children, it would make the front page no matter what, and that if it happened in Western Europe it would get prominent display with only a slightly higher body count. Dead Slavs—like the Bosnians, Croatians, Serbians and others getting slaughtered in the ethnic conflicts in Eastern Europe—were only one step on the scale above dead Africans, the argument went. It would take many more dead for them to end up on the front page. Therefore, a massacre of a half-million people, including hundreds of thousands of children, over several months in Rwanda, would not make the front page, while sixteen dead Scots would. By the same logic, the argument continued, it would take, at the very least, hundreds of dead Slavs or Bosnian Muslims to garner the front page. I had been taught that a life was a life, but was learning that when it came to American newspapers, the matter was a bit more complicated.

"So, how many dead Bosnians equal one dead British or American kid?" I asked Peter.

"I don't know. I am still trying to figure this all out."

"Lord knows how many dead Africans it takes to get onto the front page," I said, frowning.

"Oh, we know," Peter said as he looked up. "About 800,000 in three months."

He was referring to Rwanda, where even more people were killed in an even shorter time period of ethnic clashes backed by surrounding governments; where the events were ignored even more than Bosnia and the rest of Yugoslavia, where in over ten years less than half that number died. At least the stories about Yugoslavia would occasionally get prominent display in the paper.

Maybe it was journalism, not Peter, that needed more seasoning.

I held on to my dream.

CHAPTER SEVEN
HITTING THE GROUND RUNNING

My enthusiasm and energy had always, perhaps oddly, been both an asset and an enemy.

It was the summer of 1997. I was in the glass-walled office of Louisa Williams, the assistant managing editor in charge of recruitment, hiring and interns at *The Boston Globe*. I was about halfway into the twelve-week internship. Editors had been praising me for being enterprising, intense and coming to work early and staying late, but I could tell that this conversation was not going to be pretty.

I found Boston fascinating, even though it seemed to be the most ethnically segregated city I had ever been in. "I have never see so many shades of white," I used to quip.

Charlie Ball, the former public relations man who *The Globe* hired to help mentor interns, was also in the room. I was sitting in a wooden chair across from Louisa.

"We have had some complaints from fellow interns about you interrogating them about their assignments," Louisa started in.

I looked plaintively at Charlie, who was nodding, his bald head shining in front of me. Louisa continued, saying that several other interns had complained that I was asking them questions about what they were working on, intimidating them, and that editors were unfairly handing me big stories. I didn't know what to say. I just stared at Louisa.

"Wait, hold on," I said finally, bracing myself on the arms of the wooden chair I was sitting in. "Look, I don't have a problem about asking the other interns what they are working on," I said. "I was just trying to be friendly. I find it absurd that they were intimidated by it. I thought I was just being encouraging."

"Some people did not feel that . . ." Louisa continued.

"Not a problem," I interrupted her. "Not a problem at all. But I really have no say in what assignments the metro editors give out, and you are basically telling me to stop working so hard. Right?"

"What I am saying," Louisa continued, "is that you should have a life outside of the newsroom, perhaps take a few days off, don't come in so early, don't leave so late, because it's making your fellow interns uncomfortable."

"I don't know what to say," I said, on the verge of tears. "I realize that I have only twelve weeks here and that I need to make the most of them. I am working my rear off and you are telling me to stop working so hard because it's hurting the other interns' feelings?"

"Yes."

The debate continued, and I was in tears before it was over. I just thought to myself that I had to keep on working just as hard, putting in double the time, to get any credit. The summer ended with little change in my behavior, other than being slightly deflated and much less likely to communicate with the interns who I knew were the source of the complaints. I took great interest in writing about Megan's Law, the sexual offender registry that had been established after seven-year-old Megan Kanka was raped and killed by a repeat offender a few blocks from her home in Hamilton Township, New Jersey. I had changed the password on my e-mail account to "meganslaw" and wrote a story about it for the national pages of the paper.

The other notable feature of that summer was the number of dead bodies I had seen—being fished out of rivers, pulled out of lakes, lying on streets, and hanging out of the window of an apartment. *The Globe* is a big-city local paper and gives its readers a bird's eye view of death that is further encouraged by its competition for readers with the tabloid *Boston Herald*.

The next semester of school was consumed primarily by classes and drinking. My editorship of *The Diamondback* left me little choice but to drop some classes, a move that set me behind. I was nourished journalistically by writing for *The Globe*, but much of my time was spent partying. I had set my sights, professionally, on either returning to *The Washington Post* or getting an internship at *The New York Times*.

I lifted my opposition to formal wear in the second semester of college when an assistant dean at the University of Maryland journalism college called me and told me that he had scheduled an appointment for me with a recruiter from *The New York Times*.

At the University of Maryland, I was becoming a bit of a journalistic boy wonder. I came, I saw, I had a bunch of front-page stories in the campus paper. I ran it my sophomore year and worked for both *The Boston Globe* and *The Washington Post*. My writing was not beloved by editors as much as my enthusiasm and energy were considered unmatched; so was my reporting; so were some of my more odd behaviors, which were not limited to wearing flip-flops and sweatpants to my job. They also included habits like eating McDonald's cheeseburgers without any meat in them. My strange behavior was excused, for the most part, because I was talented. After all, Ross Perot taught us in his run for president that nutty people who were homeless were crazy, and successful people who were nutty were eccentric.

I was eccentric.

"I don't want you to interview for their internship this summer," I recall the assistant dean saying. "I just want you to get to know the recruiter, so a couple of years down the line, when you are ready, you will be on their radar screen."

"Sure, whatever you say," I replied.

He gave me the number of his secretary who would give me a time slot for a meeting. I was not one to question adults I admired. So off went the flip-flops and sweatpants I was so fond of wearing, and on went the tannish-gray suit, unmatching brown loafers and the white socks that would just have to do.

The recruiter was dressed in a black suit and she spoke carefully, accenting all of her syllables in a slight New York accent.

"So, why, Jayson, do you want go into journalism?"

I replied with my standard line about wanting to help people.

After two more interviews with the same recruiter and a collection of clippings from *The Globe, The Post* and other papers, I was offered a chance to spend a summer at *The Times* during my junior year in 1998.

I wore my suit again during the summer of 1998 in my first week of an internship at *The Times*. That week, Michel Marriott, a tall and burly reporter whose light brown skin and matching suit made him look like an overgrown teddy bear, took us on a tour of New York. It included visits to a drug treatment program and community center in the Bronx where we ate hot dogs. We hit the reservoir in Central Park, the one that I remembered reading about Jacqueline Kennedy Onassis jogging around before she died. He pointed out the Dakota where John Lennon was shot. We stopped in at the Cathedral of St. John the Divine, a majestic castle-like structure that had been under construction for 111 years and counting. At the Metropolitan Museum of Art, we walked through the Temple of Dendur, which was built in Egypt in 15 B.C. by the Roman emperor Augustus and was much later given to the American government. I was amazed by the breadth and energy of New York. The tour was enthralling.

The coup de grace—at least for me—was the Pulitzer hallway on the eleventh floor of the Times Building. Toward the end of the tour, we all took the elevators up to the eleventh floor. The gold-painted doors opened up and we were greeted by a large bronze medal. It was the symbol of the Pulitzer Prizes, the most prestigious award in journalism. As we headed down the hallway, I was awestruck as I passed by framed copies of stories I remembered from my childhood and history books, and writers whose names came up in journalism classes. The Pulitzer committee citations were inside the frames, beside excerpts of the stories.

"William L. Laurence, for his eyewitness account of the atomic bombing of Nagasaki and articles on the atomic bomb," read one.

"*The New York Times,* for a distinguished example of meritorious public service by a newspaper—publication of the Pentagon Papers," read another.

"Sidney H. Schanberg, for his coverage of the fall of Cambodia, a distinguished example of reporting on foreign affairs," another one said.

"*The New York Times,* for national reporting on the causes of the Challenger shuttle disaster," read another citation.

I saw the Challenger go up in streams of smoke, then hurtle toward the ground through my ten-year-old eyes again.

I stopped as the other interns continued to make their way past the gold-framed pictures of correspondents who had won the prize when something—an asterisk—caught my eye beneath the picture of a gray-haired correspondent. Small, black, calligraphic writing followed that read obliquely, "Other writers in *The Times* and elsewhere have discredited this coverage." I turned to Michel and asked whether he knew the story behind the correspondent whose prize was marked with this interesting notion.

"No," he told me, staring at the picture of the correspondent who had been awarded the prize for "Correspondence" in 1932. The man's name was Walter Duranty.

"All I know," I said, "is that I don't want to be that guy." Perhaps I already had a fear that I was a fraud, that I was not good enough for the job. It should have been a warning to me that in a room full of ninety-eight awards, I fixated on the guy with the asterisk by his name. Months later, I read an article about Joyce Maynard that struck a similarly strange chord. Maynard had written a memoir about her life, which included a cover story she wrote for *The New York Times* magazine when she was only eighteen and an affair that began a year later with J. D. Salinger, who was fifty-three at the time. I was wondering whether, sometimes, my interest and energy propelled me ahead of my emotional readiness.

Several minutes after remarking on the Duranty asterisk, I came to a picture of a *Times* reporter who won in the 1990s. "He's one of my favorite writers," I told Michel, who responded with a smirk, followed by raising his hands above his waist and strumming his fingers like he was a high school student aspiring to be a rock star, pretending to play the guitar in front of his own mirror.

"What does that mean?" I asked, puzzled.

"He's an air guitarist," one of the reporters who was with us on the tour said, spinning on his back foot and leading us out of Pulitzer hallway. "You don't want to be that guy either."

Oh, he makes things up. I got it, but was surprised that a fellow reporter would say something like that. If he knew the correspondent made up details, why didn't he report him?

One of the first people I was introduced to at *The Times* was the metro editor. Joyce Purnick was the personification of the hard-charging newspaperwoman I had imagined, like Glenn Close in the movie *The Paper*. Joyce had all the warmth and tenderness of a petrified piece of wood. Her charm was only rivaled by her enlightenment. Her claim to fame at the moment was giving a graduation speech at her alma mater where she told the female graduates of Barnard College that she could not have achieved what she had if she had been a mother, and that's just the way it was.

"If I had left *The Times* to have children and then come back to work a four-day week the way some women reporters on my staff do, or taken long vacations and leaves to be with my family, or left at six o' clock instead of eight or nine—forget it," she said in her speech. "I wouldn't be where I am."

What Joyce left out was that she was dating the former executive editor, Max Frankel. When Max was elevated to the top post, Joyce was moved to a prestigious job on the newspaper's editorial board. The two married. She came back to the newsroom after Max retired and his protégé, Joe Lelyveld, was appointed executive editor. Joe made Joyce the metro editor.

Joyce had an amazing team of editors at her disposal, a supporting cast that was unrivaled among the others at the paper, even if they did spend a good amount of their time in tears. One of the best editors on the desk was a man named Jerry Gray, the dapper assistant metro editor for politics whose tailored suits put even senior executives at the paper to shame. Jerry had a polite manner and a gregarious laugh that was uncommon among many *Times* editors. A native of the Mississippi Delta and the son of good, gentle African-American parents, Jerry began his career in newspaper reporting writing about sports in college and had the distinction of putting people before the profession. Jerry was my mentor, and became the mother hen to the other interns at the paper that summer. He often took us out to drink at fancy Manhattan bars where he would unload the latest relevant gossip to keep us from making snafus and flood each and every one of us with encouragement.

One of my first assignments came from Phyllis Messenger, a young and bubbly assistant metro editor who was assigned to the team that covered New York's suburbs. Phyllis asked me to write a brief story about a Columbus, Ohio developer who wanted to build what he said would be one of the world's largest malls in New Jersey. The project was being completed with assistance from Michael Ovitz, the former president of the Walt Disney Company, and David Rockwell, the New York architect.

The developers' staff said it would rival the Mall of America in Minneapolis, and New Jersey economic development officials said it would most certainly draw shoppers from Manhattan. It was a Monday morning, and I did not even know how to use the voice mail system and computers when I embarked on writing the story. I made calls to the developer, economic development officials in New York and New Jersey and independent experts. By mid-afternoon, when the editors met each day to discuss what stories were going to be considered for the front page, Jack Kadden, another assistant metro editor, came over to tell me that the mall story was a candidate for page one.

"Great," I tried to say casually.

Seconds later, I was sweating as I searched through the paper's electronic archives for recent development stories that had made the front page. I wanted to know how the words were used, the styles that were employed, and how they were written. In the middle of my search, the telephone rang.

"Blair, *Times*," I said, mimicking the way I had heard Jerry answer his phone several hours earlier.

"Hi, this is Deputy Mayor Levine," the voice responded.

I had left a message for him earlier in the day, hoping to get his reaction to the Elizabeth, New Jersey government official's comments. I couldn't believe I was on the telephone with a deputy mayor of New York City. I knew that the deputy mayors of New York were powerful administrators in a city of eight million people, with one of the largest governments in the world and a budget larger than those of all but three states—New York, California and Texas. The deputy mayor was in his official car, talking on his cell phone.

"I heard you had a question for me," he bellowed.

"Yes, sir," I said, pausing nervously. "New Jersey officials are saying that the 1.3 million-square foot mall they have planned for Elizabeth is likely going to attract tourists and other shoppers from Manhattan, and I was wondering if I could get your comment on that."

He paused for a moment, and then said, "Yeah, I can give you something. Just give me a second. I can come up with something on that."

The deputy mayor's voice was muffled as he spoke with someone else who was obviously in the car. I wondered whether it was an aide, or his press secretary. Or, the mayor himself.

"Okay, here we go, are you ready?"

"Yes, sir."

"It's a real long shot to think that tourists would choose Elizabeth, New Jersey over Manhattan. I mean, who gets on a plane and says, 'Honey, let's go fly to Elizabeth?'"

Score. I had the killer quote. The passive-aggressive attack that spices up a story. It would certainly help in my efforts to ensure the story made it onto the front page. A few minutes later, as I was fashioning the first few paragraphs of the story, my phone rang again. It was Malachy Kavanagh, the spokesman for the International Council of Shopping Centers. I had called them because I wanted to collect information on the world's largest malls to make sure a graphic could be cobbled together to accompany the story. I knew that graphics and photographs always increased the likelihood that a story would capture the readers' attention. Kavanagh had found the data on shopping malls I was looking for and promised to fax it over. But he had bad news also. The developer's claims were bogus. They had not anchored tenants, so it was unlikely they would build a mall as large as they claimed. Furthermore, the Elizabeth project would be 1.3 million square feet—compared to 4.2 million at the Mall of America—which would make it only the *eighth largest mall in New Jersey.*

I got off with Kavanagh, put my head phones back on, and dialed Jerry. He was over at my desk within minutes.

"This isn't a front-page story anymore," I said.

"Nope," Jerry said, shaking his head as he read the top paragraphs of my story.

"Sorry about that," I added. I had known they were looking for something that Metro could offer for the front page that day.

"There's nothing to be sorry about. Sometimes being a good reporter is just as much reporting a story off of the front page as it is writing it onto the front page. I'll go let your editors know. Good job, Blair."

Jerry vanished. I was surprised at his enthusiasm over my discovery. Most newspapers try to pump up stories that are not worthy of front-page display, and it was nice to find that Jerry and his *New York Times* colleagues had much more integrity. I went home for the day after the story was edited and made myself a gin and tonic before heading to bed in the New York University dorm room on Third Avenue and Ninth Street that I was staying in for the summer. The next morning, I picked up a copy of the newspaper. My story ran on Page B12 with the real estate advertisements.

Outside the office, I spent a lot of time at the dorm with a cool, hippie-ish woman from Pennsylvania, a student who was spending the summer working for Jim Henson Productions, the company responsible for the Muppets. Our first date was in my bedroom, where we smoked lots and lots of pot and watched *When Harry Met Sally,* followed by Woody Allen's *Annie Hall.* It was good thing she came into my life, or I would have likely watched the movie *City Hall*—one of only two videos I owned, the other one being *The Paper*—hundreds of times that summer. We watched the fireworks on the Fourth of July from the rooftop of the dorm room building. When she wasn't around, I explored the city, visiting the South Street Seaport, which was designed by a developer I admired or gorging at dim sum restaurants. I would stare out my fourteenth-floor window sometimes at night, look at the lights and the people moving below, and just think about how I was born to live in this city. I was not making much money, and the dorm room cost about $750 a month, so my diet was generally cheese sandwiches in the *Times* cafeteria for lunch, pizza on weekends, and medium McDonald's fries and a Sprite for dinner. I lost so much weight that summer that when I returned to college in the fall, none of my clothes fit me. I kept a large bottle of gin I had bought at what had to be one of the world's largest liquor stores—well, at least that I had ever seen—to mix with the Sprite each night. I would often use the gin to knock myself out. I knew I had to be at work at ten each morning. The only good meals I ate the whole time I was in New York were with Jerry.

One of my most memorable experiences that summer was covering a black militant who was trying to hold a rally in Harlem. Khalid Abdul Muhammad was not a nice man by any measure. Jerry's wife had attended Dillard University in New Orleans when Muhammad was a student, but they had clearly taken different paths. Muhammad, a former Nation of Islam official, was seen as the leader of the next generation of radical civil rights leaders by some and as a racist hatemonger by others. Muhammad was dismissed as the Nation of Islam's spokesman in 1994 after making a vitriolic speech that railed against whites, Jews, Catholics and moderate black civil rights leaders. His separatism did not play well to my child-of-integrationists' sensibilities, and his cheap attacks on whites—which I saw simply as a marketing ploy to get attention—did not jive with my intellectualism.

He had spent the early part of his career as an assistant and then senior aide to Louis Farrakhan, the leader of the Nation of Islam. Muhammad was seen as a leading candidate to succeed Farrakhan until he gave a hate-filled speech as his boss was attempting to move into the mainstream of the civil rights movement. In that speech, among other things, Muhammad called Jews "bloodsuckers." The next year, Farrakhan dismissed Muhammad, who went on to found the New Black Panther Party. He went on to get attention with remarks like: "If you believe that blondes have more fun, ask Nicole Brown Simpson." Another charmer was: "I say you call yourself Goldstein, Silverstein and Rubinstein because you are stealing all the gold and silver and rubies all over the earth . . . we call it jewelry, but it's really Jew-elry, Jew-elry because of your deceiving and stealing and rogueing and lying all over the face of the planet Earth."

That summer Muhammad was organizing a Million Youth March in Harlem, a rally which started a public relations battle with Mayor Rudolph W. Giuliani even before it was scheduled for the beginning of September. For Giuliani, using city regulations and the police department to block the march was an opportunity to take a stand against hate and cater to liberal voters who could not stomach the fiery militant. For Muhammad, the march was seen as his chance to capture the national stage. Giuliani called

Muhammad a "hatemonger"; Muhammad called Giuliani "Hitler." On August 3, I wrote my first piece on the permit battle. Muhammad objected strenuously to the piece on the grounds that I quoted many of his critics. I was not sympathetic to Muhammad or his brand of hatred, and I suspect I made it clear in our first encounter on a crowded street in Harlem.

"So, *you're* Jayson Blair," Muhammad said. "I am surprised by the color of your skin."

I grinned at the ground and then looked up.

"I cannot believe," Muhammad said in his booming voice, "That *you*, a brother, work for the White Devil *New York Times*."

"Look, Mr. Muhammad, you don't need to like me," I said. "I get my love at home. I am just here to do my job."

That was a bit of a lie. If home was the *Times*'s headquarters on 229 West Forty-third Street, I was not getting much love there—at least not from the metro editor over my Muhammad stories. Joyce could be one of those editors who gets under my craw, the ones that think they know the story before any reporting had been done. She did not believe Harlem blacks would support Muhammad. Times had changed, as we would find out later in the year, when thousands of participants would violently clash with the police at the end of the rally. Outside the building, I was getting attacked by Muhammad and his people for doing the bidding of the "White Devil" *New York Times*, and inside the building I was being accused of carrying water for the Black Devil Khalid Muhammad. I wondered whether a white reporter's work would be scrutinized for latent sympathies? I didn't think so, and that made me uneasy. It is not an uncommon vice to be caught as a black man living within the white world, being truly accepted by neither.

I was excited after I was told that, based on Jerry's evaluation, I would be offered a six-month trial employment extension. I was also concerned about hints that some would perceive me as having received the job only because of the color of my skin.

"Some people might see you as an affirmative action hire," I remember him saying. "But you take it how you can get it. There will be enough times when the color of your skin will in no way be to your advantage."

CHAPTER EIGHT
NEW LOWS

Back at college, I had become a campus star of sorts because of my success at *The Times*. In addition to my courses, I began teaching classes for some students who were in their first year at the journalism college. The first-year journalism students were considered to be some of the brightest students in the university, because the freshman admissions program for the college had some of the highest standards for SAT scores and high school grade point averages. I taught a class on journalism basics with Greig Stewart, an assistant dean at the college who had a background in education. He liked to make class as much fun as possible while emphasizing the important tenets and skills necessary for survival in the business. I was called on mainly to offer up anecdotes, grade papers and teach basic skills, like grammar, to the students. I enjoyed teaching as much as I did writing, getting a great boost from the eagerness of students beginning their college careers.

The Times had offered me the chance to come back for a six-month extension on my internship based on my performance the previous summer, but the classes that I had dropped that semester guaranteed that I would not graduate in time to return to the paper.

"Jayson," one friend yelled from about two inches from my face as I was sitting in the office of Olive Reid, the undergraduate programs director at the journalism college. "You can't do this. You can't go to *The Times* without graduating. I am not going to let you be another black man without a college degree."

Olive swears that when I stormed out of the office she could see a tear in my eye, though I don't recall it. There was ample evidence that I was falling apart by that afternoon, though.

"I just don't feel good, Olive, I feel empty, like something's missing."

"You might be depressed, Jayson, as hard as that is to imagine."

"Oh, come on Olive, I'm just going through a rough patch. I just need to get focused again."

"Look, each semester, you get one free visit at the counseling center," she said. "You should take advantage of the free therapy."

I went home that night without making a decision on what to do. By the next morning, I was convinced I needed help. I hadn't slept at all, after waking up from horrible nightmares about demons that seemed so real that they might as well have been in the room with me. It was frightening, and I needed some help, or at the least I needed to slow down on my drinking and occasional drug use. *Jesus, I need help,* I thought to myself on that spring morning. I could see the counseling center through the trees from the windows of my apartment. It was only a short walk. I got dressed and went down the stairs of my dorm, out into the plaza that led to a parking lot and the counseling center. I walked up the steps of the building and into its lobby, where I was greeted by a busy reception desk with people flying in all directions.

A woman asked me if I needed any help.

"Oh, no, I am okay," I said, as I walked through the lobby and eventually out the back door of the counseling center. I walked down the steps and back to my dorm room, where I looked at my suit hanging in the closet. It reminded me that despite my struggles, I would soon be wearing it more often. I was going back to the city I loved and the best newspaper in the country.

And, anyway, why would someone who was successful enough to become a reporter at *The New York Times* at the age of twenty-three need therapy?

Instantly, I felt better.

CHAPTER NINE
VELOCIRAPTOR

New York is an insane town, no doubt about it. Working for *The New York Times,* though, gave me my own special place in the swirling madness.

I had long enjoyed the city because of its diversity of ideas and of people, but had been put off by its frenzied pace and urban density. It was thrilling to pick up a copy, out of a street-corner vending box, of the newspaper that I read so religiously during late nights in college. On more days than not, I could flip open the pages, and there it was, my byline in bold letters. It provided me roots in a city where it was so easy to get lost.

The Times also offered me a footing in a society, with a class of people that I had neither longed to be a part of, nor ever dreamt of joining. The paper is singular among all American news outlets for the quality of its journalism and its reputation. For all the good that comes with that, there is a certain level of arrogance.

"*The Washington Post,* huh," one editor said after hearing about my background at other major newspapers. "*The Washington Post* is the world's greatest local newspaper. We are the world's only international newspaper."

I had just returned to *The Times* as a trainee and was making my rounds through the newsroom with Jerry Gray, who was introducing me to editors that he thought I should meet. Jerry had warned me before that some of the people who were kind to me as an intern would now view me as a competitor, and the gloves would come off. He warned that some would pretend not to even know my name. Jerry liked to say that *The Times* was the "kindest and the cruelest of places." In times of personal crisis, it could be an amazingly kind employer, but in the day-to-day go-around it could be like working in a boxing ring. As an intern, I had seen much more kindness.

The photographer in my class of interns had been in the United States as a student and photojournalist for several years when he arrived at *The*

Times. He impressed editors more than anyone else in our class, consistently landing on the front page. The photographer was the first among us—the largest group of interns ever asked to come back as trainees—to be offered a permanent position, but trouble emerged when *Times* officials began reviewing his immigration status. It quickly became clear that the photographer had already overstayed his visa. *Times* lawyers attempted to work with the Immigration and Naturalization Service to sponsor him, but it did not work out and he was left in limbo. Unable to fix his immigration problems, *The Times* was unable to hire him, but they gave him two parting gifts: a promise that if things were ever worked out he would have a job at the newspaper and a big check free and clear, no strings attached. It was a moment when the kindness of the newspaper shone brightly.

The other interns who returned included Monica Drake, a Columbia University graduate who was hired as a trainee on the metro copy desk. Ed Wong, a graduate of the University of California-Berkeley, was hired onto the City section and the metro desk. Winnie Hu, who had attended the University of Maryland with me and had worked previously for the Asian edition of *The Wall Street Journal*, was also brought into the City section. What distinguished me most from the other members of my class was that I was so young. Monica, Ed and Winnie were all graduate students when they were interns at *The Times*, while I was still an undergraduate student. Before returning to *The Times*, I did not tell Sheila Rule, the director of reporter recruiting, that I had not graduated from Maryland, but I made a point of making sure that others were aware.

"I am just another black man without a college degree," was my common refrain.

The decision to return without a degree was not a difficult one for me, even though it troubled my parents and professors at Maryland. Theoretically, the door would be held open for me as long as it took to graduate. Realistically, though, I knew that once Joyce Purnick, the embattled metro editor, was replaced and a new regime began, all bets concerning my employment were off. I felt I needed to proceed and seize the opportunity.

On my first day back, Jerry Gray took me around the newsroom until it was time to meet with Joyce, who had become even more of a pariah in the year since I had been gone. Several of the editors who had been on the desk when I was an intern had fled the section in order to get a little more peace. And they would regale us with stories about the late night tirades by more-senior editors—how these tongue-lashings about the quality of their writing and reporting left them in a state of fear that sent them to the bars and paralyzed their decision-making, something that was, to them, a disservice to both their egos and the readers.

Joyce greeted me with a warm hello. Jerry had already told me what she was going to say, explaining that because I had done so well as a summer intern, the editors wanted to give me a shot at something with a little more responsibility.

"I want you to go down to the cop shop at least for a couple of months," Joyce said, referring to *The Times* office in police headquarters. "You will get a chance to get some experience writing hard news stories on deadline for *The Times,* which you will find is not like it is at other newspapers," she continued. "We demand breadth and scope, things that put matters into perspective, even in our crime stories.

"You will work with Kevin Flynn and Michael Cooper, who are both wonderful gentlemen. You will also work with Kit Roane, who you will eventually replace once the summer is over," she said. "If you have any questions, you can call Kevin at the cop shop or Gerry Mullany, who will be your editor on most stories, but you should probably go down there tomorrow, get to know the place, meet some of the police officials, and get your press pass.

"Good luck," she added, beginning to turn away. "One more thing, Jayson. Congratulations on getting the chance to write for *The Times.*"

That pride, in some employees, emerged as snobbery and arrogance. *The Times* newsroom was a place where you could close your eyes, and in the words of one reporter, throw a ball and have a good chance of hitting an Ivy Leaguer who'd pretend not to know your name. This was much more apparent upon my re-entry, and even many of the people who were kind to me seemed to be infused with the notion that *The Times* was made up of the smartest journalists working on the planet. Their arrogance, in my opinion, caused them to make frequent gross professional and personal misjudgments, like Joyce's speech at Barnard wherein she essentially told the women of her alma mater that they would have to choose between children and career. It also caused gross misjudgments of the news value of certain stories, and an unwillingness to admit that they had made mistakes. *The Times* was among the few major newspapers in the country at the time working without internal safeguards to protect against serious mistakes that were overlooked by editors. At most newspapers, the people charged with this duty were called ombudsmen, and editors at *The Times* had forcefully rejected the idea of having a sort of internal watchdog for years on the notion that the rigors of their editing system virtually guaranteed that there would be no problems.

I had moved into an apartment at the corner of Eighty-sixth Street and Broadway on the Upper West Side and went home to arrange my belongings. I took a glass of red wine out of my window and onto a stone balcony that overlooked Broadway. I watched the Manhattan skyline slowly grow brighter in the darkness. All I could think about was what a perfect city this was for me to live in and, from a job perspective, even if it did not work out, it would at the very least be a good experience.

The next morning I popped awake with the sun shining in my eyes. I had fallen asleep on the tan couch that had been left by the previous occupant of the apartment, a woman who was a graduate student at Columbia University. Her mother knew mine from teaching in Virginia. She had moved in with her boyfriend. The apartment was a little more than three hundred square feet, with two bedrooms and a kitchen that opened up into the living room. The apartment, by Upper West Side standards, was relatively cheap at $2,500 a month, given the amenities, including a twenty-four-hour café downstairs on one corner and a subway stop on the other. The apartment was located directly between Riverside Park, which straddles the Hudson River, and Central Park to the east, and was in a relatively quiet neighborhood. It was also close to areas where it was easy to party into the early morning. I quickly grabbed some clothes from my bedroom and put them on. I decided to skip my morning shower. I grabbed my bag and headed down the stairs at the end of the hallway.

I passed the doorman, waving as I walked by, and bought a pack of Camel Lights and *The Times* at the newsstand right in front of the subway stop. I went down the stairs and fumbled in my pocket for one of the subway tokens I had purchased the day before, holding up the line, as busy New Yorkers grunted, scurried and complained around me. Finally I dropped one into the machine and was able to walk through the metal bar and onto the platform. I took the train south to Times Square, only a fifteen minute ride, and popped out on Forty-second Street and Broadway, one block away from the Times Building at 229 West Forty-third Street.

It was early in the morning and I wanted to stop by Jerry's desk before heading down to meet Kevin and the rest of the police reporters.

"Hello, sir," Jerry said as I approached the front of his cubicle, which was in the middle of the newsroom alongside the other metro editors. "Are you headed down to the cop shop today?"

"Yup. I just wanted to come by the office and pick up some notepads and pens before I go down."

"Well, sir, welcome to *The Times*. I have something for you. You are going to need this now that you are a *Times* reporter."

Jerry pulled a small square plastic case out of his black leather bag and handed it to me. Inside was a casting of a claw. On the back of the case was the description of the dinosaur that it came from.

It was a replica of the claw of a velociraptor—a small, but brilliant and deadly dinosaur that hunted in packs, using its mind and deadly claws to overcome the superior size of its prey. Some velociraptors were even known to sacrifice themselves to lure their prey into a position where the rest of the pack could attack and devour their adversary. It was Jerry's welcoming—and warning.

After leaving *The Globe* in the summer of 1998, I vowed to do everything I could to come off as a team player and not be so competitive among my colleagues. I made a point of embracing the new people coming in the door, as well as the old veterans, focusing less on journalism and more on things like living in New York City. I had started visiting museums and taking long walks through Central Park and Riverside Park. I would occasionally stop at the liquor store around the corner from my apartment for a bottle of red wine and Johnnie Walker Black, which I would sip on the terrace outside my living room window.

At the entrance of police headquarters, which is located near City Hall only a few blocks from the East River, a visitor's tag was already waiting for me at the entrance. After I showed the officer at the front desk my Virginia driver's license, she entered my name into a computer and made a badge that allowed me to enter the building. The officer pointed me to an escalator that would take me up to the second-floor mezzanine of the building to the "shack"—the second name of the police bureau, which was also referred to as "the cop shop." It got that name because years ago, when the department first established offices for the police reporters, they were located in a trailer that looked like a shantytown shack parked behind the building.

The conditions inside the modern-day police reporters' offices were not much better. I followed the signs to a door hidden in a corner near the office of the deputy police commissioner for community affairs. Inside the main room were file cabinets covered with papers, notebooks, and other items that had clearly just been discarded. A giant cockroach was making its way up one of the walls behind a file cabinet, and reporters were ducking in and out of each other's offices. I passed a door for *El Diario*, one of New York's two Spanish-language daily newspapers, and one for the *New York Post*. Along the walls, I noticed cartoons and headlines that poked fun at editors of each of the respective papers and embattled Police Commissioner Howard Safir. Jerry had warned me that the commissioner hated the press almost as much as the press hated him.

"The only person the cop shop reporters hate more than Safir is his spokeswoman," Jerry said.

Inside the *Times*'s small, grimy office with a window overlooking the stairs behind police headquarters, I met Michael Cooper and Kit Roane, two white reporters who had been assigned to the police bureau as trainees. Michael was a case-study of a smooth operator, never making too much of a bang, never making too much noise, just slowly working his way up. Kit, on the other hand, was a bit of a rebel.

Kit had cut his teeth as a correspondent in the former Yugoslavia. Before that, he had worked as a freelance stringer for *The Times* in the Los Angeles bureau. In Los Angeles, Kit had spent most of his days in the courtroom filing notes from the O.J. Simpson trial while the chief of the bureau, Ken Noble, a black correspondent who had been in East Africa before heading to California, wrote the stories.

In the Los Angeles bureau, Ken was responsible for *The Times* coverage of Southern California, Arizona and Nevada. He would later say that he'd wanted to become the bureau chief in San Francisco, a plum job with little gore, until Gerald Boyd, who was then the assistant managing editor for news, had pushed him to take the job in Los Angeles. Ken left the job after a relatively short period of time, but not before making a lasting impression on Kit, who said he grew tired of doing the legwork for Ken's stories on the Simpson trial. Eventually, the two had a falling out, and Kit left Los Angeles for war-torn Bosnia, where he hooked up with John Kifner, a *Times* correspondent in the region.

One of the jobs that Kit took on was re-reporting, along with John Kifner, some of the stories that had been written early in the conflict by the Sarajevo bureau chief, who was the lead correspondent on the war coverage. Working together, Kit and John formed a tight bond. John pushed the editors in New York to hire Kit and another reporter who was with them in the field, David Rohde, a young correspondent for the *Christian Science Monitor* who had won the Pulitzer Prize after he uncovered mass graves, presumably made by Serbs who killed Muslims in Bosnia. On his second trip to the graves, an armed farmer captured David and turned him over to Serbian forces. David was eventually set free with some help from the State Department.

The two arrived at *The Times* with much fanfare, but Kit had the troubles with Ken Noble still hanging over his head. He had been pegged as a person who was difficult to deal with, even though Ken himself had resigned under fire not long after Kit's departure. In fact, Kit and I bonded in those first few days at the cop shop. He and Kevin gave me tours of news conferences and the police public information office on the eleventh floor, then took me out for an all-night fire deep into South Ozone Park, Queens.

If the claw represented dinosaurs hunting in packs, Kit was nothing of the sort. He was a gentle and kind colleague.

"Jesus, Jayson, we are never going to get the hell out of here," he said one night while we were parked outside of a hospital in Queens, waiting for Mayor Giuliani to arrive in order to comfort the family of a dying firefighter. "I don't even know why I am here, because I know Joyce is going to fire me."

"What do you mean?" I asked. "You're great. You're always in the paper."

"Ah, young man, you just don't understand," Kit said. "Joyce hates me. I am just not one of their kind of people."

I probably was not, either. I quickly became friends with many of the younger, more liberal people at *The Times* like Jenny Holland, a twenty-three-year-old clerk whose father, Jack, was the well-known Irish journalist and author. Jenny had an uncanny ability to see through many people at *The Times,* and her dry wit and sarcasm served as a sharp counterpoint to my constant smiles.

Jenny was the early warning system for reporters who wanted to know what the editors were saying about them. Editors at *The Times* had this bad habit of speaking freely and cruelly about reporters who worked for them in front of clerks, not thinking that the news assistants in the office had much more in common with us than they had with the hierarchy. Jenny had been born in Ireland and grew up in New York before returning abroad to attend college. After school, she came back to New York and got a job working as a news assistant through a connection her father had with Dan Barry, one of the senior writers on the metro desk.

The night Jenny found out she passed her drug test, I went out with her, Eric Smith, a longtime clerk on the metro desk, and Andrea Delbanco, a clerk on the magazine. We started out doing shots at Scruffy Duffy's, an Irish bar on the West Side, and ended up in Siberia, a seedy bar that was literally underneath the streets, tucked underground in the stairwell of a subway entrance on West Fifty-fourth Street in midtown. Initially, I had set my sights on Andrea, whose beautiful black hair and charming smile were warm and open. When my advances were flatly rejected, I moved to whisky and Jenny. By the end of the night we were making out on the couch in the dimly-lit bar and joking about what a miracle it was that she'd passed her drug tests.

Within weeks, Jenny visited me at the cop shop—just to check the police bureau out—and we lunched at an Italian restaurant on Spring Street. Soon, I began traveling in the company car assigned to the cop shop to the Brooklyn Inn, the bar she frequented in the Boerum Hill section of the neighborhood. Later, we would crash at her apartment in Carroll Gardens, which was only a short drive from police headquarters. We would stay up late, rapping about our lives and dreams. She would often joke that blacks were the only people more discriminated against than Irish people.

In no time at all, I had learned that clerks at *The Times*, like Jenny, were not only some of the most reasonable people at the paper, they were also some of the best sources of gossip and news stories. The clerks had to listen to all the nutty calls that came in to the newspaper's switchboard, and in the process had their ears to the ground about many good stories. In one instance, Jenny took a call that helped solve a murder case and passed the story on to me. A caller had telephoned to say that there were several similar murders in the Williamsburg and Bedford-Stuyvesant sections of Brooklyn—women who were being strangled on rooftops or on the upper floors of apartment buildings. In the end, the paper's stories helped the police link the cases and find the killers—even though it was difficult to convince editors to give some of those stories good play.

"I overheard the editors talking about your story on the Williamsburg killings," Jenny once said, providing a piece of her invaluable intelligence over the telephone. "Joyce says she does not want to run it on the front of the section because the police are not sure it is a serial killer. I heard some of the other editors saying under their breath that it was Joyce's bias, that if it were happening in the Upper East Side, or in her neighborhood, she would be pushing it for the front page."

CHAPTER TEN
A DEATH IN CENTRAL PARK

I was standing in a wooded area of Central Park, obscured by trees and green foliage, watching people make their way on the walkways around the pond.

Like any good predator, I knew what my victim should look like. I was waiting for a white woman to come by, preferably someone who looked like they were from out of town. The best target would not be wearing a business suit. I was looking for a jogger or someone in casual wear strolling along alone or in a small group of people. There was no question that she had to be white, but she also had to be young and vulnerable.

I had been behind the trees waiting for a little more than an hour, chewing on sunflower seeds. I looked respectable—my shirt, with blue, green, gold and maroon stripes, was tucked firmly into my pants, and my pager hung from the belt in front of me so I could look down and easily see the time and who might be trying to get in touch with me. I was wearing my wire-rimmed glasses. I had on new white tennis shoes I had bought a few days before. The only thing that might alarm passersby was that sweat was running down the side of my forehead, and I was hiding behind trees.

The first major crime in recent times in Central Park that captured the public fears of New York had occurred in August 1986, an era when the city averaged more than 1,500 murders a year. The discovery of Jennifer Levin's body behind a leafy elm tree in the park just behind the Metropolitan Museum of Art was one of the murders that stood out among the killings. Jennifer was an eighteen-year-old graduate of the Baldwin School, an elite private prep school on the Upper East Side of Manhattan. Jennifer's father was a successful real estate broker, and they lived together in a spacious loft in SoHo. Jennifer was extroverted—friends would later say she craved attention, like so many children from broken homes. In short, news reports at the time said that Jennifer fell in love easily. Jennifer's short brown hair, freckled complexion, and engaging smile made her look like so many of the daughters of *Times* editors and reporters. It was little wonder that the story was instantly propelled into the national headlines.

When police detectives from the famed NYPD Manhattan North homicide task force tracked down Robert Chambers on the morning Jennifer's body had been found, they had no idea what to expect. The detectives arrived at 11 East Ninetieth Street, just off Fifth Avenue next door to the Carnegie mansion, where Robert's mother, Phyllis, answered the door. The detectives had been told that Robert was close to Jennifer, that they had met at Dorrian's Red Hand, an East Side bar that was popular among Madison Avenue prep school girls, and had begun a sexual relationship.

Robert agreed to talk with the detectives at the Central Park precinct, an old carriage house in the middle of the park that had been built in the 19th century. Its dark brownstones made it look like a castle from some other era. The detectives who saw Robert that morning noticed scratches on his face at the beginning of a long interrogation that would lead to a confession. Robert eventually admitted that after an argument at the bar with his girlfriend, he left with Jennifer and went to the park, where he claimed they'd had rough sex that eventually led to her death. Robert's lawyers would finally arrange a plea deal with the prosecutor, but not before the case was dubbed "The Preppie Murder."

The next big Central Park attack came in 1990, when Larry Parnham was sleeping peacefully just before dawn on a bench along Literary Walk, a quiet area of the park known for its grove of oak trees. The shooting of thirty-year-old Parnham, who was homeless, would not likely have gotten much attention in a year where New York recorded more than 2,000 murders if it had not been for the fact that the police quickly determined that the gunman had been the Zodiac killer, who had left one of his infamous astrological notes signifying his presence. The jogger attacks further fueled the belief that the park was unsafe.

Still, it was the case of Daphne Abdela that rattled me the most.

Daphne, the fifteen-year-old daughter of a wealthy Upper West Side couple, was the perfect made-for-headlines victim. Daphne and her boyfriend, Christopher Vasquez, also fifteen, were walking in the park late one night in May 1997. A little after midnight, Daphne's father called 911 to report that she had not returned home the previous evening. The police quickly arrived at the family's elegant cooperative apartment building on Central Park West that was also home to opera star Kathleen Battle and other celebrities. A doorman told the officers that Daphne had just arrived home and had gone into a laundry room on the ground floor of the building. The officers found Daphne and Christopher there, washing blood off themselves. When questioned, the young couple told the officers that they had been in an accident while rollerblading in Central Park. An hour later, the police received a 911 call that was traced to the same apartment building, the Majestic, reporting that the body of a man named "Mike" was in a lake near the park's famous Bethesda Fountain.

After finding the body of a forty-four-year-old real estate broker, Matthew McMorrow, floating face up in the park, the police headed back to the Majestic to confront Daphne, who implicated Christopher. Detectives charged them both with murder on the theory that Christopher committed the killing and then gutted the victim on the encouragement and orders of Daphne. Matthew McMorrow's throat had been slashed from ear-to-ear, he had been stabbed at least thirty times, and he had been disemboweled.

Daphne had attended the Columbia Grammar and Preparatory School, one of the oldest and most elite private schools in New York, until the seventh grade, when she transferred to another academy, the Loyola School on Park Avenue. Christopher grew up across the park with his mother and maternal grandparents, and he attended another private academy, the Beekman School.

Reading the coverage in Maryland, I was saddened by the prospect of two fifteen-year-olds heading so far off course that they would kill a man, gut his body, and drop him in a lake. By most accounts, the two teens liked to disappear among the park's sprawling fields and pathways at night, descending on rollerblades into the world of drunks and drug addicts who frequented the park. Matthew McMorrow, who had a history of drug addiction and alcoholism, was among those who crossed paths with the fifteen-year-olds. Hours before his death, Matthew had been downing beers with Daphne and Christopher in one of the park's meadows.

Daphne was white, rich, and a young woman—a collection of adjectives that when it came to murders in New York, meant the media would go crazy on the story. Christopher was an altar boy, a Boy Scout, and was known among his friends for finding homes for stray dogs and taking care of his grandmother. Neither seemed to me to fit the profile of the typical killer. For some reason, though, the media seemed to focus on the oddity of Daphne being involved in the gruesome slaying, but not Christopher. The media search for the reasons why Daphne could have done it struck me as odd, because she had been in trouble in school. Her millionaire parents had even threatened to send her away to a substance abuse treatment program. Christopher's life showed few signs of dysfunction. Perhaps it was less curious to the television and print reporters because he was a man. Perhaps he fit the killer stereotype because he was Latino.

At times, the search for the reasons behind Daphne's involvement seemed absurd.

"CAN'T PICTURE TEEN AS KILLER," screamed a headline in the *Daily News*.

"DON'T RICH OR FAMOUS KIDS HAVE RIGHTS?" screamed another headline over a column in *Newsday*.

The coverage in all the New York newspapers focused day after day on what could have gone wrong with Daphne. It seemed that the papers and television stations had already written off Christopher's involvement, even though there was even less in his past that suggested a propensity for trouble. The search for why Daphne did it was a comical exercise that I would see replayed over and over again in the news media. Reporters and editors cared intensely about those who seemed most like them, and when they looked at Daphne, they saw someone who could be one of their daughters. Christopher simply did not look like them. The exercise, when it came to crime stories, was an obvious attempt to illustrate to readers and themselves why Daphne was radically unlike their own children.

She was adopted, they said. She may have had a chemical imbalance, they added. Was she influenced by the poor kids she hung out with, they asked, even though by all indications she was usually the instigator of trouble? Was it because she watched violent Hollywood movies like *Reservoir Dogs*?

The newspapers and television stations seemed hardly surprised that Christopher was a part of the crime, even though everything seemed to suggest that he was an upstanding citizen. Not only was he a Boy Scout and an altar boy, but he was used to breaking up fights, not instigating them. Newspapers and television stations reported these details, but did not conduct an enormous psychological expedition into why he committed the crimes. After all, he was a Latino teenager. It felt like we were not supposed to be surprised by the fact that Christopher was involved in a murder, but everyone was supposed to be perplexed by why his rich Upper West Side girlfriend, who had a troubled past, would be involved in a crime.

* * *

After covering a series of news stories—mainly shootings, fires and rapes in the outer boroughs—Joyce Purnick, the metro editor, had lunch with me at a West Side restaurant to discuss my future. Joyce said she wanted to see more high-impact stories that ran on the front of the section, and encouraged me to consider the option of going to a smaller newspaper once my trainee period was over. Joyce, who had come to *The Times* after working for *The New York Post,* noted that the paper was no place for a young person to be.

Bill Schmidt, the associate managing editor for news administration, and Jerry Gray had made the point that *The Times* was working hard to develop its own young and loyal journalists. They made not-so-subtle references to the fact that Joyce's days were numbered, and a new metro editor would be taking over. Still, I took her warning seriously, and both put out feelers to other newspapers and looked for more high-impact stories. It seemed lost on Joyce that *The Times* cop shop inherently produced stories that were of less interest to editors and readers than, say, City Hall. It did not really matter, though. I had seen what she had done to Kit. And I didn't want it to happen to me.

One of my daily duties in the cop shop was to arrive before the editors called the bureau—generally the phone call would land around nine thirty in the morning—and go upstairs to the deputy commissioner for public information's office and check the "sheets" listing the crimes that happened overnight. On my daily visits, I would also thumb through police statistic books, looking for information about where crime was up and where it was down, what types of offenses were rising and which ones were dropping, seeking clues about what might make front of the section stories.

On my visits, I became friendly with Marilyn Mode, the deputy police commissioner for public information. A bit too eccentric for the press corps and most in the police department, I seemed to bond with Marilyn out of our mutual sense of being out of place. Marilyn had been a Ron Ziegler-like, longtime aide and loyal protégée to the police commissioner, Howard Safir, who was almost uniformly hated by the press corps. Marilyn's task was often to keep reporters in the police bureaus of the various papers at bay.

"We have nothing for you," was Marilyn's usual comment to reporters who had run afoul of the commissioner.

Howard was the commissioner in charge of the department during the beating and sodomizing by officers of Abner Louima, a Haitian immigrant, in Brooklyn; the shooting of an unarmed West African immigrant,

Amadou Diallo, in the Bronx; and the killing of an unarmed squeegee-man in the Bronx. The commissioner had taken flack for attending the Oscars with his wife through the financial generosity of a friend who was an executive at Revlon.

The commissioner was not entirely without fault for the negative media attention that seemed to swirl around him. After all, he was a man who once complained to *The Times* that negative perceptions of him stemmed from his downturned mouth.

Many reporters chose to ignore the fact that under his tenure, crime had dropped to some of the lowest rates in the history of the city. There was no question that he did not get enough credit for crime dropping to its lowest point since *Dragnet* was on the air. I knew Marilyn was frustrated with the fact that the commissioner did not seem to be getting much credit for the crime drops, and the press seemed to be unwilling to focus on much of anything other than scandal and mistakes. So, when I realized that major crimes in Central Park had dropped seventy-five percent in the last six years, I knew I had a story.

For what it was worth, I had an affinity toward the commissioner. He had spent much of his career in federal law enforcement—work similar to my father's—before Mayor Rudy Giuliani called him to New York. The commissioner was the son of Russian Jewish parents who had grown up in the Bronx and Long Island. I related to stories the commissioner had told me about beginning his professional life in New York as an idealist, at age twenty-three, thinking that he could change the world by fighting crime through his job at the United States Bureau of Narcotics and Dangerous Drugs, a predecessor to the Drug Enforcement Administration. In 1979, the commissioner moved to the United States Marshals Service, where he rose up to become one of the nation's most well-known fugitive hunters. In his time there, he was widely credited with transforming the Marshals Service from a criminal baby-sitting agency into the fugitive-hunting task force of Tommy Lee Jones movies. Whatever criticisms people had about him, it was hard for me to overlook his achievements.

I told Marilyn about my idea of writing a major display story for the front of the section on crime in Central Park, and she arranged for a meeting with the commissioner in his office on the fourteenth floor of police headquarters. Howard Safir greeted me from behind the desk that another former New York City police commissioner, Teddy Roosevelt, had once used. I took a seat on the couch, and he began one of his typical mono-logues on the decline of crime in the city.

Our conversation veered to Central Park. We talked about the statis-tics. The park had not had this few crimes since the 1960s, he said. Then I brought up what Marilyn had told me about the commissioner himself spending a lot of time rollerblading in the park. "If you want to see if peo-ple consider the park safe, go by the loop around ten o'clock at night," the commissioner said. "It is wall-to-wall packed with rollerbladers and bikers."

I was in the park early the next morning stalking a perfect victim for my story when my pager beeped.

212-556-7000.

It was the metro desk calling. I called the office, expecting that the day assignment editor and my boss, Gerry Mullany, was checking up to see how progress on the Central Park safety story was going.

"I know this is going to ruin your day, Jayson, but I just got word that there was a murder in the park," he said. "Kevin and Michael are headed up there, but I want you to get to the location as quick as possible."

I dialed 212-374-6700.

"DCPI," the police officer in the deputy commissioner for public infor-mation's office answered.

Within minutes, I hailed a yellow cab on Central Park South—a task that can invariably be delayed in New York if the color of your skin is dark—and asked the driver to take me as close as he could get me to 107th Street on the West Side of the park. I jumped out of the car at the corner and followed the police detectives and officers toward the wooded area where they were congregating. I soon found myself deep in the woods, cut-ting a path through American and English elms as I walked toward the area where I saw the most police activity.

"Get out of there!" I heard from behind me. "All of you, get out of there!"

The screaming was coming from a large man in a dark-green uniform and matching baseball cap.

"This is a crime scene, you all need to come back!"

I tried to see what was happening in the area where the police were located, but couldn't. My view was blocked by a police truck that was obstructing the area where, it appeared, the woman's body had been found. I began making my way back to the voice, where crime scene tape unfurled in all directions, making it virtually impossible to tell which areas the police wanted us to stay out of and where they wanted us to go. I continued west, crossing another police line far from the crime scene, when I encountered the man in the green uniform, a parks enforcement officer.

"Is it okay for us to stay here?"

"No, you need to go over there," he said, not specifying where there was.

"Where?"

"There," he said again, without pointing in any direction.

"I am sorry, sir, I am confused, which way do you . . ."

"There," he said again.

"Excuse, I am not trying to be rude, but . . ."

Before I could finish my sentence, the parks enforcement officer lunged at me, grabbing my arm and twisting me around. The officer held my arm behind my back as he carried me, lifting me off the ground, as he dragged me down a paved hill, my press pass dangling. At the bottom of the hill, a group of reporters and photographers were clustered. Many of them began to turn toward me and the parks enforcement officer at the sound of our commotion. Michael Cooper yelled "What the fuck," and I could hear him on his cell phone saying, "It looks like they are trying to arrest Jayson." The officer was yelling at this point, "Do you want me to fucking arrest you?" and I was yelling back, still restrained, "I would have gotten out of the way if you had just told me where to go." Misha Elliot, a photographer from the *Daily News,* began snapping pictures of the circus that was unfolding.

"Shit," I heard the officer mumble under his breath.

The officer let go of my hand, took me by the back of my shirt and threw me under yellow police tape, toward the media that were staring at him.

"What just happened?" Michael asked me, putting down his cell phone.

I massaged my aching arm. "I was just standing up there with a bunch of photographers and reporters, and there was police tape in every direction. I asked the officer where to go and he would not tell me. He just grabbed me, put my arm around my back and started dragging me down the hill."

Michael looked aghast. "That's ridiculous, you were nowhere near the crime scene. You should make a formal complaint to the Parks Department or to the police. That's just ridiculous."

I looked at Michael, pondering the situation. In their haste to seal off the area, the police had placed their yellow crime tape every which way, making it impossible to tell exactly where you were supposed to go or not go. I'd been standing up on the hill with a bunch of other journalists, trying to figure out how to get to the right spot and for some reason the officer decided that I was going to be his little rag doll.

"Don't worry about it," I said. "Let's just figure out what the hell is going on."

We turned our attention to the task at hand. I compared notes with Michael. All we knew was that a thirty-nine-year-old woman had been found dead in the park. We had heard that the woman appeared to have been sexually assaulted, but we did not have a name or any other information. Michael had also heard that the police found an orange juice container that appeared to have a fingerprint smudged on it in blood. The police had also found two packs of condoms, and a used one near the body. I had heard from a detective that the woman had been found lying on her back, naked from the waist down except for white socks. Her jeans were found nearby. Her purse, which still had her wallet in it, was hanging around her neck.

"The wallet," Michael said.

"What?" I asked.

"The wallet. I saw the woman detective walk over to those people over there," Michael said, pointing to a group of three people standing near a tree. "She showed them some kind of ID and asked them some questions."

Michael walked over to the group. When he returned a few minutes later, he immediately got onto his cell phone.

"Give me Gerry," he said. "It's Michael. It's about the Central Park murder. Yes. Get him out of the meeting.

"Gerry, I wanted you to know that it is a white woman, last name is Fuchs. A detective showed her ID to some witnesses and they remember that she was a white woman with the last name Fuchs.

"Yes.

"I know. I know. Okay. Great. Thanks."

He hung up the phone and walked over to me, almost excited.

"It's going to be a front-page story," he said. "A dead white woman in Central Park, near the Upper West Side and this neighborhood that means A1. They have carved out the space on the page."

Michael stopped before I had a chance to say anything.

"Wait a second," he said, turning and then walking back to the group of people.

"Shit," he said when he came back a few minutes later. "They said the card was a welfare card. That about knocks it off A1."

Michael got back on his cell phone. I could hear that he was having a conversation with an editor on the metro desk, but could not make out what was being said.

"B1," he said, using the internal phrase for the front of The Metro Section. "They want one thousand words just like I thought."

I could tell he was disappointed at the news. Later, Michael found out that the woman was homeless and made his next prediction. "B3," he said. "Nine hundred words."

Earlier in the day, when I was summoned to the northern tip of Central Park, I was convinced that this was going to be a huge story. After all, given how safe the park had become, it was hard to imagine a bigger crime story than a sexual assault and murder in Giuliani's Central Park. It could be a front-page story, an editor told me, "given the type of people who live in that area." Michael had concurred after learning that the woman was white. Now, moments later, when Michael learned that she was on food stamps, he had revised his prediction and had it confirmed by the metro desk—the story would likely run on the front of the section. But when he found out she was homeless, he took it back, judging the killing to be third-page, local-section news.

That he could guess so accurately shocked me. I wasn't naïve, exactly—I knew that some lives were considered more disposable than others—but I had to wonder if the murder would have been mentioned at all if the victim had been black or Hispanic. After taking a call from Henry Stern, the parks commissioner, about my story about safety in Central Park and listening to his assurances that the officer had been mistaken to attempt to detain me, I decided to call the metro desk and ask where the murder story was running.

Michael was only a little off.

The story ran on B3 at 926 words.

CHAPTER ELEVEN
SINS OF THE FATHER

There are very few New York City reporters who do not encounter the Hasidim at some point in their careers.

Often it can occur at a crime scene or fire near their neighborhoods, sometimes at political fund-raisers, or even in the office of a high-ranking city official. New York City's Hasidim are made up of several groups of Orthodox Jews who came to Brooklyn from Eastern Europe during and after World War II to resettle their communities, which had been largely destroyed by the Nazis and looked down upon by the Communist governments that followed.

Their animosity toward *The New York Times* seemed to me to be fueled by an unreasonable amount of paranoia. After all, we were just there to report the news, and occasionally something regarding one of their communities became of interest. That's what happened in the fall of 1999, after a construction worker (an illegal immigrant from Mexico) was killed in an accident in one of the many Hasidic housing complexes going up in Williamsburg, Brooklyn. I had my own form of hypersensitive paranoia as well, assuming when I could not make headway reporting in a neighborhood like Hasidic Williamsburg, that my race was the big factor involved. Those assumptions were proven wrong more than once.

I was standing outside of a yeshiva, not far from the Williamsburg Bridge, with a photographer who had come with me to the Hasidic neighborhood on the Brooklyn side of the East River. We had spent the morning visiting construction sites and schools, me filling my notebook with details and him taking pictures of anything that seemed interesting. I had waited for the photographer on a Bedford Avenue street corner, across from a kosher deli. I started going through a pack of Camel Lights as I watched the men in black hats and black coats go by, and the women with strollers and little children in tow.

I stuck out like a sore thumb in Williamsburg's Southside. Most of the Hasidim were Russians, Poles and Hungarians who had come over after 1945, or their descendants. *The Times* was looking into the construction work of one particular builder, a man named Eugene Ostreicher, himself a victim of the Holocaust, who had come over from Hungary.

We drove in the photographer's company car over to 26 Heyward Street, the site of a building that Brooklyn District Attorney Charles Hynes was investigating. Rumor had it that Orthodox Jewish builders in the neighborhood were getting preferential treatment from City Hall. Everyone was staring inside the car, while I was staring at everyone outside. I felt like we had been magically transported into some previous century.

I had stumbled onto the story the same way Hynes had stumbled onto his investigation, when Eduardo Daniel Gutiérrez, a twenty-year-old illegal immigrant from San Matías, Mexico died in a construction accident on Middleton Street. He had plunged three stories into a thick and wet pile of concrete, where he died of suffocation. Investigators wanted to know whether the sixty-nine-year-old developer, Eugene Ostreicher, was able to skirt city building code and construction rules because of ties to the top aides of Mayor Giuliani and $87,000 in campaign contributions made by his wife, daughter and a friend of the family.

I had come to Williamsburg to look into allegations made that the builders were damaging the property next to theirs and had lied, telling the city that the apartments were faculty housing to avoid certain zoning regulations, while all along they were selling the apartments as expensive condominiums. My examination that morning clearly showed that the construction of 26 Heyward had caused the foundation of a neighboring building to crumble.

I walked to the front door of the five-story, red-brick building and examined the mailboxes. I had a computer printout in my back pocket that listed the residents of the Heyward Street building. I also had the Department of Buildings records, where the developers told the city that they planned to use the structure for faculty housing for the Bnos Yakov Educational Center, a yeshiva connected to the small but influential sect of Hasidim known as the Pupas. The only problem was that the developers had also filed records with the State Attorney General's office, listing the proposed sale of nine condominiums at 26 Heyward for between $267,000 and $310,000 each.

In the building's lobby, there were only five names on the mailboxes. Two were the last names of the developers, and another was that of their construction company. Through the windows, though, I could see children's toys and other items that suggested families were living inside.

I rang a couple of doorbells, but no one replied.

A woman peeked out at me from behind the curtains of her third-floor window as I walked back outside, waiting for someone to come by and walk toward the building. Within minutes, a man dressed in Hasidic garb walked quickly toward me, his cell phone glued to the side of his right ear.

"Who are you?" he yelled, in a tone that suggested more of an order to vacate the sidewalk than a question.

I wanted to say that I was a citizen of the United States legally standing on a street corner, but I didn't. I might, after all, need the man, I thought to myself.

"I am Jayson Blair, a reporter for *The New York Times,*" I replied.

"What do you want?" he yelled again, his cell phone still in place against his ear.

"I am trying to get in touch with some of the families that live in the building," I said.

"About what?" he asked.

"Construction in Willamsburg," I said.

"They don't want to talk to you," he yelled again.

I asked him how he knew. He did not reply, at least not directly.

"They don't want to talk to you," he yelled again.

By now, more Hasidic men, armed with cell phones, were descending upon me. No amount of cajoling on my part convinced the men to tell me who they were or put me in touch with residents of the building. After unfruitful attempts at discourse that went on for about thirty minutes, I left my office telephone number with the first man who had approached me and said goodbye, so I could meet back up with the photographer and head over to the Bnos Yakov Educational Center.

I had tried, repeatedly, to get the head of Bnos Yakov on the phone so we could talk about the faculty housing that was supposed to be located within the building at 26 Heyward. Since he had decided not to return my messages, I decided to greet him with a surprise visit.

As we drove to the Wilson Street headquarters, the photographer told me about covering other stories that involved the insular Hasidim, like the Crown Heights riots. We discussed a photography project he was working on about dignity in old age, and how he became fluent enough in German to surprise many, including his wife.

"Sie müssen die Frauen lieben, um die Zeit zu dauern, Deutsches zu erlernen," he said, saying in so many words that his love for women led him to learn German.

Outside the school, as we waited for an administrator, the photographer took pictures of schoolchildren boarding a bus. Adorable as they all were in their matching uniforms, the photographer was right, the children were staring at us like we had landed in front of their school out of a spacecraft from Mars.

"They are looking at us like they had never seen a black man in their lives," he said as he snapped a few more pictures of the school children.

After several unsuccessful attempts to get people to talk, I spoke with a Hasidic businessman, the son of Hungarian Jews who came over after the Holocaust, who offered me some advice on the history of the community. He told me why it was hard for them to buy the notion that a reporter from *The New York Times* was doing them a favor.

"Your race is not your problem. It's your newspaper," the businessman said.

"Is it because of our coverage of Israel?" I asked.

"No, no, no, no, no," the businessman replied. "Look back and read your newspaper's coverage of the Holocaust," he added.

The businessman explained that there had been some recent stories in *The Times* that threatened some of the social service money that was coming illegally into the community, and that had people on edge. He added that the Hasidim did not, by any stretch of the imagination, have any regard for the *Times*'s coverage of the Holocaust. He said that among those who had the most animosity toward *The Times* were the Hungarian Jews who saw their relatives killed toward the end of the war, a time when America and its newspapers knew full well that the trains were headed toward gas chambers. Ostreicher, and many who knew him, the businessman told me, were Hungarian.

One Saturday morning, inspired by my conversation about the *Times*'s coverage of the Holocaust, I walked down West Forty-third Street, about a block away from my desk in *Times* headquarters, to the corporate morgue, which was located near Eighth Avenue. The researcher on duty pointed me to the long row of microfilm cassettes that included copies of the newspapers published in the 1940s, and I began pulling up relevant phrases and dates based on an index maintained by the archivists. My initial assumptions about *The Times* and the Holocaust were about to be proven wrong.

I found that the newspaper had never made the Holocaust the lead editorial of the day, and had run only six front-page articles in six years of war coverage that mentioned the Jews were the unique target of Hitler's extermination efforts. Not once was it the lead news story, even though there was ample credible and detailed information about what was happening at the death camps.

The Hasidic businessman's early comment came echoing back into my head. His argument was simple: *The New York Times* and other American newspapers knew Jews were being sent to death camps in 1944, before Hitler even began the extermination of the Hungarian Jews, and that more prominent coverage could have saved at least some lives.

"Now you see why the Jews of Williamsburg have a hard time believing that *The New York Times* has them in their best interest," the Hasidic businessmen said when I called him back after looking through the morgue archives. I did not have an answer for him.

CHAPTER TWELVE
HOW RACE IS LIVED IN THE NEWSROOM

One element I found wonderful about New York from the moment I arrived as a summer intern at *The Times* was the city's vast diversity of people and places.

When you are white in America, there are all sorts of factors that come into play when determining where to live, but rarely is skin color such a defining and limiting factor. One aspect I loved about New York, as opposed to Boston or Washington, D.C., were the limits to its racial balkanization. Sure, most ethnic minorities lived in the outer boroughs, but even Manhattan had Chinatown, Harlem, Washington Heights and other interesting ethnic neighborhoods. The city is a place where you could work on Wall Street during the day, listen to jazz in Harlem in the evening, and party with the punk rockers in the East Village at night.

The great size of the city made it a great place to hide, be who you wanted to be, and even have a secret life. The mosaic was one that anyone could fit into, regardless of their race, gender, interests, political leanings and so on. New York was also an interesting playground in which to observe people of different worlds interacting, like the Poles and the Ukrainians, who live side-by-side on Second Avenue in the East Village even though they had been at war with each other for centuries, and the Arabs and Jews who were neighbors in southern Brooklyn.

The Times, as a newspaper built around a community of people with similar interests and income levels, serves as a great measuring point of that contrast, whether it comes to coverage of the artists moving into the neighborhood underneath the Manhattan and Brooklyn Bridges, or whether its reporters are covering Harlem crime.

"Ten dead in Harlem on B10, and orchards growing in Central Park on the front page," was one version of the exaggerated self-mockery that was bandied about by many young people at *The Times*.

We were not so naïve to believe that editorial decisions were based on the most compelling stories of the day, and not the interests of our specific readers. Every time a metro editor would get on a high horse about serving our readers, we would start to talk about the story selections that were incongruent with those ideals. A newspaper sends a message with story placement, essentially telling its readers that the important things are on the front page and section covers, while the rest one could take or leave.

The orchards notion did not just fall out of the sky. It came from comparing the grisly and important stories that ran in the paper one day when a display piece with gigantic flowers ran on the front page of The Metro Section. The assistant metro editor who handled the boxed features had a thing for flowers and pretty pictures, often making the case that that was what attracts readers to the pages.

"The first thing people look at," she would often say, "are pictures and headlines."

One learns from their environs, particularly when it comes to the priorities. Because editors put certain stories on the front of a section or the lead of the paper, they are the ones that many of us reporters study and try to replicate, hoping most of all, more than helping people or exposing something, that we can get our name, and equally as important our writing, on some sliver of the front. The competition is intense, often with reporters checking the in-house electronic archives called TimesPast to make comparisons to each other's work. There would be interesting observations often about who was favored or not. Because managers were busy running a newspaper, they operated on impressions, while we had the stone, cold facts.

In the summer of 2000, *The Times* published a fifteen-story account of "How Race Is Lived in America," which many thought was destined to win the next year's Pulitzer Prize in the newspaper public service category. The series had been a massive effort launched by Joe Lelyveld and choreographed by Gerald Boyd, who was then the deputy managing editor for news, and Soma Golden Behr, the assistant managing editor for special projects. The series was widely praised by some for its analysis of black and white relationships since the civil rights movement, and harshly criticized by others who said that the American mosaic included many more people than it seemed from *The Times* stories, particularly Asian and Hispanic Americans.

There were some strange moments. One black reporter who was writing an autobiographical piece for *The New York Times Magazine* almost quit over what he described as an attempt by "three white editors to tell him how to run his life." Another reporter extensively interviewed a white quarterback at a historically black college and then turned in a draft of the story that did not include anything from the African-American side. When the writer balked at changing the piece, the paper had to send down another correspondent, who was only able to deliver a black band member on such a short timetable.

At the last minute, editors concerned about the lack of racial diversity in the stories commissioned an article that centered on a Hispanic businessman in Texas. Critics at the *Akron Beacon Journal,* the subject of one of the stories, complained that the writer would have been better off examining "How Race Was Lived at *The New York Times.*"

One Saturday in December, when I was in the office working my weekly weekend duty, I obtained a glimpse of an anecdote that I would have used if I were writing a story on "How Race Is Lived at *The New York Times.*"

The weekend chief on the metro desk of *The Times* had to decide between two stories. One was a feature about a white woman from Texas who had been hit on the head with a brick in midtown a year before. The other story was about the trial of a man who carried out one of the longest serial rape and murder sprees in the history of New York City. The man's rape and murder spree occurred in Harlem, and had not been mentioned once on the pages of *The Times,* a glaring omission that was all but pointed out in the lead. When I read the two stories in the computer system, I knew that the weekend editor had no choice but to put the piece on the serial killer on the front page of the section.

The piece was poignant and powerful, and the reporter did not shy away from attacking the media directly. The reporter even referenced Nicole Barrett, the woman from Texas who had been hit on the head with a brick, something I thought would insure that the weekend editor would see that she was just falling in line with the rest of the racially insensitive media by not putting it "out front."

"Families of Victims Question Attention Paid to Killings"
By DAVID ROHDE

After a jury convicted Arohn Kee on Wednesday night of carrying out one of the longest serial rape and murder sprees in the city in years, the father of one of his victims stormed up to a group of reporters.

"Where were they in the beginning?" the man, Gregory Washington, thundered as relatives of other victims struggled to restrain him. "It took another two girls to get raped for them to do anything!"

Mr. Washington went on to unleash a frustration-ridden diatribe against the police and the media: "It's because they're black and Hispanic! . . ."

An array of officials involved in the case—prosecutors, detectives and defense lawyers—agreed with part of the assessment: the Kee case received less public attention because his victims were black and Hispanic residents of Harlem . . .

What if Paola Illera, Mr. Kee's first victim, had been a young woman from Texas smashed in the head with a brick in Midtown Manhattan? What if Johalis Castro, his second, had been a missing Upper East Side socialite? And what if Mr. Washington's daughter, Rasheda, had been a young woman from Buffalo pushed in front of a speeding subway train?

I left the office feeling sure that it would be on the front of the section, and was surprised the next morning when I saw what the weekend editor had placed on the "out front" when I picked up the paper in front of my building on Broadway.

"Year After Brick Attack, Refusing to 'Tiptoe Around Life'"
By KATHERINE E. FINKELSTEIN

ATHENS, Tex., Dec. 21 — Sometime next week, Nicole Barrett, 28, plans to get back on a horse.

"The doctor said I could so long as I wear a helmet, which I'm not going to do because I'm not going to tiptoe around life," she said as she drove her red truck along State Highway 31 from her home in this small town to nearby Tyler for an appointment with a doctor who is helping her to regain some of her memory and cognitive skills . . .

. . . Ms. Barrett had been absorbed in the pleasures of a new haircut, a new coat, a new job and a new life in New York City that was beginning to make sense. That she even awoke, weeks later, amazed the doctors at Bellevue Hospital Center. After a month, she walked out the front door just days before Christmas, with a list from her doctors in hand that said: no guns, no horses . . .

The story went on to focus on how Nicole was riding a horse again.

I called up a fellow reporter who, despite his Ivy League credentials, was among my most down-to-earth colleagues.

"Um, did you, uh, see the front of The Metro Section today?" I recall asking. He just started laughing.

"I don't get it," I continued. "We've got a story on a bunch of dead black and Hispanic women whose families are complaining that no one is paying attention to their rapes and murders buried in the paper, while a year later Nicole rides a horse again on the front of the section? What year is it? What world am I living in?"

"Welcome to the real world, Mr. Blair," he responded. "This is how it's done. This is what these editors think readers care about."

Katherine Eban Finkelstein was an up-and-coming reporter covering health care at The New York Observer when she caught the attention of Joyce Purnick, who was then the metro editor at The Times.

If you were to read her evaluations by those who interviewed Katherine, you would find that Joyce was very high on bringing her onto the metro staff in order to corner the market on health coverage. Some other editors were less enthusiastic about Katherine, but Joyce's persistence won them over. Katherine's writing was considered slightly below the mark of a full-time Times reporter, but Joyce was hiring her to deliver scoops, so I hardly could understand why that mattered. In typical Joyce fashion, she turned on Katherine within months and was soon agitating to get her out of the paper. This left Katherine, a sweet woman with thin skin despite the tough façade, reeling without a protector, a position that no one wanted to be in within The Times newsroom.

On February 10, 2001, I was drinking a cup of the free coffee that came on carts for those of us who have to work to put out the super-early bulldog edition every Saturday morning. Nothing was really on my mind other than the really bad cup of coffee and the apricot pastry in front of me. One of the more ridiculous logistical endeavors of working at The Times was putting out the early edition of the Sunday paper that landed on newsstands nationwide Saturday afternoon. The deadlines meant that editions of the paper had to be written, edited, closed and sent to the printers at eleven in the morning, a little after two in the afternoon, and then in mid-evening before the staff even got to the normal nightly deadlines.

For the earliest of those deadlines, *Times* reporters are often asked to do insurmountable, Herculean tasks of writing stories from scratch early in the morning, with less than a few hours to get their jobs done. If you were not drafted into the Saturday morning nightmare, you often had nothing to do as a reporter into the early afternoon—after the two p.m. edition closed. This was one of those mornings of boredom for me. One frequent practice on my part during these slow Saturday mornings was to read the next day's paper in the electronic queues that held stories. Once I finished reading the major stories out of Washington, National and Business, I would move to Metro. By about eleven in the morning I had made my way to the queue in Metro where backfield editors review stories.

I received a text message from Eleanor Volstad, an energetic metro copy editor who was a partner on breaks to the *Times*'s fifth-floor smoking room. Ellie, as she went by, wrote a text message that flashed on the top of my screen, asking me to take a look at a file called Y21NOTE that was being edited. Katherine had been holding onto her job by the skin of her teeth, and had been given a chance at rebirth through writing about the trial of Sean "Puffy" Combs, the hip-hop star and producer who had been charged with gun possession in connection with a shooting that occurred across the street from *The Times* inside Club New York. I was around the corner at Robert Emmett's Bar and Grill, enjoying some Scotch, when the shooting happened a little after three in the morning. Katherine became the lead reporter on the trial once the Manhattan District Attorney's office chose to indict Combs on gun possession charges.

Jon Landman, the new metro editor, had been fascinated by the Combs trial, even pulling out the race card once to argue that he felt the stories were not making it onto the front page because they were about a black man in the metropolitan area. Jon and his deputies clearly saw the stories as a chance to give readers some insight into the world of hip-hop and black culture.

Katherine got on the bad side of many blacks in the newsroom while trying to give her editors what they wanted. In a January story previewing the trial, Katherine wrote, "Mr. Combs and his entourage, known for their display of wealth—called 'bling bling' in the rap world—made a clear attempt at moderation yesterday. Mr. Combs' mother, Janice, tucked her long, platinum-blond hair beneath a dark broad-brimmed hat. And her fingernails, often silver and frosted, were now clear and pale. There were few furs, spiked heels or leather pants to distract the jurors.

"But it was impossible not to notice the hand-tailored suits, expensive ties, cuff links and manicures at the defense table, where seven lawyers, including Johnnie L. Cochran Jr., sat with the three defendants. Also visible was a tattoo on Mr. Combs's [sic] neck, just above his shirt collar, that read, 'God's Child.'"

The intimation that *The Times* was somehow shocked that a black man might have a defense team filled with men in nice suits—as if she had expected them to show up in their warm-ups and clubbing clothes with jukeboxes on their shoulders—would not have been so bad were it not for a story that came less than a month later. It was headlined "These Days, Even Puff Needs A Mommy."

There was the reference to the "fruit juice and chicken sandwiches for her son" that seemed to come out of the manual on black stereotypes. Then there was the line about "the quixotic and violent world of rap music," as if everyone in rap was foolishly impractical or violent. Katherine felt she had to translate that Mrs. Combs' diamonds were known as "ice" in the rap world, as opposed to the Jewish jewelry world, the South African diamond world, or movies starring white people that referred to them by the same name. There was Katherine's use of the word "gangsta" as opposed to gangster when it was coming out of Mrs. Combs' mouth. She was eating chicken and drinking lemonade by the end of the story.

If the story about Mrs. Combs was insensitive and silly, Y17NOTE read like a safari into black culture for *Times* readers on the Upper East Side. It was a reporter's notebook, the space-filling features the paper often ran on trials and other continuing events. In the story, headlined "Scenes From a Courtroom: Hip-Hop and Unhipness Collide at a Rap Star's Trial," Katherine wrote about courtroom spectators' "gold teeth," noted that in the rap world it was a sign of disrespect to throw money at someone's feet (as opposed to other cultures where it's okay), and that parka bubbles were primarily used to hide weapons, and used the word "buff" to mean muscular and then explained that was unique to black culture. The story went so far as to call Combs' lawyers, among them Johnnie Cochran, "gangstas in suits." And the story went on and on and on.

After reading the story and conferring with Ellie and another copy editor, I decided to bring the story to the attention of the assistant metro editor for weekends. The weekend editor had one of the toughest jobs in the building. Being the weekend editor on the metro desk meant that you were not only in charge of that section's very large report, but you had to provide support to the various other desks that are grossly understaffed on the weekends.

To her credit, the weekend editor agreed to give the story a read when I walked over and suggested that some of it might be insensitive, but when I saw she had moved it to the copy desk for layout onto the page without making any changes or mentioning to me her reasoning for letting it go forward, an active run of messages began flying back and forth between myself and copy editors. Several of the editors agreed that the story was widely off the mark and that it would take massive rewriting—essentially reconstructive surgery—to make it publishable. Among these editors were two Irish Americans, a Wasp, and a black copy editor. It was a diverse group in agreement that the story would be an embarrassment to the metro desk and the newspaper.

I had sat in too many committee meetings and had too many conversations with people about why *The Times* had been unable to penetrate into the rising number of ethnic middle-class communities in New York. My basic thought was that *The Times* hardly covered the issues that mattered to those people when they were not middle-class, and that going on safaris into things like the rap world sent a clear message that the newspaper was written for someone other than them, to translate their world to the real readers. Stories like Katherine's did not help the cause.

Carolyn Lee, the assistant managing editor for weekends, was known as a champion for women and minorities inside the newsroom. Carolyn was one of only two women in the top ranks of the newsroom's management—known as the masthead, the leaders whose names appear in the box on the editorial page. Nan Robertson, the Pulitzer Prize-winning former *Times* writer who wrote *The Girls in the Balcony,* a book about women at the newspaper, had told me about Carolyn when she was teaching at the University of Maryland.

After graduating with a degree in physics from Tennessee Technological University and working at newspapers in Texas and Kentucky, Carolyn joined *The Times* in 1978. That was the same year *The Times* settled a lawsuit brought by several women at the paper that alleged systematic discrimination in hiring, promotions and job placements. As a result of the lawsuit, *The Times* created a plan for hiring and promoting women. Along the way, Carolyn became the first female picture editor, the first woman assistant managing editor and, perhaps, the first *Times* assistant managing editor to publicly reprimand her boss when, at least according to newsroom lore, Max Frankel congratulated her as the latest "adornment" to his masthead.

"Thank you, but I have not worked so hard all these years to be called an adornment," Carolyn supposedly said.

I wonder whether Max would have said that about a man. By the way, his comment was not made in the 1970s, but in 1990.

Michel Marriott had also told me about how, as assistant managing editor for news administration, Carolyn had recruited some of the top talent, particularly minorities, to the newspaper. Michel emphasized that Carolyn was among the best managers in the newsroom when it came to understanding issues that minorities and women faced. That's why I decided to approach Carolyn with my concerns about the reporter's notebook. In several weeks, Carolyn was going to be turning the reins of the weekend operation over to Nicholas Kristof. The two of them were sitting at the news desk, the department at the center of the *Times* newsroom that was essentially the brains of the operation.

The *Times*'s news desk was rare in that it provided a second check on editors, reviewing stories for fairness, accuracy and balance and doing special checks on the front page and stories running on the front of sections. All major decisions at night were cleared through the news desk, which was run by the best of the best *Times* editors and headline writers. I waited for Carolyn and Nick to finish their conversation before approaching them at her desk.

"I know you are busy with deadline," I said, holding a printout of Katherine's "bling bling" story, as it later came to be called. "But I am a little concerned about this story, and I don't want to say anything specific, but there are a number of things that I think might be considered insensitive."

I was trying to be careful with my words. I had asked several of the white editors on the metro copy desk to review my conclusions before walking over. I wanted to make sure that I was not the one being too sensitive. Ellie had offered to come over, but I knew that the collateral damage of going over the weekend editor's head on this one could not be underestimated. So I took it over and brought it to their attention. Several minutes later I saw Nick walking quickly past the staircase in the center of the third floor that separated the metro desk from much of the rest of the newsroom, heading straight for the metro weekend editor's desk. Even though it was a very late hour when it came to the afternoon deadline, Nick had the story pulled out of the newspaper and massive revisions made for later editions.

Colleagues on the metro desk saw the move as a victory against a boss who sometimes seemed to be mailing it in, almost always taking the path of least resistance, in this case by allowing a story that would have made *The Times* the laughing stock of many rap aficionados—not to mention all those opposed to referring to black defense lawyers like Johnnie Cochran as "gangstas in suits."

I thought it only fair to send an e-mail—albeit a bit of a zealous, self-righteous one—to Katherine to let her know that I had objected to the story. The next week, though, when Jon Landman spoke with me about the incident, it was clear that he had not agreed with the decision to revise the story. I cannot remember his exact words, but while agreeing that "gangstas in suits" was too far, he did not get the idea that he was sending the wrong message to black readers by suggesting that The Metro Section was there to provide readers with safaris into their culture.

Jon said something like, "It's a really interesting subject that we don't get a chance to write much about."

I tried my best to explain that while it is an interesting world that *The Times* does not get into, a safari into the rap world was not the type of thing that was going to win over black readers. If that was his goal, perhaps he should consider covering the communities and topics they were interested in reading more about. My words were to no avail, and it was not the first or the last time that I clashed with Jon over the racial tone of coverage.

Winning the Pulitzer in 2001 for a series called "How Race Is Lived in America" was vindication for some at *The Times*. Others, including me, were hardly blind to the reality of the way things worked on an everyday basis in the news media.

CHAPTER THIRTEEN
THE GAME

My bad relationship with the editors on the metro desk started not long after I arrived in the office. I suppose there are many things to blame, chiefly among them the fact that I am less impressive in person than I am over the telephone.

I am short. I am black. And I refuse to wear suits. I laugh loudly. Obnoxiously loud. And I did not mind skipping—yes, literally—around the newsroom. I tend to break all the minor rules, like the ones about returning the company car after assignments and filing expenses in a timely manner. And my passion for people, as well as my disdain, can be gleaned from a quick glance at my sleeve. If I seem a bit contradictory at times, it is because I am. I could be so nice to people I liked that they would conjure up feelings only associated with long lost members of their family. And I could be so cruel and cutthroat that my friends, at times, felt they did not recognize me.

"You are one fucking walking paradox," my best friend from college, Daryl Khan, who was a freelance reporter at *The Times,* liked to say to me. "In one day I could see you hand a homeless guy twenty dollars, and the next afternoon, I could see you spit in his face."

My first full year back at *The Times* after my internship was spent working hard, focusing on the task of doing my job well, and rising up through the ranks from a trainee reporter to my goal of being promoted to the full-time staff. I spent a lot of time marveling at the culture of police reporting in those early months when I was assigned to the cop shop. The crude jokes and gallows humor in the cop shop were enough to make a man sick. Jokes about rape victims and black-on-black crime were intertwined with the standard fare of racist, homophobic and cruel slams on just about anyone who was not one of them.

One of the favorite jokes among the cops and a handful of reporters was about two police officers, a veteran and a rookie, going into a bar in

East New York, Brooklyn in the middle of a brawl. Setting this scene in East New York is simply a euphemism for saying that the crowd is black. The rookie cop moves to break up the people who are fighting as the brawl spins out of control. Just as the rookie is about to wade his way into the crowd, the veteran grabs his shoulder and pulls him off to the side. "Just sit back and watch," the veteran says.

Everyone in the bar hits the ground except two men who are left standing, and the officers watch in silence as they continue to fight until one man knocks out the other. Then the veteran officer comes up behind the cheering man and pummels him on the head with his baton, knocking him out. He puts handcuffs on the man and then takes him to the cruiser. "Might as well let them kill each other on their own—we'll sort it out in the end," the veteran officer says.

I was getting knocked for leaving my cigarette ashes in the office and taking the company car on extended trips. Some things were reasonable or understandable, like the time I took the company car to Maryland to help take a friend who had been raped to the doctor. Others, like the times I would just park it outside my apartment on the Upper West Side and accumulate tickets, were much less acceptable.

One of the perks of being a *Times* police reporter was that in situations like the time my friend was raped I could call Linda Fairstein, the famed sex crimes prosecutor in the Manhattan District Attorney's office, to get advice. The downside was that I had to cover crime, like the rapes that were going on in the Bronx. I was working a customary seven-day work week this June weekend, spending both Saturday and Sunday in the cop shop.

On Saturday, I wrote about how the Special Victims Squad detectives believed that an attack on a twelve-year-old girl who was choked and then dragged under a South Bronx apartment building staircase was linked to one that had occurred several weeks before when another twelve-year-old girl was attacked under a staircase and then raped on a rooftop of a building in the Fordham section of the borough.

It was the standard cop shop formula: overview of the newsworthy incident in the first paragraph, followed by a summary of events or the names of the victims or accused in the second graph; descriptive information in the next few graphs followed by a chronological retelling of the story, with quotes from relatives, neighborhood residents and the police sprinkled throughout. This story just seemed to be filled with particularly salient facts.

A lot of high-profile crimes capture the imagination of residents because of newspaper stories. A member of the Citizen's Crime Commission once told me how when crime was dropping dramatically in the city, residents became convinced that there was a crime wave because of the tone of advertisements for new security systems that were running in *The Post* and the *Daily News*.

Stories on a crime would not always be accompanied by crime statistics. This was often the case because the public information office at the New York Police Department, particularly in Mayor Giuliani's release-no-information days, made statistics hard to come by. Still, for those of us in the dreary cop shop, there were no excuses. We could walk upstairs, pull out the stats booklets and find out what was happening in the major crime categories citywide—by borough, by section of the city, or by precinct.

I decided to go upstairs with coffee and pastries—my Saturday morning ritual for the hard-working weekend shift in the deputy commissioner's office—and drop off the eats, while looking through the stats on rapes in the Bronx. According to the statistics, there had been two hundred and forty-seven rapes in the borough from January through June, compared to three hundred and fifty in the entire year before. The borough was well on its way to surpassing the previous year's numbers. I could not get my mind off of how many victims there were, how many lives had been changed by each attack, how much trauma was left behind.

Walter Burns, the detective on duty in the public information office, was able to tell me that investigators were planning to canvas the neighborhood, distribute copies of a sketch of the suspect, and re-interview the victims. Walter told me that the Special Victims Squad was looking at anyone who lived close to the area of the attacks who was on parole and registered as a sex offender under the state's Megan's Law, adding, "but of course, there are always people who are new to the game." Walter told me that DNA samples had been collected from some of the crime scenes, but he could not say what the results were, other than the fact that they supported the police theory of the assaults.

"This is some weird shit," I said to Walter.

"Indeed, it is Mr. Blair," he replied, staring down at the stack of papers on his desk that always seemed infinitely high.

"Since this is such weird shit, I think I could take a quote on safety prevention or something along those lines," I added.

Most people who read news stories think that quotes come from interrogation-like interviews conducted by reporters and their sources. In fact, most quotes, especially on a beat like the Police Department, came about from talks like this. I wanted a quote because the rapist was on the loose, but I also knew that Walter would get points with his bosses for getting a couple of inches of valuable *New York Times* real estate for some crime prevention tips.

"How about something like this?" Walter said, going into his Mr. McGruff-the-crime-prevention-dog voice.

"'People need to be cautious, especially young people. People need to be alert when they see people in their building. When you see someone, we encourage you to confront them, don't leave him there for a twelve-year-old, because a twelve-year-old can't defend herself, much less confront him.'"

"How's that?" he asked, coming back out of character.

"Masterful, Walter, masterful. Really eloquent. Simply amazing. Perhaps you should be on stage on Broadway?"

I picked up a copy of the sketch of the man who was the suspect in the attacks and went back downstairs to file my nine hundred-word story. I got out of the office at about nine o'clock that evening and headed to my apartment on the Upper West Side. That night I sat outside on the ledge of my window, staring at the traffic on Broadway, looking uptown toward the Bronx, wondering about what little twelve-year-old girls were doing in those neighborhoods tonight. I was sure they weren't sipping a glass of red Merlot wine while sitting on a window ledge outside their $2,500 a month apartment overlooking a median full of trees, a French Roast café and the dressed-up crowds of Broadway on a Saturday night.

I retired to bed early, preparing to get up for work the next morning. I made it into the office a little bit before noon, the appointed time for the cop shop to get into gear on Sunday mornings. I had called into the deputy commissioner's office from home before arriving to check if there were any major crime developments and see if detectives had advanced on the rape story.

There was nothing new, but I knew enough to know that the assistant metro editor for weekends was going to ask me to deliver an eight to nine hundred word story, essentially on nothing having happened. It was time to "make chicken salad out of chicken shit," as Rick Bragg, a national correspondent, was fond of saying in the face of a ridiculous assignment. By the end of the day they had caught the Bronx rapist and linked him to two other rapes, including an attack on another twelve-year-old girl.

"What does this guy have, twelve-year-old-girl radar?" asked a reporter from *Newsday* who was also stationed in the cop shop.

The case was a "red ball." The term was often used by city police detectives for cases that were given high priority and had to be closed fast because of political considerations. Depending on who told you the story, the phrase either came from the Red Ball Express, the name of the World War II truck units noted for quick delivery of gasoline to the front; the types of trains that had top priority right of way on the tracks; or the fire that would be under a detective's rear end if they did not close the cases fast. In other cities, such cases were known as "heaters" because of how warm it got, or A.P.E.S., which stood for "actual political emergencies." In New York we had red balls.

For a reporter, a red ball meant a lot of running around scrounging for facts, anecdotes, statistics and anything to fill a crime story at the point when the police were most sensitive to any criticism. It was a moment of great tension, until, of course, the suspect was caught. Then, the red ball would turn into a love fest. We loved them for giving us a closing arc to the narratives of our stories. They loved us for putting their names in print and making them look good. On your garden-variety arrest in a murder in a poor neighborhood, a reporter gets to talk to a spokesman or spokeswoman in the public information office. If the arrest is a big deal or was prominent in the news, a reporter might get to talk to a detective, detective sergeant or a lieutenant running a squad. If it was really big, the commanding officer for detectives in the borough might call on the "hotline" telephone line that was wired into the offices of all the newspapers at the cop shop. If it was a white woman hit with a brick in Midtown Manhattan, media attention demanded the police commissioner.

Since this was four Hispanic women getting brutally raped by one man over a short period of time, it was in between the police commissioner and much above the commanding officer for borough detectives, so we got the ever elusive man, his majesty himself, William H. Allee Jr., chief of detectives of the New York Police Department. The NYPD was a balkanized place of more than 40,000 civilian and uniformed employees who competed based on political allegiances and ethnic origins, and measured themselves by the number of stars on their badges, the grades of their rank and the bureaus where they worked. No bureau was more prestigious than the detectives.

The chief did not have the most enviable position in the department when it came to publicity. When he was not catching strafe from the mayor, the police commissioner, the first deputy commissioner and the chief of department for cases not being closed, he was catching flak from detectives in the field and their commanders, who felt they were not getting the support they needed. The chief was not particularly well-liked among reporters, but that meant little about his job performance. After all, how does one measure performance in a job that is impossible anyway?

Allee took the grand occasion of the arrest of Rayshawn Aikens, the twenty-six-year-old rapist, to invite us to his conference room on the tenth floor of One Police Plaza. It was a Sunday, so the department big wigs were not around to hold a news conference in the press room auditorium on the second floor that was reserved for such occasions.

The chief detailed how detectives from the Bronx Special Victims Squad fanned out Saturday to the homes of friends and relatives of Aikens who lived in the borough, Manhattan and Staten Island after matching one of his fingerprints to one found at a scene of one of the rapes. Aikens was staying at his parents' Osgood Avenue house, near Silver Lake Park, on the northern tip of Staten Island. When detectives showed up at the front door, Aikens bolted out the back, over a fence into neighbors' yards, through a grocery store and onto several rooftops before he found a hiding place for himself underneath a bed in a house that he broke into on Gordon Street.

Police helicopters and additional units joined the chase, which went on for ten minutes, before SWAT team members found him hiding under the bed and took him into custody. Allee told us that his detectives believed Aikens targeted girls and young women "who looked very young." Allee also described the two new rapes that Aikens was charged with committing. In one instance, a twenty-three-year-old woman was attacked after she heard a noise and walked into the hallway of her apartment building in the South Bronx. The last one occurred on Friday night when he attacked another twelve-year-old girl, choked her and dragged her under an apartment building staircase.

"Every rape is heinous and vicious," the chief said. "But these seem to be even more vicious in their intensity and the fact that he picked on such young people."

I could not have agreed more.

The chief continued, telling us that they believed that Aikens was involved in several more similar attacks on young women. Aikens had been working as a truck mechanic at a tire repair store in the Longwood section of the Bronx. He had previously worked as a barber and tattoo artist in Manhattan.

The clincher, though, was that Aikens was married and had three daughters, ages four, three and two. That last fact stuck with me. I tagged it onto the end of the story.

That night, a little after eleven o'clock, I walked out the front door of headquarters with my black bag hanging over my shoulder. As I made my way in the darkness through the dimly lit Police Plaza, I noticed an object underneath the twenty-foot red sculpture near the entrance to the United State's Attorney's office.

At first I could not make out the object. I was exhausted, it was after eleven and I had been working tirelessly for seven straight days. I stared at the object. It was white. I looked closer. I squinted. I looked closer. I could see it now. It was a white sneaker. A little girl's sneaker.

I glanced closer as I continued to walk, but caught something else out of the corner of my eye. It was another sneaker, a little more than a dozen feet away on the steps of the plaza. It was the matching sneaker. I spun around, my bag slapping my back, and that's when I noticed the black tights. Black tights that had to have been a child's, lying right here in the middle of Police Plaza. I felt my heart sink. I yelled at the top of my lungs for one of the police officers standing sentry at the front of police head-quarters. I yelled again, and again, and again. By then, tears were streaming down my face. I was still screaming, but I couldn't hear my words anymore.

I woke up the next morning in my apartment overlooking Broadway. I walked over to the kitchen, which was wedged neatly into the side of the living room, as is common when you are not a millionaire or don't have rent control in an expensive neighborhood in Manhattan. I could not get the images out of my head from the previous night. I could not figure out why those shoes and tights were lying in the middle of the plaza, and why the police officers I had called had not looked around to see if there was more information. I also couldn't understand why the incident was kick-ing up so much in me.

The obvious explanation was the fact that I had been covering rape stories all weekend. But something about the attacks struck a chord deep within me. I pondered the previous night, when seeing a pair of shoes and tights caused me to start weeping underneath a statue. Flashbacks of my own sexual abuse came rushing into my head. At this moment I knew I needed to leave the cop shop and write about something else for a while. Empathy had always been one of my strengths as a journalist, and now it was eating me alive.

I wanted out of the cop shop, even though I did not dare vocalize that to anyone, but felt slighted by the transfer to metro business. I'd had a good run in the cop shop, and had just finished the investigation into builders, so I could not make heads or tails of the metro business move.

Many cub reporters get decent assignments to help propel them, but I was obviously not among the chosen, an outsider, for whatever reason—my personality, my lack of faith from the higher-ups, or race. *The Times* was a cutthroat culture that leaves no rivals standing, and I redoubled my efforts to figure out the rationale behind the move.

I quickly grew unhappy with my new work and fell back on the familiar pleasures of eight-hour shifts of drinking and cocaine parties. I did not realize at the time that I was setting myself up to fulfill the prophecies of those who did not trust me. My first assignment for metro business came from Arthur Ochs Sulzberger, Sr., the chairman emeritus and former publisher of the paper, but it was hardly high-profile. Arthur had been staring out the window of his fourteenth-floor office one day when he looked east and noticed the new, giant cylindrical NASDAQ screen that had been placed on a building in Times Square.

Arthur wanted to know how it worked, so he jotted off a note that he sent down to the newsroom that ended up in the hands of Jon Landman, who gave it to Chuck Strum, who assigned the story to me. The story on the eight-story cylindrical sign that wrapped around the recently constructed Condé Nast Building described everything from the 16.7 million distinct colors that could be displayed to the history of signage in Times Square. I wondered what happened when Arthur sent down a note about the paper's coverage of the Middle East.

Jenny Holland mastered a level of sarcasm and cynicism that would have made her brethren in Armagh, Antrim, Londonderry and the other Northern Ireland counties proud. After our night of foreplay in the dimly-lit bar underneath the subway, Jenny and I became fast and furious friends. We'd meet at Robert Emmett's, the local bar around the corner on West Forty-third Street that was quickly becoming the watering hole for young people at *The Times*. I would head back to work and she would usually head home, and we would meet up again late at night, often at the Brooklyn Inn, one of the popular bars near her apartment in Carroll Gardens. I would often take the company car.

On Saturdays, when I was able to get out of work early, we would go on adventures to see parts of New York that she had never seen before, from the Brooklyn neighborhood underneath the Verrazano Narrows Bridge to parts of Staten Island. Jenny would be left in the awkward position come Monday mornings of being asked by an editor to track down the company car, knowing full well that we had been driving around the city in it all weekend.

"Jayson, the car," she would say when I returned her pages.

When we were getting along, I usually got a free pass on the car. When we weren't, all bets were off. Often we would stay out drinking at the Brooklyn Inn until three in the morning and return to her apartment before four. Jenny would have to get up to be at work by eight in the morning, and I would give her rides to the office in the company car, dropping her off a few blocks from the Times Building so people would not ask questions about what we were doing together so early in the morning. I would be at my desk by eight in the morning and on some days did not leave until nine at night.

Jenny was the first person to point out how different I could become when I was drinking. Mean, possessive, and pathetic at times. An incident around this time seemed to reinforce her point, although I would not remember it until much later.

Daryl Khan and I were meeting Jenny and two other clerks at a bar below the ground floor of a building on Houston Street, just south of Greenwich Village and north of SoHo. Inside, we all sat in the corner as I shuttled back and forth from the table to the bar. Daryl was the only one who was not drinking. Long ago, he had had forsaken alcohol for reasons that still remained unclear to me. Years later he would be the one who vividly retold the tale of this night when I blacked out. Apparently in the course of the night's events, I pushed Daryl several times, choked him around his neck and traveled all the way home to the Upper East Side with another one of the clerks, Andrea Delbanco, to make sure she made it to her apartment safely, all the while crying hysterically about something no one could really put their finger on.

I was a bad drunk. I was a mess, but I knew that alcohol not only made me feel good, but it was about the only thing that put me to sleep at night. Others marveled at times at my ability to consume large amounts of Scotch, go to bed at four in the morning and pop back up to make it to work in time. I was usually groggy, and often it would be difficult to sort out my thoughts, but generally I was functional enough to survive. As my job became more boring, I became less engaged with work and more engaged with partying. When I was bouncing off the walls, there was alcohol to bring me down. When I was depressed, there was cocaine to make me high.

Everyone seemed to know about my drinking, even the metro desk administrator who was used to signing off on the frequent multi-hundred-dollar tabs from Robert Emmett's bar. Life was turning into a big party on the corporate dime. Some might call the amount of *Times* money I spent on alcohol excessive. What I was not out in the open about, at least at this point, was the fact that I was dabbling with cocaine and other stimulants to pick myself up when I was down.

Since high school, I had endured short waves of depression followed by long extended periods of mania. Alcohol during the insomnia-inducing highs and stimulants during the depressive lows were a way of life that only became more acute when I was stressed about my work life.

In this time period, I also dabbled in office politics to fit in and as a means of survival, collecting the best stories of *The Times,* like the editor of mine who got his mistress pregnant with twins, the reporter who plagiarized a story on plagiarism, another who got away with inventing characters out of whole cloth, and the correspondent who was caught by the Secret Service having sex with a White House press aide in the bathroom on Air Force One. Like everything in my life, I seemed to take gossiping to great extremes. I bonded with the mail clerks, news assistants and copy editors—as well as any-one else on staff who felt marginalized, disaffected or hated. If they were not going to let me in the club, I was going to start my own.

Covering media and technology, I learned that there were many unde-niable perks of being a *Times* reporter. If you needed tickets to a New York Knicks game, call Fern in the sports department. There was a woman in the culture section who could get you into most Broadway plays, assuming the public relations person involved in getting out the word about the show had not gotten tickets to you already. There were always clothes and free food in the Style department. Some public relations executives were straight-up and honest, but a handful would bend over backwards to obtain a brief mention of their company or product in *The Times.*

Those public relations people substituted theater tickets, free meals and drinks and, sometimes, even sex for mentions. Journalists at *The Times* were considered to have a weak spot for sex, just like the nerds so many of them once were in high school. There were many stories.

The arrangements with public relations people would start out with the normal barrage of telephone calls. In the end, I dismissed most of them because of their ill-conceived ideas or an ability to annoy that was high. In some rare cases, I became friends with public relations executives, usually the ones who were very good at what they did. They loved me and hated me. Loved me because I would listen and often plug their clients. Hated me because I had this bad habit of not showing up for meetings and not returning phone calls.

One public relations executive from a small Internet company had an in to me because of a working relationship that we had developed while she was working as a spokeswoman in the mayor's office. One night, the woman invited me out to drinks at Emmett's with her and some friends and colleagues. On the second floor of the bar, we ordered round after round of drinks to accompany the chicken wings, mozzarella sticks and normal assortment of fatty foods that went along with it. I had yet to write about their company, though I was considering several feature stories where they might be mentioned, but most of the talk centered on life in the Giuliani administration and what it's like to be young, hard-working and in high-pressure jobs in New York, a city that truly never sleeps.

My friend, the former Giuliani official who was in charge of communications at the Internet company, brought along her twenty-three-year-old deputy, a young woman who had just graduated from college and gone into public relations. I hit it off with the woman, who was blonde and whose parents were the children of immigrants who came to the United States from Russia at the turn of the century. After several glasses of Scotch, we moved to red wine and her stories of growing up in Larchmont, New York. It was a Friday night, and the two of us stayed at the bar long after the others left, consuming more and more glasses of wine. At three in the morning, we decided to jet onto West Forty-fourth Street, where we jumped into a yellow cab and headed downtown to her apartment.

We got out on Second Avenue near her apartment close to Stuyvesant Square, and I lifted her off the ground and walked her to the front door of her building on Nineteenth Street. In all candor, I must admit that along the way I dropped her once or twice, but we drunkenly laughed it off. At the front door I put her down, and we made our way up the staircase to the front door of her apartment.

We both got into bed with our clothes on and laughed and joked for a while about the night. Somewhere along the way, we started kissing and she complained about the cigarette smoke coming out of my mouth. After returning from the bathroom, we were back at it again. I slowly pulled her shirt up over her head and put it on the floor beside the bed. We kept going until she pulled up her hands and stopped me.

"Jayson, are we going to get a mention in *The Times*?"

We both laughed for a few minutes, continued, and eventually fell asleep for the night.

When it came to ethics it was hard to know where to draw the line, but there is no doubt that the night had an impact. The Internet company received several mentions in my business stories for *The Times*.

CHAPTER FOURTEEN
SECRET LIFE

The ringing in my ears seemed like a part of a dream. The next one made me wonder whether it was real. By the third, there was no doubt, and I searched for my phone, with my eyes half closed, in a groggy, half-awake state.

I slowly pulled myself together, adjusting my senses to the surprising darkness. I glanced out of the bay windows of my bedroom in the apartment I was renting in the Clinton Hill section of Brooklyn. I gravitated to Clinton Hill after deciding that I could no longer afford to live in Manhattan. I also liked the racial diversity of much of Brooklyn, although if you were to ask me the main reason I decided to pick up and move to Clinton Hill, I would be deceiving you if I did not say that it had a lot to do with the parks and rows of tall trees.

The back of my apartment had bay windows overlooking a garden that runs back forty or fifty feet to the next set of buildings. Clinton Hill, located in northwest Brooklyn close to the East River, was named after the family of former New York Governor DeWitt Clinton. The area was farmland for hundreds of years that was parceled and sold in the mid-1800s, primarily to merchants who had been forced out by the aristocrats who moved to Brooklyn Heights.

Clinton Hill is located at the highest point in Brooklyn, and many prosperous businessmen in the 1800s and early 1900s considered it a luxury to live far above the stacks that sent smoke billowing over the city. The businessmen built beautiful brownstones and large mansions. The families that settled there included the Pratts, the Pfizers and the Underwoods, and the leafy promenade of Clinton Avenue soon became known as "Millionaire's Row" or the "Fifth Avenue of Brooklyn." Many of those wealthy families had abandoned the neighborhood by the 1920s, but a revitalization began in the 1970s when black middle-class families began to take refuge there.

I had found the apartment on the third floor of this Clinton Hill brownstone with Daryl when he was making plans to move to New York from Pennsylvania, where he had worked at a newspaper in York. Small-town newspapering did not mesh with Daryl, and soon after we moved into the apartment, we held a house-warming party where he met Gerry Mullany, the deputy metro editor for nights, who told him to call about working as a freelance stringer for *The Times*. Daryl got a call the next day, and soon he was working for sixty hours to eighty hours a week for *The Times* metro desk, often doing all the reporting on stories that others would simply do a light rewrite on and put their bylines on.

The *Times*'s rules discouraged double bylines and giving credit to free-lance reporters. An article with one byline on it would often have notes from four or five reporters, contributions from stringers and a researcher, not to mention the work of copy editors and other editors. The rationale stemmed from the simple fact that *Times* management did not want people to realize how much work from so many people went into any given story. People assumed that a dispatch from City Hall or on the campaign trail was written and reported primarily by the author whose name was on it. That was not the case, and Daryl had stacks of notepads and computer files to prove it.

I did my best to pick up more exciting assignments in the afternoons and evenings after I had finished my metro business work. Sometimes I joined Daryl, popping out of bed for a midnight call to ride into battle together covering something like the massacre at Wendy's on Main Street in Flushing, Queens. The Wendy's massacre, as we called it, had all the elements of a Shakespearean urban blight drama, or at least a good cliché version: a black con man convinces a mentally retarded black friend to rob a fast food restaurant at closing. They break in. Something goes wrong during the hold-up. They march the seven employees downstairs and into a walk-in freezer. They kill five of the employees with bullets to the head. Two more are shot and left for dead, only to live and identify their assailant as a man who used to work at the Wendy's.

Daryl eventually moved across the street and into an apartment with his girlfriend, Lili Zarghami, a beautiful half-Persian/half-American medical student at Columbia University. I had become a bit estranged over time from Daryl and Lili, primarily because of my drinking. One mid-afternoon drink fest I had with Charlie LeDuff, a *Times* reporter, led to a loud shouting match with Lili while Daryl was out of town. The writing was on the wall. Within a month, Daryl and Lili had moved to the apartment across the street. We remained out of touch, for the most part, other than work and occasional moments when Daryl and I would get together at one in the morning and sit on the steps of the nearby church and rap about philosophy.

This summer night, whatever it was that was coming my way, I was riding solo. As I struggled to wake up, still looking for the ringing telephone, I noticed the red numbers on my digital clock read 8:15 p.m. I thought, for sure, it was the morning.

"Oh, Jesus," I said as I tried to lift my head, which was throbbing with pain from an afternoon of partying that had begun earlier at Robert Emmett's Bar and Restaurant with reporters, theater types and others on West Forty-fourth Street. The drinking began at four o'clock. I returned home after downing several glasses of Johnnie Walker Black and scarfing down a meal of fried mozzarella sticks and calamari with my colleague, Lynette Holloway, an aggressive, sarcastic and unhappy education reporter.

I thought about the last comment Lynette had made before we left the bar. "I am done talking about that stupid porch monkey, and now it is time to get the sniper rifle," she said about Boyd, alluding to a statement she had once made about climbing to the roof of the theater next to *Times* headquarters and shooting him in front of his seven-year-old son, Zachary. I laughed as I heard the telephone ring, musing to myself that Lynette had probably done it, and they were calling me in to either cover the story or get some understanding of her angst.

"Jayson, could you please hold for Gerry Mullany?" the news clerk on the other line asked.

"Oh, shit," I mumbled under my breath as the clerk put me on hold, not waiting for me to answer his question.

Gerry Mullany was the senior person on the desk at night, and when he was calling, any reporter knew that a big story was waiting. I put my shoes on and a black shirt, tucking in it and pulling it out of my white khakis as I paced nervously around my apartment. I grabbed my black bag filled with pens and notepads from the bathroom floor and grabbed my press pass off the neck of the bottle of Johnnie Walker Black that stood on my glass coffee table.

"Jayson, where are you?" Gerry asked when he picked up the phone.

"My house in Brooklyn," I said.

"Can you get to a house in Boerum Hill?"

"Yes, I have the car," I said.

Borrowing the company car was a bit of a sport for me, and I am sure that Gerry was hardly surprised that it was parked outside the public school next door to my apartment. Generally, I would take the black Grand Am. My drives often involved outings to the Coney Island amusement parks or other hard-to-reach places like the Greenwood Cemetery. My mileage in any given week would strike pride in Robert Moses, the legendary power broker and parks commissioner who promoted the construction of most of the city's major highways. There were certainly moments where I would use the car to search the city for cocaine and other drugs when I could not reach Fernando, my Dominican dealer who lived in the projects on Manhattan's West Side. One time, I took the Grand Am for a spin down the Westside Highway, that took me to the Holland Tunnel, out to New Jersey and then, all of a sudden, south on Interstate 95. Most of the time, like this night, I just took the car—often drunk, usually high—to make my commute into Manhattan more comfortable than a 45-minute ride to Times Square on the C train.

My use of the cars had become such a joke, an open secret, that there was a story about it on a mock page made up for the desk's administrator, Ken Meyn, an affable man who had been in his job for years and was as diligent as he was well-liked, and who'd been reassigned to the business section. What his replacement did not factor in was that the editors who were not flaky enough to let the car pass slip out of their grip were often intimidated by *Times* reporters, and the ones who were not intimidated could often be schmoozed, and the ones who could not be schmoozed, often needed rides. Gerry was one of those editors who often needed rides. He, more than anyone else, knew that it was the rarest of times when I was using the car on assignment.

Gerry gave me the address and a quick run-down of the events that were unfolding. A house less than a mile away from my brownstone had blown up for no clear reason, and there might be people dead. He needed me to get over there quickly to file whatever I could get by the early deadline, which was less than two hours away. Within five minutes, I was parking the company's black Pontiac Grand Am just south of Atlantic Avenue, only a few blocks from the scene of the explosion.

Red fire trucks were still responding to the scene, thick white-and-gray smoke filled the air, and lightly dressed women, children and men were being evacuated from the surrounding blocks. Crossing Atlantic Avenue, one of the craziest thoroughfares in Brooklyn, was a difficult task even when I was not hung over and hurting. Still, after nearly getting hit by a white van traveling in the westbound lane, walking the residential blocks gave me time to clear my head and figure out the questions we needed to have answered most rapidly.

The scene was a mess. Red fire trucks lined the street. Reporters were lined up to the right of them, attempting to ask the Fire Department official questions. I was happy to spot a friendly face. It was Sunny Mindel, the mayor's rambunctious communications director, whose gravelly voice was clearly worn by the skinny cigarettes that she constantly smoked when the television cameras were out of sight.

Sunny, who could put on a good stereotypical Jewish New Yorker comedy act, and me, a black man from Virginia, became friends when I was in the *Times* police bureau, where I would come over to her cramped office overlooking a park to smoke and gossip about other reporters, particularly the *Times*'s City Hall bureau chief, who once asked with a straight face what FY stood for while writing about the budget. The paper's coverage portrayed Giuliani as arrogant, which he was, and at times, a racist, which he probably wasn't. I had a more nuanced analysis from being a police reporter in many of the poor neighborhoods where crime was dropping sharply under his tenure, recognizing that while many of the tactics his Police Department used raised serious questions about race, they were also making black and Hispanic neighborhoods throughout New York much safer. "Ebony and Ivory," she used to sing, elongating the "n" and "r," when I would show up at her City Hall office.

Sunny had a tough job. Not only did she have to keep one of the most unpopular mayors with the news media in the history of the city in good standing with its citizens, she had to serve as the boss of dozens of public relations officials at agencies across the government who ran their departments like little fiefdoms. We found comfort in each other's wry senses of humor.

"Thank God," I said to Sunny as I approached her from the other side of the yellow police line. She motioned to a police officer to allow me alone to come to the other side.

"Mr. Blair, how the hell are you?" Sunny said, spreading her arms to give me a bear hug as colleagues behind me puzzled at the special treatment.

"So, what the fuck is going on?" I said, motioning toward the smoldering rubble to our left.

"Here's the deal," she said. "We are not sure what the hell caused this. KeySpan is at the scene over there checking to see if it was a problem with one of their lines. We got one dead, an older gay guy, and the elderly couple who owns the house is dead. The gay guy's lover, who also lived in the house, has been taken to the precinct just so he can calm down, so everyone can make sure he is okay.

"The guys from the FD," she said, using shorthand for the Fire Department, "are digging in the rubble, trying to figure out if there is anyone alive in there."

"Can I use any of that?" I asked Sunny, explaining that our deadline was rapidly approaching.

"Yeah, just say a senior Giuliani administration official told you," she said.

"Are we hopeful?" I asked, about saving anyone who might be in the rubble.

Sunny looked toward the smoldering remains of the house, surrounded by firefighters attempting to cool the rubble so their specially trained search and rescue teams could enter without being cooked alive. She shrugged her shoulders.

"The mayor's en route," she added, "and we are hoping to have some answers by the time he arrives. He's planning on touring the scene and giving a press conference at ten."

That would have been great—just in time for our deadline—if Mayor Giuliani ever gave a news conference on time in his life, I thought as I stared aimlessly around Sunny and looked into the street at firefighters who, oddly, seemed to be collecting white papers that were falling out of the sky.

"What the hell are they doing?" I asked out loud, wondering why firefighters would be assigned to pick up papers while someone could be potentially trapped in smoldering rubble. It answered my question about the odds the Fire Department was putting on anyone being alive, but raised some questions about the papers. Sunny just smiled in response to the question.

"If you find out, Mr. Blair, don't print it," Sunny said.

"Print what?"

"Print that they belong to the gay guy," she responded.

"Print that what belongs the gay guy?"

"The papers," she said with a smile.

"What are they?"

Just as she was preparing to answer the question, or maybe further obfuscate, the mayor's bullet proof, black Suburban appeared.

"I got to go, Jayson, but let's talk sometime soon," she said as she walked toward the mayor's car, her driver, Herb, in tow.

"Okay, Sunny, it's always a pleasure doing business with you," I said, fixating on the papers. The good thing about when the mayor arrived at the scene was that all eyes—at least those from the city government—focused on him. It was often the perfect opportunity to escape, sneak into somewhere undetected and collect tidbits of information that other reporters were unable to capture. I had seen that Sarah Kershaw, a friend and fellow *Times* reporter with hair as fiery red as her sense of humor, had arrived on the scene several minutes earlier. I figured that she could dog the mayor and make sure we had any of the tragic, sobby shit that he tended to repeat at every crime, fire or disaster that he appeared at, and I could do a little hunting.

First I called the office and was transferred to Andy Newman, a young, charming and eccentric reporter who had been sent to the late night rewrite job, a reporter's gulag, by Jon Landman. Jon forced him to hold onto the job longer than anyone else in years after Andy refused to take a job as the paper's correspondent in Hartford, Connecticut. It probably would have helped if Landman had not asked Andy to take the job on Halloween, a day he came to the office dressed as a clown, with orange tights clinging to his lanky legs and a black Afro wig atop his head. Still, the time on night rewrite made Andy one of the fastest, smartest reporters in The Metro Section, and knowing that he was on the job guaranteed that this difficult situation would be that much easier.

"Newman, it's Blair," I said, recounting the details I had observed and the information that I had just received from Sunny.

The throbbing in my head told me that before I could turn my attention to the light snowfall of white papers, I needed to take care of a more pressing matter. As the news frenzy continued all around me, I walked away from the action, several blocks south to a corner deli where the clerks, noticing my press identification card, asked whether I knew what was happening at the scene. I answered the question with a shrug of my shoulders and ordered a cup of black coffee, sweet, and three packs of Advil, hoping that some combination of smoking, caffeine and painkillers would make my headache go away. I noticed a lanky police reporter from *Newsday* who had just arrived at the scene and knew I still had some time to nurse my self-inflicted pain.

I walked slowly back to the crime scene, daydreaming about one of the new waitresses at Emmett's. Constantly daydreaming, and not always about women, I tried to do whatever I could to get my mind off the regular throbbing that came from either being hungover or not having enough nicotine or cocaine. Minutes later, as the *Newsday* reporter made his way back to the action, I decided to slosh back up the streets to the other side of the crime scene. The police officers near the entrance to that side ordered me back around the block to the side where the flyers had been dropping.

This was ridiculous, I thought to myself as I walked over to the other side. I have less than two hours to figure out why some brownstone in some tony neighborhood in Brooklyn blew up for a front-page story in *The New York Times,* and no one is going to say anything until after the mayor talks. That's the way it works: the mayor gives his news conference, and then the officials give you the truth. But no one talks before Mayor Giuliani. Jesus Christ. As bad as my headache was, I knew it was only going to get worse as I stood outside until two in the morning on yet another warm summer night.

By the time I had made it to the other side, the circle of reporters, cameramen and others had grown to at least five deep. I drifted back to the papers. One piece landed on a low hanging branch of a nearby tree, only a few feet from my grasp, but as fast as I noticed it, a firefighter came from the other side of the yellow police line and grabbed the sheet. I decided to return to Plan A, with everyone distracted by Mayor Giuliani and Sarah chasing him down for comment. I propped myself up against a tree only ten feet or so away from the police line, slowly sliding around its round body, disappearing into the darkness of an across-the-street-neighbor's lawn. I tucked in my black t-shirt and placed my pink New York Police Department press pass underneath it, stuck my notepad and pen in my back pocket, and walked slowly and confidently, lifted the yellow tape just high enough so it brushed my head as I made my way underneath. After making sure the police officers, dressed in the thick bulletproof blue vests and caps of the elite Emergency Service Unit who were guarding the perimeter had their attention focused elsewhere, I made my move for one of the sheets, which at closer glance appeared to be a contact sheet. I grabbed it and slowly shuffled my way back to the safe side of the police line, folded it up, and slid it into the pocket of my khakis. I made it around the corner, about a block away, before I pulled it out. The partly singed contact sheet dropped to the ground as I stood with my mouth wide open.

"Oh, Jesus Christ," I said, betraying a slight grin that began to overtake my face.

I went toward Sunny, who was busy preparing the mikes for the news conference. Behind the phalanx of cameras, microphones and notepads I could see her just-a-little-too-shiny blonde head bobbing up and down. I moved to the right.

"Hey, Jayson," Sarah said as I bumped into her chest, nearly taking her thick-framed glasses off, rolling around with a motion similar to a basketball move I remembered making in high school.

"Sunny," I screamed, clearly not capturing her attention.

Making my way back to my left, I felt almost out of my drunken stupor as I spun around the television cameraman who hurled obscenities in my direction seconds before the mayor was about to go on FOX 5 and UPN 9.

"Sunny," I screamed again, capturing her attention for a brief second as I lifted the photograph above my head just as the camera lights went on in front of her boss and the fire commissioner.

She looked shocked, and then smiled.

After Mayor Giuliani finished his news conference, Sunny walked over and was all smiles.

"Jayson, you are not going to put that in the *fucking* newspaper," she said loudly, but smiling, using her most endearing voice. "I mean, you're the *fucking New York Times,* and I mean this is just the type of shit that only the *fucking Post* would run," she added, following it with her wheezing laugh. "I mean, I wouldn't be surprised if Jon Landman, or whatever the *fuck* that asshole prick Ivy Leaguer's name is, was into that kinky shit, but . . ."

"Jesus *fucking* Christ," Sunny said, breaking out into cackles as she looked at the glossy. "That's a pretty bad one. We think it came from the ground floor."

"Okay," I said.

"Do you know what this means?" she asked.

"Not a fucking clue," I said.

"That's probably not from them," she said, pointing to the air where the upper floors of the brownstone once were and where the gay couple lived.

"How do you know?"

"'Cause we know," she said, a big smile filling her face.

"Jesus Christ," I said.

In my hands was part of what once was a photograph, a picture that had been professionally produced on an 8 x 10 inch piece of high-quality contact proof. Someone's camera somewhere had captured the image of a pre-pubescent boy giving what appeared to be a middle-aged man a blow job, and it had somehow ended up in a box or something inside a brownstone that mysteriously blew up in Brooklyn. Now Sunny Mindel, the mayor's press secretary, was telling me that it probably did not belong to either of the two gay men who lived in the building, but more likely the elderly couple in their late-60s that owned the house.

I was off the story the next day, so luckily the mystery of the floating pornography was not left for me to solve. I found myself increasingly frustrated with either having no editor to report to or reporting to people who were being shoved to the side by management. It was a recipe for failure, particularly for a young person in training. Metro business was such a backwater that one of my editors, who could not type because of carpal tunnel syndrome, made all of her changes by hand and had her reporters insert them. The other had been booted out of the newsroom and into human resources, where she was again jettisoned when that department was forced to make cutbacks.

The primary battle in my work life was between Jon Landman and Gerald Boyd, who was then the deputy managing editor. It was becoming increasingly clear that Landman was opposed to my being hired by *The Times*. I was not privy to Landman's argument, but was able to glean enough of it from other editors to know that he believed that my writing was not up to the level of full-time *Times* reporters. Landman thought that reporters should be well-rounded jacks of all trades, tools that their editors could plug into holes and use to fix anything. I had a more practical view of things. Some people were writers. Some people were reporters. Some landed in between. My specialty was volume and ubiquitousness—I would go anywhere, anytime, to cover a story. I would never say no.

In the eighteen months from the point of returning to *The Times* as an extended intern to my promotion from the reporter trainee program, I wrote 311 stories, an average of about one every workday. I frequently contributed to the business section, the Week in Review, and The Metro Section of the paper.

One day in late 2000, Gerald approached me in the smoking room and asked how things were.

"Good," I said, lying through my teeth. "I can't complain."

"Well," Gerald said, pausing to take a puff from his Marlboro Light. "They can't be so good, you're all over the paper and Landman hasn't hired you yet. I wonder why."

"I don't know why," I said.

That was the end of the conversation. The implication was, of course, that Jon was wrong and Gerald wanted me to know in no uncertain terms who was behind the fact that I had not been promoted yet to full-time. I suspected that Gerald knew I would agitate, and I did. First, I took a look at the number of stories I had written since returning to *The Times* and their placement, comparing them to colleagues who had been promoted or were on the verge of becoming full-time reporters. The analysis could be debated on several different fronts, but it was clear that I had dozens more stories than anyone else in the trainee program. While I had landed a number of stories on the front page and The Metro Section cover, several people were ahead of me in those two categories. What I lacked in front-page stories, I more than made up for in volume.

In the first half of September 2000, for example, I wrote stories about the *New York Post* halving its newsstand price; Ralph Nader's presidential campaign swing through Manhattan; a museum in a battle with its neighbors over a planned expansion; how online deliveries made life easier for the disabled; ethical questions about a faked photograph showing President Clinton and Fidel Castro shaking hands on the front of the *Daily News*; a review piece about the increasing difficulties of accommodating all the things that college students bring to their dorms these days; a business story about the raging tabloid war between the *News* and the *Post*; the real estate implications of the merger of two big banks; layoffs on Wall Street; and the rise in the number of construction jobs in the city.

In the second half of the month, I wrote about the popularity of fish tanks in the offices of prosperous dot-com companies; a review piece on what kids were watching these days on television; Hillary Rodham Clinton's campaign against Representative Rick Lazio for a U.S. Senate seat in New York; a new dot-com offering real estate ads online; the growing ratings of a Spanish-language newscast; an online grocer that was being forced to postpone an expansion; the discovery of the name of a child who was murdered in Queens and the man police believe killed her; the growth of access to high-speed Internet connections; Senator Charles Schumer's attempts to cultivate support in the technology world; a new Spanish-language radio station; a publisher listing commercial real estate space online; Sally Ride's resignation from the board of Space.com, and a Long Island company president pleading guilty in a stock scam.

And that was not even my busiest month.

Those, or any of the 311 stories during those months did not include the many stories I contributed to without a byline.

I went to Nancy Sharkey, the assistant to the managing editor for staff development and the head of the trainee program, and made the case. Nancy is never one for confrontation, but she makes it her job to know what is happening in the background. She explained that I was being blocked by Jon, and then told me the story of a young Hispanic reporter from *The Washington Post* who had come in for interviews with senior members of the paper. We called interviewing at *The Times* the "fourteen stations of the cross" because of the number of section editors, deputy section editors, assistant managing editors, and others a person had to interview with before getting promoted.

The candidate, who had been found by the recruitment committee, did not end up getting hired, but Jon put a note on his clips that railed against the affirmative action policies at the paper. Jon wrote that minority candidates were always sub-par compared to others, and that *The Times* could not drop its standards in the name of diversity. Nancy pointed out that members of the recruitment committee thought Jon's philosophy was flawed and noted that all of the hires he had made without their consultation had been white. The major flaw was that discrimination meant that some of the top minority candidates would be less seasoned than white ones, who had been given certain opportunities because of the families they were in or the schools they attended that were not always as open to blacks, Hispanics and others.

The Times, Nancy said, wanted to correct that problem by nurturing talented minorities. Nancy explained that despite my successes, I had not landed enough front page and Metro Section cover stories to make Jon happy, an idea that seemed curious since he was the one who decided what got offered for A1 and what ended up on B1, as the metro front was called. More striking to me was that Jon was the one who decided which reporters got the most prestigious beats, and it was the topics of stories that drove things "out front" as much as the writing.

I can't remember my exact words, but I said something like, "I work for metro business, Nancy, it's not exactly the place where stories go sailing onto the front page." She agreed and said she understood, but that a war was afoot between Jon and the recruitment committee, some of whom believed he was holding up my promotion to make a point. I told her that regardless of the politics of the place, the intramural squabbling was driving me crazy. I had to make some choices in life, and could not emotionally afford to sit in the low-paid purgatory of the intermediate reporting program.

By the time Jon called me into his office to tell me about the promotion, he had already lost me. I hardly remember the conversation, or the subsequent meeting with Joe Lelyveld, who, per *Times* tradition, handed me a bottle of cheap champagne. I knew by then that I had become some pawn in a racial game, and that my work mattered less than the political points my success or failure gave to two grown men, Jon and Gerald, who were in an internal fight. I was being treated like a rag doll, a toy, and neither seemed to care if I got ripped up in the process.

By the summer of 2001, only a few months after my half-hearted promotion, I was well on my way to fuming anger. One sign of my dissembling could be found in the increasing amount of time I was spending on the second floor of Robert Emmett's. Almost every night, I was there with someone from *The Times* or a source.

I was looking forward to the paper's takeover by a new executive editor, Howell Raines. I hoped that under that new regime, people as insensitive as Jon would be knocked off track, and more compassionate people would rise up the ranks and become the top *Times* leaders. The only question was whether I could make it that long before self-destructing.

CHAPTER FIFTEEN
A NEW LEADER

Howell Raines had a lot of things in common with me.

He was a big believer in rapid social change. As a reporter, he was the one that management would go to if they were having a problem with the worker bees. Colleagues throughout his career had said he had an air about him that left the impression he had been around forever even though he had not been.

His relatives were from the South. Like mine, they were farmers who tilled the fields that created great economic successes that many historians say contributed to America's ability to become one of the world's most powerful nations. People would describe Howell as an unforgiving man, particularly when it came to class and race. Howell would later say his ancestors were farmers who owned neither plantations nor slaves. That was, perhaps, one area where we diverged. Many of my black ancestors were slaves and many of my white ones owned them.

In his 1993 memoir, *Fly Fishing Through the Midlife Crisis,* Howell wrote wistfully of Franklin Delano Roosevelt for having "brought electric lights and the best crappie fishing in the world" to the South, an obvious reference to his appreciation for the New Deal president's social programs. My father's middle name was Delano, in response to my grandmother and grandfather's admiration for the 32nd President of the United States.

Howell's father moved to Birmingham, Alabama in the late 1930s and opened a lumber and woodworking business, known as Raines Brothers. The success of the business would help pull the family out of poverty, in very much the way my parents' ability to pull themselves up by the bootstraps and make it into college prevented me from having to suffer the plight some of my cousins faced.

Howell was strikingly different than me in one clear respect, other than being white, of course. He was one of those people who tripped across journalism by mistake. I had been a zealot, almost born to write for news-papers. He, on the other hand, had taken a job working at the Birmingham *Herald-Post* as simply a way to pay the bills while he worked on writing nov-els and teaching English. Somewhere along the way, covering his favorite coach Bear Bryant and watching Alabama Governor George Wallace with great irritation, Howell took a career in journalism. Actually, perhaps, it took him.

Howell rose quickly, jumping from the *Herald-Post* to the local WBRC-TV station, to *The Birmingham News*, to *The Atlanta Journal-Constitution*, along the way writing an oral history of the civil rights movement in the South called *My Soul Is Rested*, and a novel, *Whiskey Man*. By 1976, Howell made it to the *St. Petersburg Times*, where he was eventually recruited in 1978, two years after I was born, to *The New York Times*, where he began his career as a correspondent in Atlanta for the paper.

 Soon after Howell's May 2001 promotion to executive editor, I read an award-winning piece he had written called "Grady's Gift." One universal line from the piece stuck in my head: "For while some of the benefits of psychotherapy may be dubious, it does give us one shining truth," Howell wrote. "We are shaped by those moments when the sadness of life first wounds us."

Much like my own life, I could see how Howell's existence had very much been shaped by race. I could not agree more with his statement. Then some people in the newsroom complained that Howell was handed the feature-writing prize by the Pulitzer board as a favor to the Sulzberger family. No one in recent memory had become the executive editor of *The Times* without winning the Pulitzer Prize before their ascension. Joe had won the award for general non-fiction for his 1985 book *Move Your Shadow: South Africa, Black and White*, which chronicled apartheid in his years there as a correspondent. Max Frankel had won for his coverage of President Nixon's campaign visits to China in 1972. Abe Rosenthal had won the international reporting award for his 1959 reporting from Poland. Howell won for his story on Grady.

Howell was promoted to editor of the editorial page the same year he won the Pulitzer, and soon took an office on the tenth floor, located in a room off the side of the brown-wood-paneled, Victorian-designed library. Howell was recognized for nurturing columnists and editorial writers, like Maureen Dowd, Frank Rich and Brent Staples. Howell would be known for his fire-breathing editorial page, his liberal positions on most issues and his obvious disdain for Bill Clinton, the young man he had written about long before he became President of the United States. Howell's disappointment in President Clinton jumped off the page.

It was so clear from everything I knew about Howell that he was governed very much by his heart. Many journalists marry other journalists, sometimes out of desperation, sometimes out of convenience, sometimes for political considerations. Soon after meeting Krystna Stachowiak in 1996, Howell made a move that I decided was not just apolitical, but one that, in the name of love, could harm his chances of becoming executive editor. Krystna, a public relations executive, was visiting the paper for a meeting with the editorial board and her client, Aleksander Kwaniewski, the president of Poland. Soon afterwards, Krystna and Howell started dating. It did not take long for people in *The Times* newsroom to begin using the fact that Howell was dating someone in public relations against him as he tried to become executive editor of the paper. In the face of the risks, Howell did it anyway.

Later, after my resignation, *Times* staff members would suggest that I had begun a romantic relationship with Zuza because of her mother's relationship with Howell and Krystna. The assumption is wrong. I began a friendship with Zuza in September 2002, long before I knew about Howell and Krystna, much less her family's connection to them. And I began it for the same reason Howell did, for love. Few things made me angrier than seeing someone I loved not only dragged into the situation, but also hearing the suggestion that my heart could be moved as a simple matter of convenience. It amazed me how, in general, the news media would turn Howell into a caricature. They could not see the young white man who grew up in the most virulently segregated part of the South, whose family rose up from poverty and who, against all odds, became executive editor of *The Times*.

All I could see during the long summer of 2002 was hope in the name of a man named Howell Raines, hope that he would bring a new order to the newsroom, an order where I was not a pawn in a game because of my race. Still, I was going through a transitory phase, a moment in which my comfort with the institution would diminish so rapidly that I could barely hold on, a moment where life would change so quickly that I could hardly recognize myself in the mirror.

CHAPTER SIXTEEN
NEW YORK DIXIE

One day in May, Charlie LeDuff and I were sitting at his desk making plans for the *Native Voice*, the newspaper put out by students each day at the Native American Journalists Association annual convention. This summer's convention was being held in June in Buffalo, New York and its theme was "Journalism Without Borders," a particularly poignant theme for Native Americans, many of whom live on reservations, which some compared to the Jewish ghettos of 1940s Europe.

Bill Schmidt, the associate managing editor for news administration, put together the delegations of people for the summer conventions. Bill had asked Charlie to help out with the convention, and Charlie had asked me to join him. Charlie is a talented writer and reporter, but his work was more art, whereas mine was that of a yeoman of breaking news and analysis. I also understood technology, production and other issues that could be vexing while putting out a student newspaper.

Charlie saw himself as the emotional, creative and inspirational fire behind the project. My job was to deliver and make sure the ideas made it onto the page. We were also a good complement to each other's personalities. He played the bad cop, and I played the good one. Before the end of the convention there was more than one young woman student who would catch Charlie's deliberately ramped-up I-am-going-to-scare-the-life-out-of-you wrath, only to be comforted by my gentle explanations of how much Charlie cared, and that he was really pushing them so hard because he wanted them to do well. It was all choreographed. We made a hell of a team.

Charlie had gone to bat for me over and over during my time at *The Times*. When I was an intern, he was encouraging. When I began to feel like an outsider, he helped me find paths to get stories I cared about into the paper. When Jon Landman was resisting conclusions I had come to in a story, Charlie marched into his office and raised what can only be described as hell. I had developed a friendship with Charlie and his wife, Amy, although at moments it was testy. Charlie was all heart and liked me, but Amy sensed that something just was not right.

We played together. We partied together. We threw footballs around the newsroom together. We critiqued the way the paper covered everything, including Native Americans and blacks. We did journalism together. When he left the metro staff to become a national correspondent, Charlie put a reporter from *The New York Observer* on the phone and told the scribe that I was his spokesman. I believe that he is among the most talented journalists I have ever met, someone whose name someday will go in the canons of writing right beside E. B. White, H. L. Mencken and Joseph Mitchell. Charlie, Ed Keating and I were perhaps the worst-dressed reporters in the newsroom. Ed and I could be easily described as slobs, while Charlie was all about eccentricity—whether it was his long flowing mane of hair, the boots he wore, or his leather vest and scarf. His fashion tastes were not in the *New York Times* mainstream.

Minutes after walking away from Charlie's desk, I ran into Jon Landman.

"So, Charlie's Native American?" Jon said, in the form of a question, obviously in reference to the Buffalo convention.

He stood, staring at me with a half-smile, as if he did not believe it.

"Yeah, I think his ancestors are from a tribe that has a reservation in Michigan," I replied.

"That's interesting," he replied. "So, what, are you Native American too?"

"No," I said. "I am just going to help out, in solidarity."

Charlie was proud of his Native American roots, advocating for them and educating people about their history. It was interesting that Jon considered Charlie white. Charlie was one of the few minorities who had garnered a measure of respect from Jon, who had inherited the one black editor on the metro copy desk and the Hispanic assistant metro editor. Of the black reporters on the metro desk during my tenure, all were inherited, or their hire came on the recommendation of the newsroom recruitment committee managed by Gerald Boyd and Bill Schmidt, who was the internal champion of Arthur Sulzberger, Jr.'s clear commitment to diversity.

Charlie had grand plans for the Native American Journalists Convention. He recognized that stereotypes, overt discrimination and insular experiences were things Native American journalism students had going against them.

Instead of spending time just covering the convention, Charlie wanted to expose the young journalists who would be in attendance to the broader world of journalism, sending them into downtown Buffalo and Niagara Falls, as well as reservations in Canada and New York State. Charlie believed that experience, hard work and simply getting into the game were the key steps for leveling the playing field.

One weekend morning in early June, Charlie and I left his home in the multi-ethnic neighborhood of Astoria, Queens, took the Triborough Bridge over Randall's Island into the Bronx, and eventually made our way north onto the Palisades Parkway in New Jersey and then the New York State Thruway. It is a scenic route through the north, whipping through roads cut out of the sides of mountains, with views of fields, streams and lakes along the way. We entered Catskill State Park on Route 23A, and headed west along the road, which twists through the mountains and greenery that had served as the inspiration of so many Hudson River School painters.

We were headed there to meet a fifty-five-year-old friend of Charlie, a man whose current fixed address was the fourth floor of the bookstore at the University of Michigan in Ann Arbor. We arrived at a run-down house in Tannersville, New York that was owned by the man's brother, a British playboy. The house was far off the main road, surrounded by acres and acres of fields, swampland and imposing views of mountains. I remember something about a missing cat, three guys, Charlie and a lot of alcohol and a lot of pot wafting through the air. I have a hard time recalling the details, other than it was a relaxing time in which we tried to do things like build a raft out of discarded trees and use it in the lake.

We may have failed at that, but we succeeded in having a relaxing weekend. I hung out with Charlie and the friend of his who lived on the floor of the Michigan bookstore, who went by the nickname Uncle Herb. Charlie, Uncle Herb and I made our way west through the Catskill Mountains and eventually to Otsego County. We were only a few miles from Cooperstown, the home of the Baseball Hall of Fame, when I noticed a Confederate flag hanging outside a brown store to our left.

"Stop, Charlie! Charlie, stop!" I yelled.

"What the fuck, man," he replied.

"Look," I yelled back, pointing at the flag.

"Oh shit," he replied, slamming on the brakes. "Right here in the middle of New York State. Whoever said New Yorkers weren't racists?"

"Not me, never," I replied. "We gotta stop and go there, and find out what the hell is going on."

Partly frustrated and partly bored by my job covering local business, I was always up for a little excitement, whether it was covering a subway derailment in the city or stopping for lunch at a store and restaurant with a Confederate flag hanging outside. We parked the rental car in front of a red shack in the lot behind the building and went inside. The back part was a restaurant and bar, where patrons could order meals like swiss cheese hamburgers and fish sandwiches. We planted ourselves at the bar. Charlie had a beer in front of him within seconds. My Johnnie Walker Black arrived soon after. I can't remember what Uncle Herb was drinking. What I do remember, though, was that Uncle Herb was smitten with one of the waitresses, an innocent-looking woman, a country girl, probably in her late teens, maybe early twenties.

We were loud. We played pool. We goaded Uncle Herb to say something to the young waitress. Uncle Herb made an awkward approach as Charlie and I giggled at the pool table like two high school girls who had just set up their friend for failure. We chatted up the bartenders and waitresses. The drinks flowed. We helped bring life to this seemingly docile place. On our way out, we laughed and remarked about how kind everyone was in the face of our initial presumptions about them—due to the Confederate flag and all—about the place. Then Charlie noticed something.

"What the hell is that?" Charlie asked, pointing to the tire of the driver's side of the car.

The air was rapidly deflating out of the tire and there was a gash on the side, as if we had driven over a sharp object, or, perhaps, that someone had driven a sharp object into the tire. We never solved the mystery of the Confederate flag restaurant tire. Perhaps it was something innocuous, like a large metal object that we had not noticed running over, but lingering in the back of our minds was whether someone had slashed the tire while we were inside. Either way, we hobbled along until we reached the Wal-Mart Superstore just off of Route 23 in Oneonta. Uncle Herb was nowhere to be found while the car was being fixed and Charlie and I played basketball, running from aisle to aisle with passes in between, through one section of the store.

I was back in the office for about a month before I headed to Orlando, Florida for the National Association of Black Journalists Convention, an annual event where black journalists from around the country come to talk about race in newsrooms, learn skills and recruit, or be recruited, at the job fair. For me, it was a chance to see former colleagues at other newspapers and friends from the University of Maryland, while doing time at *The Times* recruitment booth, which always attracted an interesting collection of underqualified people with a tremendous amount of moxie. It was my second year, so I expected it to be somewhat boring. The day before leaving, I bought a copy of *The Hobbit* at the Borders bookstore in the World Trade Center complex. One of the main reasons I was at the convention this year was to listen to Gerald Boyd's speech when he accepted the National Association of Black Journalists award for being the journalist of the year.

I had come up with the idea for nominating someone connected to the "How Race Is Lived in America" series, which had won the Pulitzer Prize for Public Service the previous year. After e-mailing a suggestion of nominating him for the award to Joe Lelyveld and Bill Keller, I was assigned to work with Soma Golden Behr, the assistant managing editor who handled, among other things, contest entries. Soma wrote a powerful letter with my help, that I signed, as a member of the association, and months later we heard that he would be receiving the award.

Gerald gave a good speech at the convention, and his friends and several *Times* colleagues gathered for a dinner to honor him. Howell Raines had already said that he intended to make Gerald the managing editor when he took over the newspaper in early September, so it was a festive event for everyone involved, including Arthur Sulzberger, Jr., who joked about his attraction to Gerald's wife, Robin Stone, a former copy editor.

I spent several hours at the recruitment table, but most of my time was spent reporting on a story about a planned community that was created by the Walt Disney Company, a town called Celebration.

Howell had mentioned me and several other black journalists at the newspaper during a breakfast speech he gave at the convention. Bill Schmidt had given Howell the names and biographies of several black journalists at *The Times* who were attending the convention, and he made sure to mention almost all of us. He mentioned several minority reporters in the context of their attendance at historical black colleges, and myself and Greg Winter, a friend and business reporter, as examples of those who had joined *The Times* as a part of the paper's "commitment to the development of young people as journalists."

"In recent years," he said, "we have broadened the way we identify and recruit talent, and have worked harder to spot the best and the brightest while they are still on their way up."

Greg and I were sitting at a table discussing newsroom matters, including issues that he was having with some of his editors. Greg was the rare example of a young person at *The Times* who could really take it or leave it. A counselor for many years before going to graduate school for journalism at the University of California, Berkeley, I could have seen him just as easily return to the world of social services if things did not work smoothly at *The Times*. Greg knew that I had been feeling depressed in recent months, and had recommended over the summer that I consider seeing someone.

What prompted the conversation was me mentioning that I had been dealing with depression all of my life, but that it was always okay as long as I could at least see the light at the end of the tunnel. I had not been seeing it lately. The summer had been tough, and I felt the new metro business editor who had been installed was a text-book example of having a borderline personality.

The woman had worked on the foreign desk, before being involuntarily sent to the Human Resources Department, in an unusual move. Nancy Sharkey had warned me about her, saying that Joe Lelyveld wanted to give her a chance to get back into the newsroom before he retired. I was, again, getting sloppy seconds as an editor, someone who was so valued by the newsroom that they did not mind watching her head upstairs to Human Resources.

Reporters who had worked with her in a technology section and on other desks almost uniformly agreed that she was difficult to work with, and her arrival was unfortunately timed for that moment when my depression hit the next stage, when I could not see the light at the end of the tunnel anymore and I was beginning to wonder whether there would be one. Greg had been counseling me to consider talking "with someone," a euphemism for seeing a professional with a background in psychotherapy. We did not have much time to talk about my issues with life and his issues at work, at least not at that moment, because Howell arrived at our table.

We chatted briefly about the types of stories he likes and things that would be happening in the newsroom come September 5 when he took over the paper. I would not sit down again with Howell Raines until much more than a year later, one morning in late March 2003 when I was vying to push my career forward and take a job as the paper's correspondent in Nairobi, Kenya.

Upon my return to New York I filed my story on Celebration and then planned a trip upstate to write about a town that had the unfortunate position of being a victim of the technology booms in both the 1980s and the 1990s.

It was after coming back from doing some of the reporting on Celebration that Olive Reid, the director of undergraduate programs at Maryland's journalism college, remarked that I seemed out of sorts.

I had come up with the idea of writing about Celebration, Florida, while sitting with an editor from the Week In Review section on the second floor of Robert Emmett's, which I was frequenting so much that *Times* copy editors had taken to posting it on the internal list of staff numbers and calling me there first before trying my cell phone.

More than a decade before, Disney executives decided to create a neighborhood by carving 10,000 acres of land out of the empty property that was a part of the Walt Disney World theme park, south of Orlando and just west of Kissimmee. The idea was to create a planned community where the ideals and philosophy of Walt Disney would be able to prosper as a social experiment. As a man who was born in Columbia, Maryland, Celebration had always piqued my intense interest, and even more so after I read news stories about American demographics that suggested that natural integration was on the decline in most of America.

James Rouse had created Columbia to go against the grain, but in many ways he was aided by the tail end of the civil rights movement, when blacks who were once shut out of white neighborhoods were looking for new homes, and whites who appreciated ethnic diversity were more open to embracing them. The Lewis Mumford Center at the University of Albany, a research concern that specializes in demographics, had just published a report I had read about that piqued my interest in how successful Disney had been in Celebration. The report said segregation had increased from 1990 to 2000 in almost every large suburban area in the country. The trend toward integration, it seemed, was waning, a notion that I found disturbing given my affinity for Columbia and its model.

I looked up articles in news databases on efforts by Disney officials to ensure that Celebration was as integrated as the workforce at its theme parks in California and Florida. Disney placed advertisements in newspapers and magazines that catered to blacks and Hispanics. They hired minority brokers for the real estate office. They held a lottery for homes to ensure developers did not discriminate based on race. They printed brochures featuring minority members of the community.

Still, according to the 2000 Census estimate, only one percent of Celebration's residents were black, in a county where African Americans made up six percent of the population. The Hispanic population of the neighborhood was seven percent, in a county where Hispanics made up twenty-nine percent of the people. Celebration was eighty-eight percent white in a county where whites only made up fifty-nine percent of the population. Blacks owned only twelve of Celebration's 1,093 homes. There was no question that Disney's purported efforts at integration had been an abject failure. I went to Florida hoping to do a story on the social reasons behind why Disney's tireless efforts at integration had failed. It was the anti-Columbia.

There too, I was disappointed once I discovered, at least in my opinion, that the efforts to integrate Celebration were a sham. I was able to obtain access to chat room conversations about race between residents of Celebration that were found on the Internet by my friend Liz Kelly, a researcher who had left the paper for the research department at NBC. The chat room postings referred to some type of payment Disney officials had made to the local government to finance subsidized housing in exchange for not having to build any in Celebration. After a few quick phone calls from my room in the hotel, I discovered Disney had given Osceola County more than $900,000 in order to not build subsidized housing in Celebration. Given the county's socioeconomic and racial demographics, subsidized housing in Celebration would have guaranteed integration.

Olive, who was attending the convention, lived in Columbia and knew I had been late coming to the realities of the racial dynamics in America. She knew that I had a hard time acknowledging racism until it hit me squarely in the face, smacking me so hard that it nearly knocked me over. Olive also knew that when I discovered it, my anger would well up quickly and passionately. She knew that, like Howell had said in his story about Grady, that I was shaped by that moment when life first wounded me. There was no question that it was race in America that first pierced my armor of innocence, dictated the battles I would fight most ferociously and emotionally. Emotion was my journalistic friend; it was my personal enemy.

A deputy metro editor asked if I could put in a few extra days and spend September 11 working poll sites in black neighborhoods in Brooklyn—even though I had vacation time approved. The Florida elections of 2000 had *The Times* prepared to be super-vigilant about problems within the election booths in New York State. I agreed, but said I was going to take Monday off in order to prepare for my vacation, so he or Chris Drew, who was coordinating the coverage with Joe, would have to leave the precinct map on my desk and I would pick it up early Tuesday morning.

At a party on Saturday we hung out with my colleague's interesting collection of friends, including a metro desk copy editor who always seemed to be stoned and, at the same time, wrote some of the best headlines. The man was the creative case for marijuana legalization, I thought to myself. About seven or eight of us smoked a joint in a bedroom and I brought a little cocaine that a few of us shared.

My cocaine use had been up in the recent months since I had been depressed. Even though I had used the drug often, I was careful to make sure my colleagues did not see that part of my world. One night at Emmett's, a friend who was a reporter came by and asked if I wanted to go meet his brother-in-law, his wife and some of their friends who were at the Waldorf-Astoria. I said sure. I had been to the hotel to cover officials and other dignitaries, but rarely as a guest in anyone's suite. We were the guests of a wealthy widow whose husband had died several years before in a freak accident while on the job.

The woman's husband was one of the nation's highest paid corporate lawyers when he died, making more than $2.5 million a year and leaving behind an estate worth nearly $200 million. The wife was in a battle with his children, a common situation after the deaths of America's most wealthy, over the estate and the home they owned that bordered a golf course and a lake. The woman sent her black driver and limousine, which had been parked outside the Waldorf at her beck and call, to come pick us up at Emmett's. After a short ride crosstown on Fiftieth Street, we were on the East Side of Manhattan, walking into the Waldorf's side entrance, only a few blocks from Saint Patrick's Cathedral.

The widow was in the suite with the brother-in-law of my colleague. The two had been dating for a little while and he was discussing the suit he had bought recently with her money. My colleague's wife was also there, and we greeted each other with a kiss and a hug. Another man, whom we would later refer to as the "sycophant," was in the bedroom, organizing some clothes. The woman, who seemed to be in her mid-40s, was blabbing rapidly about the Greek astrology books she bought even though she did not speak Greek, and the jewelry she had, items she had picked up that day during her Fifth Avenue shopping spree.

I picked up a large necklace covered with giant precious stones. Moments later, the $50 bottle of Johnnie Walker Black I had ordered arrived. I had placed the order, almost inadvertently, when the sycophant had asked me what I wanted to drink.

"That cost $150,000," the widow said in a high rate of speech before unleashing what could only be described as a diatribe on how jewelry just wasn't what it used to be.

As she continued, I stared at the necklace in my hands and thought about how it would take seven years of my mother's salary as a teacher to make enough post-tax money to purchase this little necklace with its precious stones. It flashed through my mind how easy it would be to take it, buy my mom a house, and set her for life. No pawnshop owner, though, would pay $150,000 for a necklace that would cause so much potential trouble that could lead to a knock on the door from the police. Still, I was reluctant to let the necklace go, because the only other thing to focus on was the woman's babbling.

Sitting across from me, the sycophant put a bag in his lap and then pulled out a circular silver plate. He then put the plate in his lap and started to push white powder out of the large bag and onto the tray in front of me. He broke lines across the plate, using some kind of instrument I could not make out, and then passed it across the room. When it got to me, I found myself self-conscious. I did not want to seem too experienced with the drug in front of a colleague from work.

I took my finger and dabbed it onto one of the edges of a line, and immediately felt it racing through me, my heart already clipping at a faster beat. My blood pressure was already rising. The veins in my upper thigh were beating. The blood in my arteries was quickening. The nerves in my brain were screaming "yes"—they knew they were about to be flushed with dopamine. It must have been pretty pure cocaine, not stepped on, diluted, or cut with additives like baking soda, baby powder, laxative, or lidocaine. Cocaine is usually one quarter-strength of what it should be by the time it hits the average retailer selling on the streets. Dealers like mine didn't step too hard on the cocaine reserved for their best clients. A reward for paying your bills was getting the best stuff.

Drug use was rarely about friendship or bonding for me. I was never a social smoker, a social drinker, or a social drug user. I was not attracted to drugs, like so many, out of decadence or novelty. For while it ravaged my body and my ability to function properly in society, cocaine did something within the four walls of my skull that no emotion, pat on the back or sexual experience could accomplish. It made me normal. I knew something was wrong with that, but at the time my mind just did not translate it as an illness. It was a gift to be able to go to the places that cocaine took me, I thought, not a disease.

Paying was rarely a problem for me. The job generated enough cash to provide several hundred dollars' worth of cocaine a week. During this depression, I was spending more than $500 a week on cocaine—sometimes as much as $1,000. When I could not come up with the money, I brought friends in on my purchases or dealt some of it for a profit to people I knew at *The Times* who were coke fiends.

I knew how to play dumb as I sampled the cocaine. It didn't take much for it to make my head start pounding. I had heard a number of recovering drug addicts give speeches about how they hated cocaine, the bloody noses, the pains throughout their bodies, the feeling that death was creeping up on you as you sat on the toilet, only to think the moment you knew you were in the clear that perhaps one more line could be done. You always told yourself it was risky. I felt that those types of recovering addicts were telling themselves they hated cocaine so much as a psychological game to convince themselves not to pick up.

There was a physical addiction to the drug, of course. For me, though, it was a wondrous thing what a few lines of blow and a glass of Scotch would do to my mind. Cocaine was one of the few drugs that could be mixed with alcohol and offer the experiences of both highs, the mind stimulation of blow and the calming effect of Scotch, that were somewhat of a refuge for me. When I was manic and could not stop from racing around all of God's creation, alcohol took the lead. When I was down, it was cocaine and me. When my two mistresses came together, it almost felt like cocaine was speeding my metabolism, allowing the alcohol to make it there faster. Call her by any name: Star-Spangled Powder, the All-American drug, blow, bouncing powder, or Carrie—cocaine was the woman for me.

I had heard people talk about how their drug addictions had made them lose control. I had never felt more euphoric, reinforced and in control than I was when I was high on an alcohol and cocaine cocktail. I'd read enough about cocaine to know that when mixed in high doses with alcohol, another drug was manufactured. Cocaethylene, as the combination is called, took me to a psychotic place where I felt at peace and in harmony with the world as my mind was racing. It was almost as if I could feel cocaethylene increasing the dopamine in my synapses.

In a cocaethylene induced state, ideas abounded, depression vanished and I felt like nothing could stop me. I might become a little more extroverted, but I was just as happy to sit on my couch and drink and do blow on the coffee table in front of me in my Brooklyn apartment, which was beginning to look more like a dumpster filled with magazines, newspapers and bottles of Scotch and beer.

That night at the Waldorf, in the summer of 2001, was the first time I let it be known to a colleague that cocaine was a friend of mine, one that would send me to Astoria, Queens or the Lower East Side in the middle of the night; one that would have me walking the halls of Manhattan housing projects with armed dealers; one that would send me to seek out dealers on Classon Avenue in Bedford-Stuyvesant and Roosevelt Avenue in Queens.

I had decided not to drink or do cocaine on my vacation, at least, after the Saturday party at Ellie's house. Two other friends who did not do cocaine gave me and another journalist rides home to downtown Brooklyn, where the car was damaged when we went over an Atlantic Avenue pothole. In my weed, cocaine and alcohol induced state, I could hardly stop laughing. On Sunday, I had this feeling we were due a "big one" as reporters liked to call stories, like the Wendy's massacre, that would consume days or weeks of our lives. I thought nothing of it.

I stayed at home drinking.

CHAPTER SEVENTEEN
WHEN THE DUST SETTLES

Tuesday morning, I left my apartment on the leafy block in Clinton Hill, Brooklyn. I went to the deli around the corner for my normal coffee, with milk and sugar, and egg-and-cheese-on-a-roll sandwich. Coffee was necessary each morning to wake me, although I was such a mess that I didn't even have a coffee machine.

I drove across the Brooklyn Bridge, crossing the East River, and, once I was in Manhattan, took the exit leading north on the FDR Drive. I loved driving on the FDR, wedged beside the tall Manhattan buildings to the left, the East River to the right and the Brooklyn and Queens skylines off in the distance. Once I reached the office, I checked my e-mail and picked up a map that had been left on my desk. I went back downstairs and jumped in the Grand Am, speeding down West Forty-third Street.

I took a hard right onto Ninth Avenue, then another right onto West Forty-second Street, which led me to the Westside Highway. Cruising down the Westside Highway was always a treat, with the beautiful waterfront and the views of Lower Manhattan.

That morning I took a left turn on Chambers Street and made my way past the Tweed Courthouse, City Hall and took a right where the road dead-ended at the neo-classic Municipal Building located in front of One Police Plaza. It was a quick jump before making the left onto the Brooklyn Bridge. Charlie and I had decided to meet up for lunch. He was in Brooklyn, and in typical Charlie fashion, hanging out with the one guy in the city who supposedly was on call to fix broken voting machines. I got a call from him while on the bridge at 7:52 a.m.

So, I decided to quickly pop off the bridge and make a quick hit by heading to Vinegar Hill, a Brooklyn neighborhood encircled by a housing project, the East River, the Manhattan Bridge and the Brooklyn-Queens Expressway. I took a right on Tillary Street in downtown

Brooklyn and passed Flatbush Avenue. That's when I heard fire truck sirens.

Most people panic at the sound of fire sirens. As a cub reporter, it is easy to learn that firemen were called to all sorts of strange things, including gas leaks and medical emergencies. What causes your radar to go off was the crush of sirens, loud and long, that keep on going and going. The noise this morning seemed unrelenting, like the sirens were coming from every direction and they were not stopping.

A fire truck had just passed me when I noticed that everyone on the street seemed to be gazing and pointing toward Manhattan. I looked over and beyond a set of trees and saw that there was smoke billowing out of the northern tower of the World Trade Center. I ran a few feet to get a better view, and it became obvious that the northern tower was on fire. Any fire in a World Trade Center tower, even a minor one, would be a journalistic "red ball," a "big one," with all hands on deck. Trade Center officials closed the streets around the towers when they were simply removing windows for fear of harming someone. A large fire in either of the main buildings meant the city would have to be cleared for dozens of blocks. The last time I had been in the Trade Center had been just before going to Florida. I had gone to pick up a copy of *The Hobbit*. The time before that I was giving a speech to Silicon Valley business people in the Marriott that was attached to the towering buildings.

The upside of the fires would be that many of the metro reporters who hardly got a chance to see each other would be grouped together on the blocks around the trade center complex, covering the fire, being fed quotes from witnesses, government officials, firemen and the police. The downside was that it was going to be a long night of reporting and many would be dead and wounded. I had not even contemplated the possibility that hundreds of people were already dead, but the loss of life would be high in any fire in a New York skyscraper.

I immediately started analyzing the ways they'd go: smoke inhalation, flames, falls down stairwells, being trampled, trapped in elevators and backdrafts that could blow people out of the buildings. I started to think like an editor and divide up the parts of the story that would need to be covered: impact on the elections, the response from City Hall, fire headquarters, the scene of the fires and the neighborhoods where the victims lived.

My mind covered the possible rescue efforts: rooftops would be too hot, trucks would be surrounding the buildings and perhaps they would try to bring a fire barge up the Hudson River side to shoot down the flames. Those were all possibilities.

I called the metro desk and an editor picked up the phone.

"Hey, it's Jayson," I said. "There is a fire at the World Trade Center. I am just across the bridge doing elections stuff, and am going to head in."

"No," the voice on the other line said. "Stay where you are and continue to do the election coverage. We need you to stay there."

I couldn't tell whose voice was on the other end, but I could tell they were in a panic that led to a partial loss of their senses. A fire in the World Trade Center was going to disrupt all of downtown and send people into a frenzy. There is no way the election is going to be finished today, I thought to myself. They were going to have to cancel it. That's when I saw the second plane slam into the side of the south tower, a giant plume of smoke and fire billowing into the sky.

My mind immediately flashed to several weeks before, when I had been driving down Fourth Avenue in Brooklyn with a colleague. We talked about Tom Clancy's novel *Executive Orders,* where Japanese terrorists flew a fuel-laden 747 into the east side of the U.S. Capitol, killing the president, the Supreme Court justices and most of Congress during the State of the Union speech. We talked about how easy it would be to do the same thing to the World Trade Center.

It was then that I saw a giant explosion that appeared between the two towers. It looked as if the fire had leaped from the northern tower to the façade of its southern twin. I had seen something that looked like a jet or a helicopter approach the south side of the buildings. I wondered whether they were consumed in the flames. I went back to my car and turned on the radio to see what they were reporting about the second explosion, and a woman from Greenwich Village was on screaming that she had seen a "second plane" slam into the southern tower.

I knew in that moment that the Trade Center buildings had been hit in a terrorist attack, but I tried to suppress that notion by coming up with other rational explanations. Perhaps the second plane got lost in the smoke and then struck the south tower?

My rationalizations disappeared once I got out of my car and started talking with people on the streets of downtown Brooklyn, where almost every person I encountered said they clearly saw the second plane slam into the southern tower. I talked with a woman who was crying because her son worked in a building next to the trade center towers. I talked to a man who was angry that he could not get to an appointment in the Trade Center buildings.

As the towers burned, I drove to the Brooklyn Bridge, where an officer told me that only emergency vehicles were being allowed into Manhattan. Just as I pulled my car off to the side of the road so I could interview the people who were running across the bridge from Manhattan, I heard a United States Marshal's radio crackling. I stepped closer to get some idea of what was being said.

"They hit the Pentagon, they hit the Pentagon," she screamed to her shotgun carrying colleagues. "There has been an explosion outside the State Department and the military is tracking another plane headed up the Potomac. There has been an order of an evacuation of all government buildings."

In an instant, my reporting professionalism gave way to a complete sense of personal panic.

I thought about my family. My father was in a Smithsonian Building just off the mall and near the Department of Energy's headquarters in Washington. My mother was at the high school where she taught, which was near the headquarters of super-secret National Reconnaissance Office, which managed satellites for the Central Intelligence Agency and Defense Department. My brother was at work in Northern Virginia not far from the Pentagon. We were all under siege. I tried to call my father at the Smithsonian and could not get through.

I drove to the thin, wooden pier in industrial Red Hook, Brooklyn that Jenny Holland and I used to walk out onto late at night to catch views of the moonlit light, the colorful Verrazano-Narrows Bridge, and the lit-up towers of the World Trade Center buildings. Papers were floating down from the clouds of debris pouring out of the trade center building. I was covered in white ash and papers that went flying. I found a picture, burnt, of a little girl, the other side obscured—it looked like a memento from someone's desk. I found a virtually intact copy of an agreement between Merrill Lynch and one of its employees.

I knew that the pier was about three-and-one-half miles away from the trade center. I imagined the force that it must have taken for the papers to have flown that far and still remained intact, stapled together. I thought about what that force would have done to a human body.

That's where I watched as one tower collapsed in a plume of smoke, and then the other followed suit soon after, the fallen ash and debris creating what could only be described as a dry snowfall. Just then, I received a call on my cell phone from Charlie, who had been in Far Rockaway, Queens when the buildings were first hit. He had received a call from an assistant metro editor asking him to check out grocery stores to see if people were stocking up on basic supplies.

Charlie had convinced the editor that we should make a run for either getting into Manhattan or traveling up New York Harbor in a boat to get to another location that I had not even thought about. Charlie had discovered that officials had ordered body bags sent to Governor's Island, which was just south of Lower Manhattan, and that it might be used as a temporary morgue or refugee center. Charlie asked me to meet him out near the Queens-Nassau County border.

I used back roads where I had covered fires and shootings to find my way around the snarling traffic. Along the way, I picked up an Orthodox Jewish couple who looked alone, stranded and in the wrong neighborhood. I gave the couple, both of whom had walked from Manhattan to downtown Brooklyn, a ride to Grand Army Plaza. They had come across the bridge from Manhattan and then become lost as people screamed for them to just get out of downtown Brooklyn. To them, it was unclear whether people were screaming for them to get out of downtown because of its tall buildings or because of the predominantly Arabic business district along Atlantic Avenue. It was a day where every fear and paranoia seemed more than justified. We had been hit, out of the blue, by the totally unexpected.

After dropping the couple off, I made the twelve-mile drive to the Nassau County-Queens border to meet Charlie. There was hardly any traffic headed toward the city, other than fire trucks and ambulances. It was strange to look at the entrances to the humongous John F. Kennedy Airport closed. I passed the airport and made my way south through back roads to an inlet along the Queens-Nassau border.

Charlie and I were unable to make it into Manhattan because of the closures and had come up with two back up plans: one, trying to get a fisherman friend of his in Jamaica Bay to take us into New York Harbor and then the southern tip of Lower Manhattan, or getting a raft and then making our way across the East River. The fisherman, who had already been stopped out on the water by the Coast Guard that day, was unable to help us proceed, but he did offer me a cup of coffee and some food. We tuned in to the radio to listen to the latest reports from Lower Manhattan.

The estimates were that thousands of people had been in the buildings when they collapsed, and hundreds more had been on nearby streets. Entire fire units were missing, according to the radio reports.

We decided to head back toward Manhattan, and if worst came to worst, make a stab at crossing the East River on an inflatable raft. We dropped off our cars in the tree-lined neighborhoods of Cobble Hill and made our way toward the bridge on foot. We met Daryl, who had been working the story from the riverfront underneath the bridge, on a main street in downtown Brooklyn.

That's when one of us, and I can not remember for the life of me which of us, saw a city bus across the Manhattan Bridge. We talked to the police, who told us it was taking people who lived in Manhattan home and escorting rescue workers toward the scene, and that medical command centers had been established on the west side of the island. We came up with a plan to disguise ourselves as rescue workers and boarded the next bus into Manhattan.

As we crossed the bridge, Charlie struck up a conversation with one of the real medical workers about whether, and how, we should retaliate against whoever was responsible for the attacks. Daryl and I stared at the windows facing the Lower Manhattan skyline. The first thing that struck me when we came off the bus was the deep smell of the remnants of the buildings and the people who were in them. I could not take my mind off the idea that my nostrils were inhaling what was left of hundreds, if not thousands, of dead people.

At Canal Street, we split up, and Daryl tried to find ways to get closer to whatever was left of the trade center buildings. Charlie and I headed west toward the end of Canal Street, where the medical workers were assembling in the darkening evening. We surmised from a call from an editor on the metro desk that we were within "the red zone," an area that had been closed off to anyone other than emergency personnel and residents.

"Where do we head?" I asked Charlie.

"Toward the action," I recall him saying, as he nodded toward an area along the Westside Highway where the medical workers were gathering.

On the way, we ran into Department of Corrections buses that had been lined up along the street. The inmates had been evacuated from jails and detention centers in Lower Manhattan. The inmates were whistling and hollering at the women who walked by, and yelling "Kill the Sheik" in unison. The chants about the Sheik referred to the mastermind behind the first World Trade Center bombing that had happened several years earlier. Charlie approached one of the buses and started shouting back at some of the inmates as we made our way down the street.

As darkness began to consume New York on the first nightfall after the attacks, I made my way to the piers along the Westside Highway, where I had begun driving that morning. I looked into the faces of the police officers and fireman. Normally, no matter how deadly the disaster, the police officers and firemen on the scene seemed confident. Not tonight, though. They seemed almost panicked, and it was their panic that gave me shivers.

"What are the estimates?" I asked an officer, as I lit one of the last Camel Lights in my pack.

"Some people think that there are 5,000 to 10,000 casualties," he replied. "They have no idea how many of those people are dead."

"Hundreds of firefighters alone are missing," he continued.

I scribbled his words into my notebook and then called them into the bank of transcribers who were working the phones on West Forty-third Street.

"There are at least a hundred people who jumped or were thrown out of the building," he continued.

I had noticed earlier what I thought were birds flying in the skies above the trade center buildings. The images flashed back into my mind. They were all descending too quickly. Those must have been people jumping, or being thrown, out of the buildings. I imagined them landing on the sides of streets and on the fire trucks below.

Soon, newspapers would be criticized for showing in gruesome detail the images of the jumpers cascading out of the buildings. The public had no idea of the even more shocking images being hidden from them. One lesson of September 11, at least for me, was what the news media held back. There was a man impaled on a traffic sign. What appeared to be a pocketbook was a flattened head, the black strands of hair still recognizable. There were images from that day, and ones that followed, so horrific that they were hard to imagine, particularly if one had seen most of September 11 on the safe side of a television.

One pier along the Westside Highway near Canal Street had been converted into a makeshift medical facility. Prisoners who had been evacuated from downtown parked in buses on the streets. I could not help but think about the hurt and fear that would cause a group of men to commit suicide by flying planes into the World Trade Center buildings. Anger as a byproduct of hurt and fear was not a foreign concept to me.

"How many people are you thinking?" Charlie asked a police officer who was at the scene.

"They have no idea," the officer said, "but we are speculating tens of thousands of people could have been in there when the planes crashed into the building."

"Holy shit," Charlie said as he worked his way over to me. "This is fucking, holy fucking shit."

I had never seen Charlie stuttering-over-his-words speechless.

I talked to a handful of people that afternoon. The conversation I remember most was with Amie Parnes, a friend who was my age who had worked as an intern in *The Times* bureau in Miami, under the tutelage of Rick Bragg, the Pulitzer Prize winning feature writer, who was the envy of many a reporter writing on West Forty-third Street. Amie was twenty-five at the time and had moved to the East Village in Manhattan to attempt a freelance career. Amie was among the most hardworking of my peers, and landed a freelance gig with one of the business editors at *The Times*. Like Daryl before her in the Middle Atlantic states, she took on a gig writing as a national correspondent in New York for *The Boston Globe*.

Amie had tolerated many of my worst moments, drunken stupors and episodes such as the time that summer—to this day I can't remember what it was that caused it to happen—when I called from work for her to meet me on the park benches across from her apartment on Ninth Street and Second Avenue. We had dated briefly, but remained in constant contact about story ideas, and a mutual love of journalism. We imagined what it would be like when our generation of reporters took over the business. We wondered whether, by then, our youthful enthusiasm would have faded, whether we would have had to stab so many people in the back to rise that we would become as cruel as our predecessors, and whether our stories actually did make a difference.

Amie, like me, had spent her entire day reporting.

"Jayson, when the dust settles, pardon the pun, let's get together for a drink," she said.

The dust never settled for me.

Late that night, I returned to West Forty-third Street with Charlie.

The newsroom, even at that late hour, seemed still embroiled in confusion. I went upstairs to the fifth-floor smoking room to take a break. I turned the lights on, and noticed that two police officers were sleeping in the green chairs. I wondered whether they knew about the latest reports suggesting that many of their colleagues were trapped inside the burning rubble.

Back downstairs, after my cigarette, I noticed some people huddled in corners crying, but for the most part this was a news story. It happened in our city, and that only furthered the obligation for us to put out the best report, while others were focused on delivering an authoritative product that could provide people with much needed, helpful information, to separate fiction from the facts of what was already, by that night, being called September 11. People were coming in covered in dust. There were more faces filled with shock than there were those crying. Executives were on the phone trying to get a special escort to ensure the newspaper trucks would be allowed into the now cordoned-off city. Regardless of our emotions, the newspaper train had to keep on moving.

The nobleness, though, was not universal.

One photographer put on a United States Bureau of Alcohol, Tobacco and Firearms cap and tried to sneak into the closed area around the World Trade Center that had already taken on the name *ground zero*. Another photographer put an orange traffic cone on top of a severed hand, waiting until daybreak when he would have the natural light to shoot it.

That night, I led a group down to Robert Emmett's, which was closed to the public. The owner and his girlfriend were behind the bar. The owner, Brendan, invited me and the handful of people I was with in, to find refuge in the free drinks that were flowing. *Times* people trickled in that night, and Brendan would ask "Friend of Jayson?" before allowing them in. As crazy as life had been, I felt at home at Emmett's that night drinking pint-sized glasses of Johnnie Walker Black.

Within days, matters quickly moved to bickering, although the tone was somewhat different. In the coming days, several metro reporters would voice their concerns to Jon after he sent out an e-mail praising one reporter for his act of heroism on September 11.

That act, apparently, was to write the main scene story in the paper that day relying on notes from all of us reporters who were in the field. His act of great bravery, apparently, was enhanced by the fact that the reporter did not know where his dog was and when he went downtown to check on him, the police would not let him into the cordoned off area, which on the first night was impenetrable, even though it extended, in some respects, all the way to Fourteenth Street. Bickering over credit had not begun yet. Instead it was over some of the more insane ideas, for the front-page headline, for example, that came from some of the editors who normally seemed so confident and cocky.

Not tonight, though. There was no bickering.

We, as journalists, were used to making seemingly intensely emotional decisions about the value of life and even at times the deaths of hundreds of people, but normally the numbers were so small or the events so small, or happening so far away. This one, this time, this was in our backyard. It was hard to escape the rotating feelings of helplessness, shock and insecurity. People called it a tragedy, but it was no tragedy.

Those are when someone attempts to save something or accomplish some positive goal, and their actions themselves achieve the opposite. A tragedy would have been if someone were attempting to stop the attacks and their actions led to them occurring. This was no tragedy. This was a deliberate act of violence that caught us by surprise. That was the hard part to stomach. New York had gone from the city of tolerance to Pearl Harbor in this newest war, in one instant.

I spent that night at the bar with editors and reporters going over our recollections of the events. One colleague read out loud from E. B. White's *Here Is New York,* reciting a seemingly foreshadowing passage about how "a single flight of planes no bigger than a wedge of geese can quickly end this island fantasy, burn the towers, crumble the bridges, turn the underground passages into lethal chambers, cremate the millions. The intimation of mortality is part of New York now: in the sound of jets overhead, in the black headlines of the latest edition."

White wrote that line in 1949.

I was still not prepared for the possibility of annihilation.

CHAPTER EIGHTEEN
RWANDA ON THE HUDSON

The night began with a conversation with Jerry and Pete Khoury, a metro desk copy editor, who showed me how journalists could be basically put into two camps at this time period. There were journalists, like Jerry, who had been in war-torn areas who had never expected New York to become a battleground, but were able to put the 3,000 deaths in the trade center in perspective with other events that they had witnessed or reported close up on. Then, there were people like Pete and me, who also never expected New York to become a battleground. We, however, could not get our heads around the up-close view of death and destruction of this magnitude.

Jerry told us about traveling to Zaire and Rwanda in August 1994 to cover the ethnic massacres occurring there. Jerry left New York with $60,000 in cash from *The Times* to cover his expenses, and some equipment, including a cellular telephone and a laptop. Jerry had covered African conflicts before as the Nairobi bureau chief of The Associated Press. I had read his stories, and those of other *Times* correspondents covering the conflict as an intern, and had a hard time indicting the newspaper in my mind and grouping it with others who had ignored the 1994 massacres.

Some human rights officials had argued that if the news media had shown what was happening in Rwanda in all of its horrific details, it would have been hard for the Clinton administration to ignore the conflict and not step into the fray as it would do later in Kosovo. The news media at large had virtually ignored the massacres as they were occurring, but not *The Times*, which poured resources into the region.

Jerry told us about coming across a truck soon after arriving that was filled with dead bodies. One colleague, who was with him, he said, noticed that a man in the back of the truck was still alive. When they spoke with the driver, they were told that all the bodies had been picked up off the side of the road and that even if there was a man alive in the truck, the choice was whether he would die on the side of the road or die in the back of the vehicle. He was going to die, the driver said, no matter what. It was not a simple matter of not having the resources at hand to save the lives of the starvation victims of the conflict—it was just impossible to get the resources, the food and the doctors, safely to them.

Jerry told us about visiting a village in Zaire where there were thousands of refugees from the Rwandan conflict, many on the verge of dying. He told us the story of a physician at an orphanage who was forced to choose which ten of the more than 4,000 children under her care would be given the chance to live by being sent with the team of Israeli doctors who had arrived. The decision on who would live and die, Jerry told us, was cruelly Darwinian by necessity in the Rwandan conflict. The very young and the very old tended to be the weakest, making them the least likely to receive help because they were the least likely to survive. Jerry told us of having to watch doctors make these difficult and intensely emotional decisions.

Jerry said that Rwanda was one of the few things that he found personally analogous to the September 11 attacks as a reporting experience.

"It just has not hit me, emotionally," Jerry said of the September 11 attacks. "I don't know why. I don't know whether it will eventually. I think about something like Rwanda, where more than 4,000 people were dying a day, and I don't know whether it has given me thick skin, but for whatever reason, September 11 just has not hit me in that same emotional way."

Then again, Jerry told us, Rwanda did not hit him emotionally until long after returning home to Princeton, New Jersey, where he greeted his wife, daughter and son.

"I saw my children and that's when it hit me," he said. "I just broke down. I couldn't stop crying."

Jerry did not have to explain that so many of the victims he had watched die in Rwanda had been his own children's age. He did not have to explain that if his children had been born in another place, they would have undoubtedly perished. He did not have to explain that the 3,000 victims in the trade center could not compare to the 4,000 victims a day in Rwanda. There was little he had to explain.

I was in the second camp. I had never seen or covered anything like this. The closest I had come were fires with multiple victims, crashes or accidents where several people were killed, or the summer I spent in Boston where I had seen more than my share of dead bodies. To me, it was hard to get my head around September 11. It was even harder to get my head around Rwanda. And there was no question that I was not doing well emotionally.

On the night of September 11, I went to Emmett's to drink with colleagues. On September 12, I was back there with an even bigger group. On September 13, the group hit its apex, with correspondents and editors from all over the building joining us at our watering hole. We, in so many words, needed a drink. And as someone who drank a lot already, I felt like I needed ten or twenty. The depressive affect of alcohol, at least after its first ounce, was lost on me, but in retrospect, it made sense why I gravitated so fiercely to cocaine in the months after the attacks. I needed something to lift me out of the sadness of a story I didn't want to cover and a new world I didn't want to live in.

One night I was sitting at the bar crying. My mother had called to inform me that Dr. Norma Steuerle, a family friend whose daughters I knew as a child, had died on the plane that hit the Pentagon. I concocted a story about one of my cousins being among the victims so I would not have to write the "Portraits of Grief." I went so far as to find the one Blair among the victims, and gave their name to Bill Schmidt in my explanation of why I wanted to stay away from writing our profiles of the dead. It frustrated me that talk had already begun on the metro desk in early October, not a month after the attacks, about how we were going to win a Pulitzer for them. They were called "Portraits of Grief," an apt description for what I was. Perhaps if at that moment I had been honest about my emotional state, alarm bells would have gone off in the ears of those listening, and something could have been done to help me. I just wanted to be left alone, given a chance to disappear into my world of drugging and drinking.

I also concocted a lie about The Times sanctioning the drinking that was occurring around the corner at Emmett's. The sessions became our own version of counseling, something to take the edge off the anxiety and sad emotions that seemed to be swirling around like frosty demons. My life, in the three weeks after the attacks, centered on four blocks. The Times Building on West Forty-third Street, Robert Emmett's around the corner on West Forty-fourth Street, the Times Square Hilton I was staying in, and the Gap on West Forty-second Street. The cycle went like this: leaving work late at night for Emmett's, staying at Emmett's until three or four in the morning, making my way to the Times Square Hilton, and then walking to the Gap in the morning to buy a new set of clothes. This went on for three weeks.

I was so distraught one night that I asked Judy Tong, a news assistant at The Times who needed a place to stay, to join me at the Hilton. There, she read aloud portions of The Hobbit from the copy I had bought just before heading to Florida, until I feel asleep.

Another night I stayed at Emmett's with the staff until long after closing, and took a cab ride with one of my favorite waitresses, Karolyn. The plan was to stay with her that night at her apartment in Woodside, Queens. That plan was foiled, though, when we reached Woodside and she was too drunk to respond to the cab driver's requests about which building she lived in. I decided to reverse directions and head back to Emmett's, where I could put her in the hands of her co-workers who would know how to get her home. That plan too was foiled by the fact that it was past four in the morning, and everyone had left. So, I took her to the Times Square Hilton, where the concierge was able to get a wheelchair and we were able to take her up to a room in a tower overlooking Times Square. For many of us who drank a lot already, running from September 11 had given us a reason to flee reality altogether.

I spent another week at the Times Square Hilton before I headed home for the first time since the attacks, arriving in my Brooklyn brownstone late one Saturday evening. I walked up the flight of brown stairs and then opened the glass door, relieved that I would finally get a chance to sleep in my own apartment. Mail that had been waiting for me was stacked up outside my door, one level up from the elevated entrance to the building. I opened the door to my apartment, which was dark, and flipped the switch. I found myself confronted by my long horizontal, framed picture of the Manhattan skyline taken at night from New Jersey. Right in front of my eyes, almost as if they were staring at me, were the World Trade Center towers. I started crying as I turned away, and walked toward my bedroom.

On October 13, though, the morning I was out with Jerry, we made our way to the Times's corporate apartment he had been staying in. As the editor of the Continuous News Desk, the team of reporters and editors who write onto the Nytimes.com website twenty-four hours a day, Jerry could not afford to make the long trek back to Princeton each night in the middle of the war on terrorism and coverage of the aftermath of the September 11 attacks. Jerry gave his wife a wakeup call in the Midwest, where she was on a business trip, and then went to sleep.

I couldn't sleep, so I arrived in the office a little before 8:30, set up at my desk and began working. Since September 11, I had worked non-stop, but not gotten many stories into the newspaper. The paper had begun to clean out and publish its inventory of stories in the "advance" hold queues of The Metro Section, the national section and the foreign report. Stories would often sit there for weeks, sometimes months, as editors would pick and choose among the new arrivals. Choice is what gave editors power, and there was little time for such games. The sheer volume of resources dedicated to the Afghan war and the September 11 attacks dictated everything be emptied from those queues to fill the pages dedicated to general news.

The pressure had become intense to even get your name in the paper. While it was not the most important thing occurring, in retrospect, it was clear that many reporters needed some validation, their names appearing on a piece of paper as a testament to history that they were there, that they saw these devastating and painful things. Our editors did not seem to understand this need. My story from Kingston was cleared out of the queue on September 16 and ran on the front of the national section.

On Saturday, I went back down to ground zero with Charlie Bagli, the *Times*'s top real estate reporter, the one who would most likely lead the charge in covering the rebuilding of Lower Manhattan that was about to begin. I ran into Jenny Holland's parents as we were ushered by the police with hundreds of others along pathways that led to one of the few streets where the average New Yorker could get a clear view of the twisted rubble, piled hundreds of feet in the air. Later, Jenny's parents would tell her that the look of shock and numbness on my face stood out in comparison to other New Yorkers.

Two days later, on September 18, my first shot at a byline came in the form of being assigned by the business section, to the chagrin of the metro business editor, to write about a day trader. I was so desperate to get into the paper that I took the assignment to interview a day trader at the E*Trade office on East Fifty-fifth Street and Madison Avenue on the first day of the New York Stock Exchange reopening. I interviewed scores of people, none of whom at the end of our conversations would give me their names. One man, though, gave me his first name as Andrew and, back in the office, I improvised by creating a last name for him. I had lifted quotes from other papers before, but never made something up.

It was the first thing I had made up. A name: Rosstein. I do not know where it came from or how I got the name or even what I was feeling at the moment—other than a desperate desire to get into the newspaper. Emotionally, I know, I was drained and had had very little sleep over recent weeks. I also knew that getting a byline in the paper had turned into an arduous task, even for me, in the days after the September 11 attacks. And I knew I wanted one. Hindsight is 20/20, and it was obviously the wrong thing to do. My motivation, as grotesque as it sounds, was plain and simple. I wanted to make sure the story made it into the paper and was not incorporated into one of the many other business stories running that day.

On September 20, I was able to get in a story about the costs of computers and other technology destroyed in the trade center—a story that was researched and reported based on solid figures and interviews. I felt back on track, both at work and in my personal life. On September 21, I was able to get in a notebook item on the damage the attacks had had on the West Thirtieth Street heliport, and a day later I was able to get in an item about television reception problems that were leaving many people worried and wondering that the next wave of attacks had begun each time they heard a strange noise. As a city, we were in post-traumatic shock, and the immediate answers of television were something that put us at ease as much as their gruesome images unnerved us.

My story about Celebration, Florida eventually ran under the headline "Failed Disney Vision: Integrated City" on September 23. Each day was a battle to get into the paper, though. My first knockdown, drag-out fight with the new metro business editor came over a story, oddly enough, about real estate. Barbara Corcoran, the founder of the Corcoran Group, the powerful Manhattan real estate firm, had decided to sell her company and told us about it nine days after the attacks. It was one of those stories destined for the back pages of the paper that no one was going to read, particularly in the middle of a major local crisis in New York and a war brewing in Afghanistan.

I told my new editor, after Andrew Ross Sorkin and I had filed the story, that we both thought it should carry two bylines because we both did an equal amount of work. She said fine, and went back to editing the piece. Minutes later, when the story was on the copy desk, I noticed that she had struck out my byline and just left Andrew's in place. I went back over to her desk, and pressed my point about the double byline, waiting for her reply.

"I did not know whether we used double bylines on stories this short, and I was going to check with someone," she said.

"Well, we do," I replied. "So, could you put my name back on the story?"

People often make some version of this mistake when they meet me. They assume, because I am nice at first blush, that they can roll over me.

They think I am "Webster" or Gary Coleman, and that I will just laugh at their stupid jokes as they drive their trucks over me. I was never a doormat. I was never passive-aggressive. I was straight-up aggressive, if anything. It was my way of protecting myself. If a person feared having to deal with my shit, they were more likely than not to go my way if they were sitting on the fence about something.

By this point, my editor had been driving me nuts for months. Before the attacks, she negotiated her return from exile in the newspaper's Human Resources Department, where Dennis Stern, the vice president, was making cuts to come into budget. She was trying to read tea leaves. "Hey, Howell wants more fashion coverage," someone would say. All of a sudden someone was covering fashion. She tried to fight battles like the one over the byline to send the message. I once fought with her for nearly a day over the question of whether the September 11 attacks could be called "the September 11 attacks" on first reference, or whether we had to do what she wanted, and insert the word "terrorist" between "11" and "attacks." As if there was any confusion.

I had to go to Allan Siegal, the assistant managing editor for standards, to get the dispute settled. September 11, like Pearl Harbor, was just fine, he said. I think it surprised my editor that I was willing to push back this hard, but I had long ago lost interest in being so eager to please.

What I was doing, from this point on, I told myself after the summer trip to Florida, might not be for myself, but it sure as hell was not going to be to please my editors. That jig was up. Years later, people would tell me that my troubles at *The Times* seemed to coincide with the September 11 attacks and the appointment of my new boss. Something about ego-centrism and careerism—someone talking about "how you need more front-page stories," and how that "will help your career"—something about it just was not the right tonic to chase the September 11 attacks with; well, at least not for me.

CHAPTER NINETEEN
ANTHRAX IN THE NEWSROOM

"**O**h, my God, oh, my God," Claudia Payne, an editor in the investigations pod yelled as she ran past my desk in the newsroom.

It was a little after 9:15 in the morning and I had had a long night. It started at Robert Emmett's at about seven in the evening and ended at about six in the morning at a diner on Eleventh Avenue and Forty-second Street, where Jerry Gray and I watched a man on a bicycle pick up a transvestite prostitute and disappear for a few minutes. Soon, they biked back together and he dropped her off. If that was not a sign that things were getting back to normal in New York, nothing was.

It was October 11, one month after two planes were hijacked and flown into the World Trade Center towers and another was flown into the Pentagon. It was only six days after the war in Afghanistan had begun in earnest, with American bombings of Taliban forces and Al-Qaeda camps. It was a time of turmoil. The upside was that much of the things to be fearful about were shifting from New York to other places, like Afghanistan and Florida, where an employee of American Media, the company that publishes the *National Enquirer,* had contracted anthrax.

The attacks had obviously shaken me, if my drinking and aggressive tone could be used as any measurement of the place that I was in, but things began to really fall apart when Claudia Payne came running by my desk with her hands in the air. I paid her no mind until I saw *Times* security guards, in their distinctive blue uniforms, come rushing by my desk. I decamped and followed them toward the Investigation's pod. On my way, I ran into Lynette Holloway.

"Nyet," I said, using a nickname for Lynette. "What in the Sam Hill is going on?"

"All I know," she said, "was that I was sitting at my desk this morning, minding my own business, when Judy Miller came flying around the corner."

Judith Miller was the award-winning investigative reporter who had covered the Middle East and terrorism, as well as written a recently released book on germ warfare with two other *Times* journalists, science reporter William Broad and investigative editor Stephen Engelberg. Judy had been all over the airwaves since the September 11 attacks, saying that we had not seen anything yet if we thought that the plane attacks were bad. Imagine if the planes were packed with chemical weapons, she would say. Imagine how many would be dead then.

Lynette continued.

"Judy jumped into Barbara Stewart's desk and started dialing sources for some story she was working on about the Treasury Secretary and the names of some terrorists."

I knew of this story. My friend and cubicle mate, Stephanie Flanders, a former chief speechwriter for Treasury Secretary Larry Summers in the Clinton administration, had been working on some element of that story with Jeff Gerth, an investigative reporter in Washington.

"Well, what happened?" I asked, as I motioned toward the stairwell to the smoking room.

"Judy had opened up some kind of package at her desk and white powder came flying out," Lynette continued. "Then that bitch had the audacity to come sit beside my desk and keep on reporting. Then, Claudia came by and called security."

I looked at Lynette. She looked at me.

"Any suspects yet?" I inquired.

"Nope," she said.

"Well, I got one," I added.

"Who?"

"Jeff Gerth," I said, mentioning the name of a correspondent who had worked with Judy.

Lynette laughed.

"If it wasn't him, then I would guess Steve Engelberg, because not only did he work with her on a book, he has had to edit her for all those many years. I would bet against terrorists, since they are really into spreading irrational fear and she seems to be a mouthpiece for that."

My humor notwithstanding, I got a little alarmed when I saw Gerald coming by with his arms around Judy and police officers and firemen headed in the opposite direction. Soon the area near the Continuous News Desk and the investigative team was cordoned off, and then a voice came over a loudspeaker, ordering us all to evacuate the third and fourth floors of the building. I got even more worried when I saw the guys in the head-to-toe moon suits come rushing onto the floor. We knew that the anti-quated ventilation system in *Times* headquarters was a terrorist's dream. There was little ability to filter out something like anthrax spores. Half the newsroom ended up on the fifth floor of the building, and I ended up leading a pack of people from the business section out one of the back doors.

There, several officers of the New York Police Department greeted us.

"Excuse me, sir," an officer yelled as I burst out the door, ready to make the mad dash as far as possible away from the *Times*'s headquarters.

"Excuse me, excuse me, ladies and gentlemen," he yelled as he could see our group was getting larger. "Please return to the building. For your own safety, please return to the building."

"Wait, hold on. You mean to tell me that this building could be con-taminated with anthrax and you are telling me to return to the building for my own safety?"

I am sure it was not *my own* safety the officer was worried about.

Soon the officers were forcing us back through the doors. We walked through the loading docks and into the lobby where other would-be escapees were sequestered. That same day, at NBC News headquarters not far away, Tom Brokaw's assistant had contracted anthrax from powder in a letter she opened in late September. Was someone targeting the media with deadly germs, we wondered? Charlie speculated that it made sense—if you wanted to terrorize the public, get the news media scared of anthrax and that's all anyone would hear about. We were no longer covering the story. We had become the story.

"Had *The Times* planned for such an emergency, I would have been iso-lated from my colleagues and the potentially deadly letter," Judy would write in the paper several days later. "But like most organizations, we had not conducted drills for a biological or chemical attack."

The question of the day that evening over at Emmett's once we were released was some formulation of this, "How close were you to Judy?" For those who were real close to Judy, they were taking Cipro, the drug that is supposed to kill anthrax. Some people had their doctors prescribe the drug for their entire families. They took Cipro; I took Johnnie Walker. At this point, my cocaine use was coming more out into the open, and I was begin-ning to look, talk and act more like an addict, more like a victim, more like a sucker than I ever had before.

When asked at a group counseling session masked as a seminar on covering war, one colleague answered a question from Patricia Drew, the director of the employee assistance program, about what we were doing to cope. Stephanie glanced at me, and then said, "We drink."

CHAPTER TWENTY
GETTING LOST IN THE DUST

I tried to eke out a fun story every now and then in between writing about the impact of the September 11 attacks on telecommunications networks and tourism, and stories like the death of the lead detective in the case of Martha Moxley, the fifteen-year-old girl who was mysteriously murdered in a wealthy neighborhood in Greenwich, Connecticut on Halloween in 1975.

One particular story gave me a chance to go underground, into the hidden underbelly of New York to write about the billions of dollars in damage done to the cables, wires, pipes, subways and other infrastructure in the most crowded underground in the world.

There were other ones, on what was left of my media beat after my new editor decided that she did not want me to cover news organizations, like the piece on an advertiser withdrawing from the *New York Post* because of a cartoon depicting Mort Zuckerman, the chairman of the company that owns the New York *Daily News,* as the person who sent anthrax to the editorial page of the *Post,* where an assistant, Johanna Huden, contracted anthrax.

The first panel of the cartoon showed *Post* editor Col Allan sitting at his desk, with a chart behind him showing the paper's circulation rising, as he is asked by an editor, "What sort of twisted sicko would send us anthrax?" The second panel showed Mort Zuckerman in his office, with a chart behind his desk showing the *Daily News* circulation dropping, as he was licking envelopes in front of a jar marked "Anthrax."

The bulk of the work was sad, and when I was not at *The Times* or reporting from the field, I was drinking or drugging, and with a hangover or coming down, things that were already annoying became like fingernails scraping the chalkboard within my skull. My new editor was one of those people. For Jon, attitude was half the battle, and mine was getting worse by the day. I felt that the newsroom had become way too focused, in general, on winning the Pulitzer Prize rather than on the impact of the attacks on the lives of people in the city.

One night after work I headed over to Emmett's with a colleague I was deeply fond of working with and talking to. She, more than most, recognized that I was, at least psychologically, falling apart. Given her family background, she understood what it meant to be disassembling. She had worked as a reporter for several years more than I and was wise to the ways of the newsroom. I guess what I had always offered her was some measure of confidence and affirmation, which is like a drug in itself in the newspaper business.

I normally love that time of year. The air, the changing colors of the trees. I just felt at home, at least normally. We laughed and joked about my crushes on the Irish waitresses endlessly. Most of all, between my breaks in the men's room to do lines of blow, we talked about the turmoil in the newsroom. Few of us were making it in to the paper, despite working tirelessly, and it was beginning to wear on morale.

"Why so many trips to the bathroom, my dear?" she asked me.

"To powder my nose," I said, pausing, debating whether to come out in the open with my secret.

". . . with cocaine," I continued.

I had bought an eight ball, the street name for one-eighth of an ounce of cocaine, in a housing complex where my drug dealer operated on Tenth Avenue in the 50's. I had met my current dealer on Eleventh Avenue, just north of the Market Diner. I had gone searching for a score on Eleventh Avenue when my normal dealer got stuck in traffic in New Jersey. As an addict, if you walk the streets long enough, just simply making eye contact, dealers knew who you were and what you wanted.

"I know what you want, got what you need," a man whispered to me.

"Ounce of blow, powder," I replied.

"Okay, I can get it for you in half an hour," he said. "You got the money?" I nodded.

"Okay, brother, meet me here in half an hour," he said.

"Nope. That's a no-go. You can meet me in my territory, a bar called Robert Emmett's on Eighth Avenue and Forty-fourth Street. You walk in, and I will follow you to the bar in the basement."

It was my way of insuring that the street hustlers were not police. Undercover police officers operate with intense surveillance and trap teams that I knew would not move three blocks away just to bust a small-time user. They were there for bigger hits or easier takedowns, and I was neither. The dealer in front me, Fernando, a Dominican who had moved to New York from the southwest in order to get back into the drug business, did not get high on his own supply, and turned out to be a profitable entrepreneur. Street prices with high-end quality were the theme for those of us who bought a significant amount.

I had paged Fernando earlier that day and gone up to the projects where we were able to do a quick deal. I bought $350 worth of cocaine that I thought could last me through much of the week. As soon as my colleague found out, she wanted to try some. We ended the night driving around erratically in a friend's car, all us doing cocaine as we swerved through traffic. She and I ended the night at her apartment, getting high out of our minds on the entire $350 worth of cocaine until it became early morning, which meant we both had to get back to work.

I ended up calling in sick, and she ended up making it into the office in time for one of those silly meetings that some bosses hold just to justify their existence. That weekend, I was back at it again, hanging out at Emmett's on one of my two days off, a Sunday, with a bartender. That night we were at his house in Sunnyside, Queens, snorting coke on his kitchen table as his girlfriend, who'd grown averse to drugs through her brother's heroin addiction, watched us all too unhappily. Instead of staying there that night, I took the company car that was parked outside and headed home to Brooklyn.

It was November 12, a month and a day after the anthrax scare that rattled everyone in *The Times* newsroom, and two months after the September 11 attacks. I was sleeping on the dirty white couch in my living room when my cell phone started ringing.

I ignored my cell phone.

It was my day off, and only *The Times* would be calling that early in the morning.

All of a sudden, my home phone was ringing.

Now, I knew it had to be *The Times* because all my friends *knew* that I never picked up my home telephone because of the bill collectors and because it did not have caller identification.

A second later, my doorbell was ringing.

The cell phone rang again. This time I picked it up.

"Hey, man," Daryl said, "Get down here. There was another crash."

"Not again," I said, as I hung up the phone.

I did not blink an eye. I jumped out of the couch that had become my bed in recent months. Daryl gave me the quick rundown of what he knew as he sped down Flatbush Avenue, navigating his way through the emergency vehicles headed in the same direction. An American Airlines 747 with more than 200 people had fallen out of the sky somewhere over the Rockaway Peninsula in Queens.

I knew that the Rockaway Peninsula was separated into several sections. There was the predominately black part of the peninsula, with low-income housing and more than its share of shootings and drug dealing. There was a middle-class part that was aptly located in the middle of the peninsula. Then, there was Fort Tilden, once the home to Nike Ajax conventional missiles and later underground bunkers for Hercules missiles meant for the defense of the East Coast, from Providence to Baltimore. I had learned of the strangest part of the Rockaways only that summer when a colleague, David Herzenhorn, got kicked out while reporting on Breezy Point, once known as the Irish Riviera, a gated community on the western tip of the peninsula. David was writing about how Breezy Point had remained ninety-eight percent white. A beach ran across most of the peninsula.

I had not been to the Rockaways since September 1999 when an assistant metro editor for weekends came by my desk late one Friday afternoon with an assignment. Weekend editors were always desperate to fill the Sunday and Monday sections of the newspaper, but the editors responsible for the rest of the days of the week would steal the stories they had planned before the weekend came. This Friday, the weekend editor asked me to drive out to a beach on the Rockaways at four on Saturday morning to report on 1,000 black descendants of slaves making a symbolic trip there, to where the Atlantic Ocean meets the city's streets, from St. Paul Community Baptist Church in East New York, a neighborhood that had become a euphemism for danger and segregation.

Standing on the beach that morning, I watched the Reverend Johnny Ray Youngblood lead members of his church in prayers in honor of slaves taken from Africa. A candle-lit ceremony followed, where those who had gathered, dressed in white robes, walked into the waves. Being a reporter meant access to beautiful, thoughtful moments like these, but always ensured you would on the outside, regardless of your feelings. I did not have much time for emotions, though. That would have gotten in the way of my deadline. I had to make the hour-and-a-half drive back to *Times* headquarters in Manhattan to write the story for the 11 a.m. early national edition deadline we faced on Saturdays.

In our car on the way, Daryl said that there was no clear call yet on terrorism, and that was what many were speculating about on the radio, as we zoomed past cars and even emergency vehicles. We came up to a roadblock on Flatbush Avenue that had clearly been established to prevent people from making it out to the Rockaways.

"What should we do?" Daryl said, staring at the police officers in front of us.

"Drive up slowly to him, with your ID against the window, and then once he has a second to glance, just keep on driving," I said.

It was the equivalent of the clipboard trick in the movie *The Paper* where Michael Keaton's editor character tells Randy Quaid's columnist character to get past the main desk in a precinct by clutching a clipboard and walking like he is in a hurry. That trick worked in Flatbush just like it did in the movie. Daryl and I did not have to explain who we were until we were deep into the sealed-off zone, at the entrance of Marine Parkway Bridge. The officer posted at the entrance of the faded steel-blue bridge assumed that if the others had let us pass, then it was all right for him to let us go by.

Daryl pulled into a parking lot at Jacob Riis Park, and then began walking east on Rockaway Beach Boulevard toward the site of the plane crash. It was a little after 10 in the morning, and we had picked up from the radio a few more facts and details that clarified the situation. The downed plane was American Airlines Flight 587, an Airbus A-300 carrying 260 passengers and crewmembers headed from John F. Kennedy Airport to the Dominican Republic.

The knowledge of the flight destination meant that, outside of a few vacationers, most of the victims were Dominican. There was no doubt that *The Times* had already begun dispatching reporters uptown to the Washington Heights section of Manhattan, the neighborhood with the densest concentration of Dominicans. *The Times* machine was in motion. Reporters in Washington were undoubtedly calling their sources and asking in news conferences about whether the government suspected terrorism, again. The airlines and the Federal Aviation Administration had admitted in recent weeks that they were having a hard time ensuring tight security in airports. Air travel had plummeted so precipitously, that the airlines were asking for federal bailouts and Delta Airlines was even offering 10,000 free tickets in an effort to get travelers back into the skies.

I separated from Daryl at the fenced-in lot of a church where the mayor's support team had set up a command center. I ran into two other

Times reporters, and we split up the duties. One was going to try to hit the crash scene. One was going to stay at the command center. I was going to talk to people. I hit the streets.

It quickly became clear to me that the people of the middle-class Rockaway neighborhood where the plane crashed were still recovering from the September 11 attacks. Belle Harbor was still collectively mourning the deaths of dozens of residents killed in the World Trade Center attack. Rumor had it that there was a memorial service for one of the September 11 victims occurring at a nearby church or synagogue.

On the street, I ran into Amie, who was no longer freelancing for *The Globe* after obtaining a job as a reporter at *The Philadelphia Inquirer.* We chatted for a while about the enormity of what was surrounding us, and horse-traded information. Amie told me that officials in Washington were unsure about terrorism, but that bridges and tunnels had been closed, and security was increased at nuclear plants and government offices throughout the region. She borrowed my phone to call Philadelphia. Mayor Giuliani, she said, had essentially sealed off New York City, making it impossible for her flat-footed colleagues to make it to Queens.

At *The Times,* the men who got all the credit often wrote from comfortable, air-conditioned offices on West Forty-third Street while we got to see the bodies. Some agitated to get to the scenes—even just for a few minutes. Others were more comfortable doing most of their reporting by simply taking feeds from people in the field. I often wondered what they talked about at dinner with their spouses after a big story, as those of us in the field were at the bar, trying to wash the images away with alcohol.

St. Francis de Sales Roman Catholic Church had held a dozen memorial services in honor of those killed in the September 11 attacks, and the monsignor was in the middle of his nine o'clock mass when a woman ran in to tell him that there had been an explosion several blocks away. The monsignor finished his prayer and then ran outside. Soon, the rectory and nearby lot were transformed into the city command center. Outside on Beach Channel, I spoke to the United States Representative and state assemblyman who had come to look at the scene. Senator Chuck Schumer eventually arrived in the afternoon, promising what politicians promise, a thorough and complete investigation.

By the evening, as the sun was coming down, Daryl had snuck his way into the crash scene. Another reporter had dressed up as a nurse and made it a few feet away from the bodies. The ever-present Charlie LeDuff, was all over the place, on top of everything. There were at least two reporters in Washington Heights. Others were at hospitals, the airport and near the scene. In the end, of the more than thirty reporters on the story, less than a dozen received bylines for their work. It was typical *Times,* not wanting the public to realize that their reporters were not gods, that it took so many people to do solid reporting. It was essentially a policy of lying for marketing. Their deception was a message not lost on me.

I was among those credited that day. In the darkness of a late evening, another reporter and I had gone to a yeshiva for Orthodox Jewish students to borrow the pay phone to call our notes into the desk. Our cell phones, it seemed, always died on big stories. Inside the yeshiva, I met Steve Feldheim, a member of Hatzoloh, a volunteer ambulance service, who helped with the rescue efforts in the aftermath of the crash. Feldheim told me of losing five friends in the World Trade Center, making comparisons unavoidable.

The carnage. The suitcases. The twisted metal. The broken-off plane fuselage in the street. It felt, he said, almost like the same scene.

"You look in the fireman's eyes and see déjà vu—it's happening all over again," he said, adding a line that shook me.

"One thing we have in this case that we did not have in the World Trade Center," he said, "is bodies."

After deadline, Daryl, Amie and I went to a pizza shop and had something to drink before we hit the road and headed back toward our homes. Daryl and I dropped Amie off at Ninth Street and Second Avenue, and then headed back to Brooklyn. It was all in a day of work, in a world that had changed and a job that had transformed entirely since the September 11 attacks.

Some time around this period, for the first time, someone stepped up to the plate and told me to my face that they thought I had a drug problem. Stephanie Flanders had seen me go to war with Jon Landman in what would later become Exhibit C in my case against him, my push to get off the metro desk. There was no doubt that at moments I could be sloppy, but it seemed that it was more than made up for by the fact that there were good editors on the copy desk and I was a speed demon.

Soon after the attacks, the newspaper began running a section with war and terrorism and aftermath news known as "A Nation Challenged." One of the regulars in the section was a collection of brief items called

"Notebooks," where reporters would usually tell one anecdote about something. With Jon, sometimes you had to wonder whether he realized that his reporting staff had just seen a lot of dead bodies.

A tourism official had mentioned at one of the numerous news conferences I had been attending in those days that museum attendance had dropped sharply since the attacks, and the non-profits that ran them were suffering. At the same time, a colleague told me they had someone close to them working at the American Craft Museum who told them that they were in so much financial trouble that they had decided to move out of their Midtown Manhattan galleries to a location downtown, where real estate was going for cheap prices. I called the friend of my colleague who informed me that the museum was in serious financial trouble before the September 11 attacks.

I wrote a line about them in a five-paragraph piece that ran on the third page of the "A Nation Challenged" section. I did not even mention the planned move. It did not take long for Holly Hotchner, the Manhattan socialite and director of the museum to call and complain to Jon, who told me "we are going to have to run a correction on this."

"Because the museum director said it's not true and she says you never called her for confirmation," he said.

"Well, I called someone else at the museum who has knowledge of the finances," I explained.

"We are still going to have to run a correction," he said. "You have put me in a difficult situation here."

Difficult situation, I thought to myself. *Putting someone in a difficult situation is having them run around plane crash sites as you play on your office computer and make fun of the writing of those sending in reports from the scene. That's a fucking difficult situation.*

"What do you mean, Jon?" I said putting emphasis on his name.

Jon tried to explain to me why we as a news organization had an obligation to contact the director of the museum even though I had talked to an employee who was aware of the books. Jon assured me that Holly had told him no one else, other than the chief financial officer of the organization, would be aware of the finances of the organization. I explained that the person I had spoken with was by the very nature of their job aware of the museum's finances. The staff was not that big, I told him. The museum was moving to resell their lease in midtown and purchase a new location in the now depressed real estate market.

"You are essentially printing a rumor," he said, demanding that I agree to a correction or name my sources so he could speak with them.

I decided, pissed off to the heavens, to walk to the museum and meet my source for this one line in the story. The woman confirmed the details of the financial situation of the organization and gave me the phone number of another person to call to find out even more details. I compiled it all and sent it in a memorandum to Jon. Still, he demanded to speak to the source. I arranged for the person to call Jon, and she did. Holly assured Jon that the museum did not intend to move and that its finances remained strong. Jon came back even more determined to run the correction.

The correction ran on a Tuesday.

A brief article on Oct. 20 about the effect of the decline in tourism on New York City cultural institutions referred incorrectly to the American Craft Museum. While lower-level staff members spoke of financial troubles that existed before Sept. 11, the director, Holly Hotchner, says the museum's finances are strong.

I would take unrestrained glee nine months later when the assistant metro editor in charge of corrections would e-mail me a link to an article about how the American Craft Museum was indeed moving. I would take even more glee almost exactly a year later when a reporter in the arts section wrote that for the fifth time since its founding, in 1956, the craft museum was attempting to reinvent itself. I wondered whether Jon ever noticed how wrong he was when he read them. But in the moment, in October 2001, I was livid. I had to write a memorandum to the editor who handled corrections explaining how the mistake was made.

The big problem was that I refused to concede a mistake had been made. Apologizing for things I was not responsible for has never been my cup of tea. I don't remember what I wrote in the memo, but I do remember firing off an angry e-mail to another editor, saying that I "held my nose" as I wrote the memo. That night, Stephanie could probably tell that my emotional reaction to the situation was as disproportionate as Jon's reaction to the call from Holly.

I ended up leaving and returning to my apartment. For the first time, I flushed cocaine down the toilet. It was a few grams. I did not tell myself I was going to quit. I just told myself that I was not going to do any that night. To me, that task seemed a gargantuan hurdle, a nearly impossible, Herculean task, just to make it through one night without it. In the weeks that followed, others would come forward to say something. I promised I had stopped.

The days of my wistful Week In Review pieces were over. No more writing about a book deconstructing *The Simpsons* and making my own conclusions that Lisa represented American intellectualism; Homer came out of the depressing side of Aristotle's brain; Marge followed the Aristotelian recipe of a happy and moral life; Maggie is a philosophical and psychological mess, and Bart is the Nietzchean superman.

Instead, I was writing Review pieces on topics like measuring the September 11 attacks with every statistic I could find, including the cost of rebuilding Lower Manhattan, the meals dispensed on the United States Navy medical ship that docked on the Hudson River, and the rising consumption of comfort food. One particularly telling example came near the end of the story, where I noted that the federal government had given $28 million to the affected states for counseling and other mental health services and that prescriptions of Prozac, Zoloft and other anti-depressants, as well as visits to mental health clinics, were rising sharply.

One Review piece, published a few days after the anthrax scare in *The Times* newsroom and a little more than a month after the terrorist attacks, examined how American marketing, legal and illegal, had already begun to see "opportunity" in the dreadful events of September 11, with sales of everything from a $14.99 Osama "Rub It In his Face" mousepad, to a $99 Waterford Crystal flag for $99 on sale at Tiffany, and thieves selling ashes supposedly from ground zero to tourists and relatives of victims. It was ghoulish and obnoxious, as was the note that was in my chair when I came to work the next Tuesday.

"WHAT'S THIS?!" read the note, taped to a copy of my October 14 Review piece on the sales of tacky items.

It was a note from my editor who had said she wanted to be able to control what stories we wrote for other sections. I had explained to the editor, who was on the metro desk, that Review pieces were done on our own time and we were paid like freelancers. She really should not be involved in the decision-making, but she was a control freak and wanted to have the power to decide. It was a month after September 11, and the editor was already back to her control games, trying to use us to help revive her career. To do that and to be comfortable, I could tell she needed control.

"This is a story," I wrote on another Post-it note, placing it all back on the editor's desk.

My relationship with my editor was making my life miserable, and I began agitating with Nancy Sharkey, the staff development editor, to get away from her and be reassigned to someone with a little more confidence, someone who could help nurture a young reporter like myself. After receiving the note, my editor came to my desk and started in on me with her typical diatribe about writing for other sections—even if it was on my own time.

At first, she always tried the "it would be good for you" method. But that could always be deflected with, "No, let's be honest. That's not logical. It would be good for you—bad for me, because you would tell me for no reason not to write them." Then, she tried the "it is important for us to communicate and be open" tact, and my reply was standard, "Yes, but you just want to have control, to be able to say no just to exert your authority." I admit, as an employee, I was transforming from eager-to-please to a Grade A nightmare.

I took off again in October, which was coincidentally as my cocaine use and drinking were rising, but I shot myself in the foot with a colossal blunder that marked the first time that alcohol and drugs really got in the way of my writing. I wrote seventeen stories in October, including one where I made a visit to a fire chief I knew who had lost his brother in the World Trade Center attacks to write about the GPS technology that was being used to map the scattered remains found at the site.

Unfortunately, the one that got the most attention was a story I wrote drunk and high. I was supposed to attend a concert benefit at Madison Square Garden late one Saturday night. I had every intention of going, but somehow found myself at a party at an assistant foreign editor's house on the Upper West Side. After a couple of drinks, I headed downtown to go to the Garden, but realized I did not have the proper credentials to get in. So, instead, I headed to West Forty-third Street, where I watched the event on television, taking occasional breaks to go into the stairwell near the Continuous News Desk to snort a little cocaine off of a cigarette box I would place on the railings.

Writing off of television was not that odd an occurrence at *The Times*. Mayoral news events and other stories were often handled that way by editors and reporters who would tune into New York 1 or C-SPAN coverage. It was just strange to do it when you were less than ten blocks from an event and had the time to go report and then return and file.

Coke had served me well in reporting, so far, I thought. It gave me the energy and focus that Ritalin, which I took as a child, could not. I had spent many late nights in the newsroom, until five, six and seven in the morning reporting stories and writing with the assistance of a drug that had certainly become my best friend before September 11. She was turning into a jealous lover now, one that apparently did not get the fact that I could not afford her tastes without a job. Still, she wanted to be with me all the time. She made my editor go away though. She made September 11 all right.

"Was Jayson drunk when he wrote that?" Gerry Mullany, the deputy metro editor overseeing the paper that night, would later ask Lynette about the story.

In fact, I was drunk and high. Gerry's question was motivated by the 123-word correction we had to run on the story.

The correction mentioned how I had misstated the price of the most expensive tickets, writing that they were only $1000 when they were, in fact, $10,000. I misquoted former President Bill Clinton as having said that he was given the hat of Raymond Downey, a deputy fire chief who died in the September 11 attacks, when he had been given his bracelet. And I quoted Clinton wrongly again, saying that he had said in reference to terrorists, "I hope they saw this tonight, because they thought America was about money and power. They thought that if they took down the World Trade Center, we would collapse. But we're not about mountains of money or towers of steel. You're about mountains of courage and hearts of steel, and I hope they saw you here tonight." He actually said "hearts of gold."

It was the story I could not get out of the back of my mind when I decided I needed to slow down, and try to use cocaine less frequently. I had also had a run-in recently where I bought $500 of what I thought was cocaine, but turned out to be Alka-Seltzer, in a street buy. I ended up snorting most of the Alka-Seltzer anyway for the tear-flowing, eye burning high it provided.

I decided to try to spend the days before Christmas, when I was returning to Virginia to visit my parents, without picking up a drink or snorting a line. And, surprisingly, though I do not remember much of the week other than lying uncomfortably on the couch as I watched television, I made it through. I took the train from Union Station in Washington back to New York on Christmas Day, arriving a little after eight in the morning. I took a cab straight from Penn Station to *The Times*, where I was scheduled to work that day.

When I got into the office, I was assigned, as I had been for each of the past three Christmas Days, to follow Mayor Giuliani around town for his annual gift giving. It was "Christmas with Sunny," as I began to call what seemed to be becoming my annual routine of hanging out with Mayor Giuliani and Sunny Mindel, his communications director. Sunny was a born comedian and this day I decided I was going to badger her with questions about the media.

"Sunny, is it true," I asked, pausing for effect like television reporters did in City Hall news conferences, "that a City Hall bureau chief for *The New York Times* recently called your office and asked what 'FY' meant on the city budget documents?"

"I am sorry Jayson, I just can't comment on that," she said.

"Sunny, is it true that reporter thought FY, or fiscal year, was some kind of trick that the mayor's office was using to pull a fast one on reporters?" I asked, continuing the charade.

"I am sorry, Jayson, I just can't answer that," she said.

"Well, my sources say it's true," I said.

"You've got to decide whether you want to go with that," she continued, laughing at our little game.

It was our third Christmas together, and this was the first one where there would be news. Mayor Giuliani, who was leaving office in a matter of days, was trying to push through deals for a football and baseball stadium before his successor, Mike Bloomberg, took office.

That night, I went home happy. I wrote a good, solid story, and had made it more than a week without cocaine. I cannot remember what happened next, but sometime around one in the morning, I awoke in a panic. Within minutes I was on Fulton Street in Brooklyn, standing on a corner where I knew drug dealers came by. A young, beat-up looking man approached me; he could tell I was standing there for no particular reason.

"Whatchu looking for?" he asked.

"Blow," I said quietly.

"I thought you wanted a blow job," he said, running his tongue through his cheeks. "Rock or powder?" he asked.

"Powder," I replied.

That night, he and I were up in my apartment, sniffing and snorting, snorting and sniffing. I was getting high again.

After our short break-up, cocaine and I were back together again. She had me, and I was doing more than ever, an eight-ball a night. I had also pulled the unlucky straw again, assigned to work the late shift on New

Year's Eve. We were on full-blown terrorism watch. Since September 12, everyone had been waiting for the next attack. That said, bomb threats called into the Empire State Building cleared much of the southern part of Midtown Manhattan, and I found myself scratching my head as I ran toward the scene as everyone else was running in the opposite direction. On New Year's, here we were doing it again, waiting for the bomb to go off in Times Square. The lovely part is that if it ever happened, we would be dead, and dead reporters are not good reporters, and the newspaper's offices on West Forty-third Street would probably be knocked out.

If *The Times* had known about September 11 an hour before the first plane struck the north tower, I have no doubt that they would have sent twenty of us to the foot of the towers and then complained as we suffered from third-degree burns that we were not filing on time. Each of us was going to be dispatched to different locations in Times Square, to provide feeds for the overall coverage and angles on any other attacks.

Coming to the office on New Year's Day involved the normal security precautions, plus some. At Forty-third Street and Eighth Avenue, we were stopped at the corner and asked to show our *Times* ID cards. Inside the building we were given assignments. Mine was to report from the office until a few hours before being dispatched to the field. At some point, I went outside and called my dealer, meeting him on Tenth Avenue as he walked by with his girlfriend and her younger siblings. We did a quick deal for an eight-ball and I was back in the office in time to run into a colleague with whom I had done coke with before.

I went with her up to the fifth floor, back to a kitchenette in a cavernous area with no windows where the obituary reporters and regional weekly editors worked. We did coke for about an hour before it was time to head outside for our assignments. Eventually, several of us hooked up via cell phone, and decided that if we were going to die on New Year's it made much more sense to do it drunk at Emmett's than it did getting incinerated in the cold and frigid air among the crowds of Times Square. Several reporters stopped by Emmett's that night before the ball dropped and joined in our revelry.

The owners gave us a table at the top of the stairs at a window that overlooked the crowds on Forty-fourth Street. We ordered rounds of steamed dumplings and other appetizers as the countdown for the New Year began. Lorraine, the beautiful waitress with the obsidian hair, was off-duty but still in her blue buttoned-down shirt and black pants that made up her uniform, and by my side when we watched the ball drop in Times Square. Before the clock struck midnight, several of us at our table ran into a stall in the women's bathroom and did lines off of the top of the commode.

Back outside, Lorraine's boyfriend was at the bar. When the countdown hit zero, she was behind me. She turned to me, pursed her big lips, and I felt their softness against mine. She pulled back, and came down again, my lips tingling as hers touched mine again, with the slight heightened sensitiveness that comes with touch on a mild cocaine high.

"Nice, Jayson," she said. "I have never kissed a black guy. Happy New Year's."

For a long time, I had associated drugs with women, or, well, at least sexual experiences. There were plenty of times when I had enhanced my chances, loosened myself enough to make advances on women, and there were other less memorable moments where I performed, or received, a sexual favor for drugs. When I was on the performing end, it was usually implicit that it was for drugs. When I was on the receiving end, the reasons were under the surface, even if the surface was transparent and obvious.

There are women whose names I don't remember. There are apartments in the East Village, Williamsburg, TriBeCa, Woodside, Sunnyside and other parts of New York that I barely recall. It was easy to tell a woman who would get hooked by her reaction to the drug, the smile, the burning if not passionate desire, to come back at it again and again. Inevitably, though, casual coke users had no interest in being with cokeheads. And even cokeheads aren't really interested in being with cokeheads.

There was the woman I met on a cold Friday night around this time in an East Village bar with her roommate. We warmed ourselves up with a ton of coke in the bar's bathroom, made our way back to her place in Williamsburg, Brooklyn with her roommate and some guy I met that night. The guy and her roommate went to bed, while she and I did coke in her bathroom, sharing our hopes, dreams and how we should not be doing coke until there was no more left, which precipitated a livery cab ride to my place in Clinton Hill, where I had a brick stored in my cabinet. We did coke all morning until I snuck out, telling her, as I was sliding through the doorway, to let herself out as she was admiring my Georgia O'Keeffe reprints. It was Saturday morning. I had to get to work early.

There were too many moments during this time period that I woke up next to a stranger, wondering whether it was me that she enjoyed so much or whether it was the drugs. There were too many dry, bloody noses and headaches only rivaled by the headaches caused by the hangers-on who were big into sharing.

Coke is no way to make lasting friends. All roads led back to her being your only true friend. Each time I tried to get away, it was almost like she would promise that everything would be okay, and succeed at sucking me back in. To a person who is not an addict, it may sound odd to hear a drug being described as a person, but, for me, she was a very real one.

I tried to convince Lorraine and her boyfriend to come to an after-party in the SoHo apartment of the girlfriend of a young colleague from *The Times*. I was betting on the *exotic black man with the bag of cocaine* over the boring Irish guy. For whatever reason, though, I got caught up in something, and found myself with a female colleague and her boyfriend, in a car parked off of West Forty-fourth Street, doing cocaine off the dashboard.

The night ended at a party being held in the large loft apartment of the colleague's girlfriend, who had just come into a serious amount of money by selling the rights to a magazine article she wrote to Hollywood. It was mostly drinking and socializing, and the drug addicts did not take over the living room until the early morning hours. Some smoked weed, some pounded pills, while the rest of us did coke on the table until eight in the morning.

My reservations notwithstanding, I was a ringleader in this drug party. I spotted my victim. It was a young woman who said she wanted to do a line.

I said, "Sure," pouring out a gram onto a mirror that had been taken off a wall for the night's business.

Cocaine commonality. Cocaine camaraderie. I fit in.

"The MetroCard is the best thing that ever happened to casual cocaine use," I said as I pulled out one of the thin, flexible cards that the New York City subway system began issuing in 1999.

A perfect tool for cutting lines. Flexible, thin. And coke did not stick to it.

I cut a deliberately long line. It was thick too.

"Now do the whole thing," I said, laughing.

"I can't do that," she replied.

"Oh, yes, you can," I shot back, my audience looking on.

She did less than half and then stopped, and looked back up at me and smiled. My face was unwavering.

She finished the line in two more bursts, and soon was the life of my own personal party.

I had tried to break up. It didn't work.

Coke was back in again.

CHAPTER TWENTY-ONE
PRETTY LITTLE BOY

I was fantasizing about killing her.

I was sitting on my ratty white couch, soiled by cigarette burns and spilled Scotch. I had two grams of cocaine in front of me on the coffee table. I just spent the last few hours searching on my hands and knees, on the kitchen floor, on the hardwood in the living room and underneath the couch cushions. I was trying to find the third baggie of cocaine that I thought had fallen out my jacket pocket.

Crawling on the floor to find little specks of cocaine that had fallen between the cracks in the kitchen linoleum was a common occurrence, but losing an entire gram was never any fun when it was before midnight, and I knew that what I had left was supposed to take me through the night.

Howell had taken over the newsroom six months earlier and with that Gerald had risen to become managing editor of the newspaper. The move only intensified the personal battles between Gerald and Jon, and I felt increasingly in the middle. My editor and Jon had slammed me in my evaluation for the high number of corrections I clocked in 2001. I was frustrated. They would not hear my pleas that while the numbers were high, the percentage of stories were within a reasonable standard. This period was the first time I had seen Jon show what I considered genuine concern. He started using the word "self-destruction" to describe my behavior in face-to-face conversations. He wanted me to slow down. He was right. I just didn't know how.

It was a Wednesday and I was still recovering from five days earlier. I did not get home until one o'clock in the afternoon on January 1. I felt cornered. I had a choice of fight or flight, and I chose flight, to withdraw further into my own world. Howell, who came in with such promise, saw everything he planned get hijacked by September 11, and he was making a mess of the newsroom with plans to reassign the bulk of the national correspondents. There had already been defections, an unusual thing in a workplace where people generally stayed for many years. I could tell that a battle was raging in the background about me in newsroom management. A survivor can smell hostility or difficulties a mile away, and I was not even worried about pulling up to defend my rear flank. My heart was racing this night. I could not get to bed, my head and heart pounding.

I had a breakfast appointment the next morning so I decided to only do a line or two of cocaine that night on my glass coffee table. I had made the appointment a few weeks before with Susan Edgerley, the senior deputy metro editor. It was for early in the morning, at Teresa's, a restaurant a short train ride away in Brooklyn Heights. Two lines turned into five lines, five into seven and soon I was onto the third gram of cocaine, fantasizing about killing the drug that had begun to own me, doing another line to make the thoughts go away, a couple more lines and maybe it would all go away, forever. My heart was pounding by five in the morning, and now needed coke to keep me up so I would not miss the appointment.

I was tired of the five in the morning visits from the young man trying to sell himself for drugs, the endless doorbell ringing. I was tired of having to buy bottles of nose spray before heading into the office in the morning. I was tired of the office. I was not ready to give up on cocaine though. I needed it in moderation, I thought to myself. After all, some of my best stories were inspired by drug-fueled writing. It did not help my rationalizations that I got compliments on the lead of the story from across the metro desk, including an e-mail from Jon. The story began:

Along Central Park South around the winter holidays there is an economic indicator found not in tourism data but on the streets: full buckets of oats. The fuller the buckets of oats, the more the horses are eating, and the horses eat the most when business is booming for Central Park carriage drivers.

At a time when business is bad for almost everyone in New York, particularly in the tourist industry, the full buckets have been arriving along this avenue each morning by the dozens.

That is good news for Ian McGreever, 33, and his brother, Colm, 32, who have been taking New Yorkers and tourists alike on horse-drawn carriage rides through Central Park for more than a decade.

"The oats are high energy," said Colm McGreever, explaining why full buckets mean good news. "You don't want to give a horse too much if you are not doing too much business, cause then all you have is a hyped-up horse on a tightrope."

My face felt numb. My eyes were watering. Another sniff. My heart started racing again. Another sniff. It was pounding, this time ferociously. My watering eyes moved from a trickle to an outpouring. My legs started getting numb, cold. They were gently shaking. I could feel my heart muscle pounding against the wall of my chest. I went to the bathroom. As I walked in the door to the bathroom, I caught a glimpse of myself in the mirror. The black skin around my eyes had turned purple. The whites of my eyes were red, covered with a coat of liquid. I could tell how in recent months I had lost weight. My skin had grown brittle, and closer to my bones.

I had spent hours hunched over the glass coffee table doing coke, which I had hustled on the West Side of Manhattan and then in my neighborhood when I needed more. Now, I found myself staring in the mirror, wondering about something I could not put my finger on. I looked at myself as if I were perplexed, and then all of a sudden found myself wondering what ever happened to the "pretty little boy" I was once was. My heart was still pounding, but the water in my eyes was no longer simply a physical reaction to cocaine. I was softly crying.

I again flushed what was left of the coke in the toilet. I stayed up until thirty minutes before my meeting with Susan and made my way to the subway, still aching. I stopped in the corner deli and picked up a copy of *The Times* and a cup of hot tea with lemon. The warmth cleared my sinuses, and even though I was a coffee addict, the dehydrating effect was too much after a coke binge. Susan greeted me warmly at Teresa's. Whatever negative things might have been said about her around the newsroom, Susan's motherly warmth could be exceedingly powerful.

Somehow, I just blurted it out.

"I have got some problems that I need to take care of, some personal problems," I said.

Susan expressed what I believed was genuine support and asked me about the nature of them.

"Drugs and alcohol mainly," I said. "Drugs and alcohol, and emotionally I am a mess."

It was the first time I admitted needing help. It was the first time I admitted that drugs and alcohol were a problem. Even though in recent months it had become ever more clear to me that I was struggling to stay above water, my mind fought to stay on the destructive course. I had never been one to ask for help with my emotions. I always wanted to be able to rise above them on my own.

"Jayson, no matter what happens I want you to do me a favor and go up and visit Pat Drew," Susan said, mentioning the name of the woman who ran the employee assistance program at *The Times*.

Somehow, Susan made an appointment for me before I got to the building. I took the N train into Manhattan by myself. It was the longest ride of my life, at least emotionally if not literally. When I came out of the subway, I ran into Gerald in front of the building. He asked me to make an appointment with his secretary, Christine Moore, because he wanted to talk to me about something. I knew there was no way he could have known about the conversation I just had with Susan.

I went upstairs to my desk on the third floor and dropped my bags off. I cannot remember whether I called Pat or she called me, but within minutes I was in her comfortable eleventh-floor office, its windows overlooking West Forty-fourth Street. I did not speak with complete openness and honesty, to Pat about my problems with my emotions, alcohol, and drugs. She listened, her eyes focused intently on me, gently responding to questions I had, but for the most part letting me talk.

"It sounds like you need to go into rehab," Pat said softly.

I had never thought my name would be said in the same sentence with that word. The prospect scared me for a variety of reasons, but Pat said that everything would remain confidential and that we could work out a medical leave if necessary. The first and most important thing, she said, was for me to get in to see someone. She assured me that many people at *The Times* had fought their way back from emotional and substance abuse problems. She asked me if I had heard of the Twelve Steps, and I said, "Yes." I did not know them by heart, but she talked to me a little bit about them.

While I was still in her office, Pat made an appointment for me to go downtown to the Union Square East offices of the Realization Center, a drug and alcohol treatment program that offered some of the best outpatient services in Manhattan. Pat spoke with the director of the center, Marilyn White, a woman who herself had years before had her own substance abuse problems. There had to be something to what she had to offer.

At the Realization Center's seventh-floor office overlooking Union Square, the kind woman behind the desk handed me a stack of papers to fill out. They included questions about everything from substance abuse and medical conditions to family history and prior experiences in treatment. I met with a counselor named Stacey, who conducted an intake, which included a list of other questions.

Stacey and Marilyn decided that it was best that I begin outpatient treatment immediately, the following Friday.

"First day of the beginning of the rest of your life," Stacey said. "Go home, get some rest, eat some meals—meals are important to staying sober—and we will see you tomorrow."

Pat called me that night on my cell phone.

"How was it?" she asked, in a calm voice that I was beginning to already find reassuring.

"It was wonderful," I said. "I am really going to try this."

CHAPTER TWENTY-TWO
BIRDS CHIRPING?

One morning as I walked down my block of Brooklyn brownstones, I heard birds chirping and marveled at how much I enjoyed a sound that had always jangled me when I was an addict.

Most, including the bartenders at the Irish bar where I used to hang out, were strong supporters of my new habits: shots of espresso and glasses of cranberry and seltzer. But for all the small, daily improvements sobriety brought to my personal life, it seemed to take a toll on my job. My error rate declined drastically, but my section editor, to my annoyance, still kept me on a short leash.

A close friend in the newsroom had told me confidentially that being a recovering addict at *The Times* was bad enough, but that being a recovering black addict was something that many would not forgive me for any time soon. I would have to do my "time in purgatory."

I instead focused on a budding relationship with Marion Kohler, a twenty-nine-year-old assistant to a literary agent who worked for my landlord. Together, we combined my reporting assignments with our own explorations—-visiting black churches, Harlem, a Jewish Museum on the Upper East Side, Central Park, and anywhere else we could enjoy and I could write something. This lasted for months until Marion, to my great sadness, had to return to Germany.

I was looking forward to a long-awaited vacation scheduled around the September 11 anniversary in order to make sure I did not get drawn into the coverage. The anxiety in the newsroom seemed to take on palpable form in the weeks before the anniversary. Each day that went by without a terrorist attack was received with only measured relief and concern about when the next one was coming.

I had come in early one morning to work on a story that was due before I went on vacation and passed by the desks of two business editors. In less than an hour, one of them was dead, having leapt over the parapet on the fifteenth floor of the building. The editor's suicide—which seemed connected to psychiatric and family problems as well as his stagnating career— sent shockwaves through the newsroom. Five months earlier a black female colleague who had struggled with what we assumed was schizophrenia had died under mysterious circumstances.

A friend pulled me aside after the suicide to say I seemed deeply affected by the two latest deaths—as well as the newsroom reaction—and to suggest that I see a counselor from the employee assistance program. I told her I would be fine and that I was headed on vacation. When I returned after the anniversary of the attacks, I began a warm and supportive friendship with a news assistant I had met months earlier at a party. Over dinner, at an Asian restaurant not far from the World Trade Center site, we talked for hours about the similarities between the African-American and immigrant experience. My life was beginning to feel beautiful again.

Morale at the paper was dismal because of troubling actions by the executive editor—the man I had seen as my potential savior—including the purging of more than a half-dozen veteran national correspondents supported by the rank-and-file. Others who were not aligned with him saw the handwriting on the wall and quit. Most would not be replaced because of a hiring freeze, which put a tremendous strain on the rest of the newsroom employees. More and more I tried to disengage from problems at work and concentrate on my new relationship and my sobriety.

I walked to a Lower East Side club to watch several friends perform their monthly act. The trip marked the first time I was out of the house for anything other than visits to the Realization Center. My parents already knew that I drank heavily, but now I had to break it to my mother that I had also been using a lot of cocaine. The talk was a bit like telling someone that their loved one was alive after a horrible accident. I could break the news and then assure her that I was going to be okay. Still, telling your highly emotive mother that you are a drug addict is no way to end a day.

After talking to my mother, who seemed to take it surprisingly well, I received a phone call from my younger brother Todd. He had graduated from the University of Virginia, and was now working as a computer engineer for a large company. I envied Todd's calmness in the face of whatever storm he encountered, which stood in strong contrast to my emotive nature. I had envied his intelligence, which I considered more practical and useful than my brand of dreaming. Todd offered his support and confided in me that our mom was reduced to tears upon hearing the news, but was doing her best to hide that from me and trying to muster the strength to put up a wall of support.

The night ended in a bar a few blocks off of Houston Street, in a room full of friends, three of whom were cocaine addicts and two of whom seemed to be occasional users. I did not pick up. I knew that I was changing.

My relationship with *The New York Times* had dissolved to the point of becoming irreparable by the summer of 2002. They just did not know it. That's because they weren't listening, and Lord knows they were not paying attention.

There are those who have looked back and said that this was a time period when I proved that I could perform without committing a high number of errors. They have said that this was the moment when I shined once again, so brightly that I was given another chance to perform at the highest levels once more. This notion was clearly based on an evaluation of me that focused almost entirely on the decrease in the number of corrections I was accumulating, and nothing else that was happening. Journalism was just a job for me by the summer, no longer a mission.

Gerald Boyd would later tell a committee that examined my career at *The Times* that he had instructed my managers to focus on job performance and not be psychologists. Though I did not know it was coming from Gerald, it was a line I often heard my editor repeating in our long, almost daily meetings where I was asked to account for my work and explain what I was doing. If I had been paying one ounce of attention to my mental health, perhaps, I would have seen what was unfolding.

The handful who were paying attention to more than just my job performance and cared about my overall well-being, friends like Lynette Holloway and Jerry Gray, were baffled by both my appearance and demeanor. They tried in their own ways to intervene, to help ascertain what was unfolding. But in reality, I struggle even now to comprehend it entirely. At that point, I knew nothing more than that I felt disengaged from work, engaged in my life outside work, and tired of *The New York Times*. Perhaps if they had looked more carefully, people would have seen the storm raging inside me.

Soon after returning to the newsroom from two weeks of full-time outpatient treatment at the Realization Center, Gerald called me to his office. He had seen my poor evaluation for 2001 and offered me a warning.

"You know I have been a big advocate of yours," Gerald started in. "You have enormous promise and potential, but your career is in your hands."

"Gerald, as you may or may not know," I replied, adopting the flat affect I had picked up while detoxing, "I have been struggling with some personal issues and am taking the steps to better myself. It has been a long, hard road, and I think I am getting the help I need for these problems."

"What kind of problems are you dealing with?" he asked.

I froze, not knowing how to answer the question. I was less concerned about my drug problem becoming more public than I was about the background of the man who was sitting across from me. Gerald grew up in St. Louis, raised by his grandmother after his mother died following a long struggle with drugs. It had shaped much of who he was, and I was well aware from my interactions with him and research I had conducted for a profile of him for *TimesTalks,* the in-house magazine, of his emotional detachment.

"Cocaine," I said.

He nodded.

"I wish you luck," he said, presumably relying more on personal experience than he was willing to give up. "It is not going to be easy."

Easy it was not. The physical withdrawal from cocaine was tortuous, but luckily the Realization Center provided a wealth of information and ideas on how to lessen the difficulties of that process. The psychological withdrawal was equally scary, and lingered much longer than I could have imagined at the time. I came to understand what was meant by the phrase a "monkey on your back" when I would feel a bolt of recall, a simulated cocaine high in my head, and my shoulders would tighten up like I was carrying something heavy on my back.

I am glad I listened to their early tips to stay away from bars, to not walk around with $40 or more in my pocket, to stay out of the neighborhoods where I used to score drugs, to throw away all the beeper numbers, to jettison all the friends that I had made with drugging, to find fellowship with other recovering addicts, to remind myself I could write well without cocaine, to eliminate unstructured time, and to balance work and life to prevent stress or anything else that could be a trigger for drug use.

Balancing work and life was perhaps the hardest for me.

Pat Drew was working hard to ensure that some sort of balance was found, receiving permission to release certain details of my treatment to Nancy Sharkey, the staff development editor, who was then also bound by state and federal rules regarding confidentiality.

What I did not realize, and I presume to this day Pat did not know, was that Nancy, my editor and Jon had developed a plan to keep tight reins on me. The plan was presented to Gerald, who approved it. If I had known that Nancy was a part of this troika I would never have signed the release to allow her to receive information about my medical care, nor would I have gone to her in confidence if I had known that she was holding back on the details of this structure for managing me.

The one element of the plan that Jon discussed with me was to focus on quality instead of quantity. It dovetailed with what I had told Pat and Nancy about my desire to focus primarily on my drug and alcohol treatment, and that work was going to have to, like it or not, take a backseat. This meant thirty-five-hour weeks instead of the normal sixty- to seventy-hour weeks that I'd been clocking over the past few years. In the month of February 2002, for example, I only wrote seven stories and often would leave work after seven hours—a rare thing at *The Times,* even though that is what the union contract said a workday was—to go to Union Square for treatment or to attend Alcoholics Anonymous meetings.

In this time period, I also met a veteran reporter who had struggled through a cocaine addiction in his earlier years, and listened as he regaled me with stories of life on the run. I took advice from him on ways to cope with the stressors, and we provided support for each other in life, work, and in recovery. One thing that now sticks out to me is what he said about how difficult my recovery would be.

"I can't imagine trying to recover while still working at the same place you worked when you were using," he said. "Then, on top of that, the place is *The New York Times,* which is particularly unforgiving, and you are black. A black recovering drug addict at *The New York Times.* Not a position I envy."

On February 22, the news came that Monte Williams, a forty-year-old reporter who had been on a medical leave because of her struggles with mental illness, died in her apartment in Forest Hills, Queens. I had watched Monte deteriorate over the years as her condition became worse, and I saw Joe Lelyveld and Joyce Purnick, with great kindness, try to find a spot for her on the metro desk where she could write occasionally. It essentially became a way for Monte to keep her job and health care, without demanding much more than an occasional story from her. When Monte wrote, she would often write well—it would just take a lot longer than it did in her heyday.

That all changed, though, when Jon took over the metro desk. Soon after arriving, Jon provided Jennifer Preston, the editor in charge of special personnel matters inside the News Administration office, with a list of reporters that he would like to reassign to lesser jobs within his section or send out of the department. Monte was one of the names on that list. What followed could only be described as harassment. It is hard to imagine what compels someone to exert such pressure and utter such cruel comments as the ones we overheard one assistant metro editor making to Monte. Sometime in 2001 she disappeared from the office, though we all knew she was still on the payroll and on leave from the daily lists prepared by the metro administrator.

We all thought suicide immediately when Monte died, but the truth proved to be more elusive. The New York City Office of the Chief Medical Examiner opened an investigation into her death, though to this day I have been unable to bring myself to find the answer. What I knew was that Monte had died, and her life spoke of many of the horrors of *The Times* newsroom, of how if you had weaknesses, the place would bring them out in all of their grand glory.

Exhibit A in that case was Monte's funeral. The assistant metro editor who had driven her to stare at the bathroom mirror in tears for several hours stood up and gave a eulogy. Charlie LeDuff read a poem that said something about chicken wings. Lynette Holloway was the master of ceremonies between tears. And I got up and shared a story about Monte berating me while we worked together for not knowing the number of steps a man walked right before he died and the color of the walls inside an apartment building. It was a cast of insanity.

The ugliest moment came between Jon and Gerald. In his brief remarks, Jon admitted that he "had not known Monte well," and when Gerald got up to speak, it seemed that all of his rage toward Jon's callous style of management—at least that's the way my mind chose to interpret it—came pouring out.

"*Well*," he said, pausing for emphasis. "*I did know* Monte."

I hunkered down with Lynette in the smoking room and we reviewed the bizarre proceedings. "They killed her," I said at some point, overreacting, in an obvious reference to *The Times*. Lynette swung back and forth about the *Times*'s culpability in the death of Monte, but would provide the first serious suggestion that I struggled with similar issues.

At the Realization Center, Marilyn all but told me she thought I had a twisted relationship with my job. "It is a high-pressure field, and a tough place to work," she said. "Trust me, you are not the first person to succumb to the pressures of *The New York Times*. It's the same thing with our clients on Wall Street. At some point, you really have to ask yourself whether you want to stay in the profession."

Inside work, life was mundane. I had only obtained two corrections on stories since returning to work, both written on deadline. One was a geographic mistake where I had used "across the Hudson River" to describe a site that was, in fact, on the same side of the river as the place I had mentioned. In the other, I misstated a detail about a woman who was a part of a local neighborhood board. So I was a little floored one Tuesday morning when I pulled an envelope out of my mailbox that included a harsh two-page letter of reprimand.

The crime?

I had obtained the two corrections and not shown up for work one day. I had not called in. My supervisor was out of the office taking care of her two daughters, so I did not bother calling to mention that I was working from home. The letter chided me most profoundly for not meeting Daryl Alexander, the assistant metro editor for administration, for a personal lunch I had scheduled with her that day. It was obvious that Daryl told Jon that I had missed the lunch, and that it was being used as simply another excuse to pull the reins tighter on me, even though my job performance had remained steady.

The letter was written by Nancy, presumably in some misguided belief that I would respond with less force to a letter that was signed by her, as opposed to anyone I had a more contentious relationship with. They might as well have signed the names of the lawyers who wrote the letter, because there was no doubt in my mind that the fingerprints of Jon and the legal staff were all over it. I confronted Nancy, and she admitted that she had not written the letter. She would only say that lawyers wrote it. Nancy talked about others she had known in the past who had struggled with substance problems and their work, and she came off sounding like she did not believe I was clean.

To me, it was the last straw. I was out there, exposed, and they were being much less than transparent. I took a few personal days off, and over the course of that time decided that even if they were not going to be honest, I was going to be.

Soon, in what were turning into daily jousting matches with my editor, I was increasingly expressing my unwillingness to work more than the thirty-five-hour union schedule. I told her that if she wanted to make changes to stories that were going to keep me there late, she was just going to have to wait another day. No more extra days on my weekends, and I fired off a note to the deputy editor who handled schedules asking why I was still working weekends, while so many people who had come after me were not, when it was supposed to be about seniority.

I also took most of my belongings home, including the trinkets on my desk. It was enough that it led Erika Sommer, the supervisor of the clerical staff who sat next to me during my first few years, to ask, "What's going on, Jayson? Your desk is not a pigpen anymore. Are you leaving the paper?"

The same week I was cleaning up my desk, *The Times* was celebrating being awarded a record seven Pulitzer Prizes for work in 2001, five for its coverage of the September 11 attacks and two in other categories. Bill Schmidt sent a note out to the newsroom staff inviting them all to a giant party that was being held in the banquet hall at Laura Belle, a fancy Manhattan restaurant. I was pissed, so I would not have gone anyway, but something about "celebrating" our coverage of "the September 11 attacks" did not sit well with me. Obviously, it was just fine for the hundreds of my colleagues who did show up. I wondered whether they ignored the blood on those Pulitzers as they danced the night way.

I will admit that I did not walk back into work after rehab with high hopes. After all, the fact that I woke up at six on the morning of my return and watched the movie *Seven,* a film about a serial killer who uses the seven deadly sins as thematic inspiration, to prep myself was not a good indication that I expected things to go smoothly.

As I was disengaging, Howell was dismantling the newsroom in the unceremoniously cruel fashion of a man who knew he had just won seven Pulitzers. The first indication to the public that something was going wrong inside the hallowed walls of West Forty-third Street came in a late April article by Paul Colford in the *Daily News* where he wrote that Sam Howe Verhovek, a well-known national correspondent, would be leaving the paper to be a writer for the *Los Angeles Times* in Asia. The backstory, though Colford did not report it, was that Joe Lelyveld had all but promised Sam a position as a foreign correspondent after his tour as the Seattle bureau chief. Sam was a writer many others at *The Times* modeled themselves after, so Howell's decision not to send him overseas sent a shockwave through those who felt they were going to have to get new routines.

The *News* story also chronicled the long list of other editors and reporters who had left the paper for the *Los Angeles Times* over the previous two years. The Atlanta bureau chief, Kevin Sack, had left the paper several months earlier rather than accept an order from Howell to transfer to the Washington bureau. Kevin was in the middle of a particularly ugly and public divorce, and was worried that transferring to Washington would harm his chances in a child custody dispute. Many inside the building viewed Kevin's request to stay in Atlanta until the custody dispute was over as one similar to the waivers granted other correspondents in the past for lesser reasons. Still, Howell would not budge.

Howell was seen as the person behind the removal of Gustav Niebuhr, the scholarly religion writer on the national desk, even though Katy Roberts, the national editor who had quickly fallen out of favor with Howell despite having been his deputy on the editorial page, was the one who orchestrated it. Adam Liptak, a senior counsel at the newspaper's parent company, replaced William Galberson, the national legal affairs reporter. Howell had convinced Adam Nagourney, the Los Angeles bureau chief he'd appointed toward the end of his reign, to stay in New York to cover the aftermath of September 11.

John Montorio, the associate managing editor for features, resigned in the days before Howell took over. Colford missed it, but that is because he did not know that John had once supervised Gerald's wife when she was a lower-level editor at the paper, and he just seemed to be getting out of Dodge before the pair took over. After Montorio's departure to the *Los Angeles Times,* he was able to recruit the paper's food editor, Michaline Busico.

Steve Engelberg is the investigative editor who had run the much-maligned Wen Ho Lee coverage and much-praised examinations of anything else he touched. A former Central Intelligence Agency correspondent, Steve had written a book about bioterrorism that was published just as the anthrax attacks were occurring. Steve collaborated on the book with two colleagues, Judith Miller, an investigative reporter, and William Broad, a science reporter. In the last of a long list of slights, Howell did not tell Steve that his team had won a Pulitzer for investigative reporting on their coverage of Al-Qaeda and the Taliban before and after the September 11 attacks.

Steve had to hear the news in the form of pretty solid gossip from Bill Keller, who had left the newsroom to become an op-ed columnist. Steve's

team, which had turned *The Times* into an investigative paper under Joe
Lelyveld's leadership, had performed strongly before and after the September 11 attacks. Howell was pushing them to be quicker in their reports, to
not wait for all the details, and to not get beaten on stories. The message
was clear: getting it right was not as important as getting it fast; and if we
got it wrong, we would just write a story the next day that read, "In a surprise move . . ."

The message was not lost on the rest of the newsroom. Soon after the
Pulitzers were announced Steve left to take a similar position at *The Ore-
gonian,* near where his wife's family grew up outside of Portland, Oregon.

As this was going on, Howell was conducting a very public spat with
the editor of the Sunday Arts & Leisure section, John Rockwell. In a posting to a classical music website, Rockwell wrote that "Howell thought that
A & L was esoteric, boring and that nobody read it," adding that he wanted
the section to focus more on pop culture. The moves Howell was making,
this one included, seemed to lend credence to the arguments that he had
bought into the notion that we were living in a celebrity culture that did
not value truth, but hype. The stories on the front page about botox injec-
tions, Britney Spears, Mariah Carey, Gennifer Flowers, and Marshall Faulk
were not helping Howell's defense team.

In Howell's defense, though, *The Times* could be a boring read, particularly for those under forty years old, and his changes, ranging from better
display of pictures to more eloquent writing, seemed to bring the paper
alive. Still, if the newspaper was more alive in newsprint, the newsroom was
in anguish in reality. Part of it was a matter of style. The newsroom had
become so top-down in their management style that the Washington
bureau had begun to refer to the newsroom leadership as the Taliban and
Howell as Mullah Omar.

In early February, Howell dispatched Gerald Boyd and Bill Schmidt to
Los Angeles to inform three West Coast correspondents, including Sam
Verhovek, that their services in their current positions would no longer be
needed and that they should prepare for a transfer. The two other correspondents at the meeting—San Francisco bureau chief Evelyn Nieves and
Los Angeles correspondent James Sterngold–chose to leave the newspaper
instead of transferring and dealing with the public humiliation of facing a
newsroom full of people who all knew about the meeting. Only one correspondent who was asked to transfer complied. That was David Firestone,
an Atlanta correspondent who agreed to go to Washington. The other tar-

geted correspondent, Michael Janofsky, the Rocky Mountain bureau chief who was based in Denver, avoided transfer because there was little left of the national desk by the time the senior editors got around to him.

In tone and substance, Howell was changing the paper, and in the process, many people feared he was damaging what made it great.

The subtleties of *The New York Times* star system were flowing out into the open. Anyone who has spent a moment as the favored, fair-haired child in *The Times* system knows that there are pretty much three ways to end up on the front page of the paper. If you write a beautiful feature or thoughtful trend story, you can make it onto the front page. Since those terms are subjective, though, one generally makes it "out front" if he is a favorite. One can go the other route, which is by getting a beat with news events so big that they have to run on the front page, but the problem there too is that one generally gets those assignments because he is a favorite.

Section editors and mid-level editors become the kingmakers, ensuring that the most favored, not always the best and the brightest, rise. Generally, though, there reaches a point even with the favorites, buoyed by the opportunity to write the most stories for the front page, when their stardom begins to take on a life of their own, and they begin to work the system to a point where few would question their talent. Several of the correspondents who fit into that category, and would have been safe regardless of the editor in previous regimes, were under attack by Howell. At that point, examining what undercurrents were ripping the paper apart and causing so many people to leave, Howell decided to view the matter as a war with the *Los Angeles Times*.

In response to one raid by Dean Baquet, the managing editor of the *Los Angeles Times* and former national editor of *The New York Times*, Howell hired the *Los Angeles Times* correspondent in Atlanta, Jeffrey Gettleman. The way Howell and Jeffrey met sent a message to the newsroom just as strong as the attempt to kick the *Los Angeles Times* for its raids, but there was a deeper foolishness to it that would not become clear until months later.

Generally, the executive editor of *The Times* lords over coverage from the newsroom in West Forty-third Street, but Howell showed a hands-on tendency when it came to friendship and stories he cared about. That level of advocacy did not bother me much, but unsettled many of those in the newsroom who said it violated the tenets of objective journalism.

In early May *The Times* sent Rick Bragg, a friend of Howell's and a Pulitzer Prize–winning correspondent, to cover the trial of Bobby Frank Cherry, an ex-Klansman accused of the 1963 bombing of a church in Birmingham, Alabama. On top of one of Rick's early stories there was a note that said if the desk editors needed him for any questions he could be reached through Howell's cell phone. Quickly, it became known that Howell was in the courtroom with Rick taking notes when he had to step out to file or talk with editors on the National Desk. Howell was sending a message, whether he intended to or not, about who and what he cared about. On the trip, Howell met Jeffrey Gettleman, the *Los Angeles Times* correspondent he later hired. The backstory he did not know, though, was that Dean Baquet had grown furious with Jeffrey's performance and was about to call him on the carpet, a fact that was widely known within the New York newsroom.

If Howell or his deputies had been connected to the rest of the newsroom, they would have known that the message they were intending to send—that we could take the best of the *Los Angeles Times*—would not be received well when we all knew that Jeffrey was on the outs with his bosses, and would not be considered either a coup for *The New York Times* or a major loss to the *Los Angeles Times*. It was widely believed also that Jeffrey's friendship with Rick Bragg, forged while counting chads in West Palm Beach, Florida, was a factor in the decision.

It was a move that in one fell swoop sent the message that Howell thought that the retention problems were not connected to the way he was managing the newsroom but the aggressive recruitment of correspondents by competitors, that he favored certain correspondents over others, that he favored certain causes over others, that he was capable of making a retaliatory hire without checking the facts, and that he was out of touch with what was common knowledge in the newsroom.

I had little time for the bumbling politics going on at the highest level of *The Times*. I was just trying to prevent myself from losing my grip and quitting my job. After one therapy session, I drafted a brief resignation letter that I simply left in my computer queue. I was more interested in attending group therapy and attending to my personal life.

"If they want to play hardball," I thought, "I can play hardball as well."

I started terming my editor's annoying attacks, confrontational style and immature behavior—only rivaled by my own, I must sadly add—as "harassment" and "contributing to a hostile workplace."

I did not suggest that race was at play, but the combination of what I knew about Jon's stand on affirmative action and minority hires in the newsroom, and the patronizing tone that was being delivered to me on a daily basis, left me convinced that it was a factor—a black recovering drug addict at *The Times* was not going to be given the same leeway that a white one might be. After all, I did not look like their sons and daughters, their cousins or extended family. To them, the world of a black drug addict was filled with all sorts of unimaginable things and places.

Marion left to return to Berlin in early April. We had the clichéd airport hugs and kisses goodbye, and I settled nicely into sessions at the Realization Center and a broadening personal life.

On August 22, I came to work early and walked past the business desk on my way to the cubicle where I sat with other metro reporters. I had picked the desk several months before because I felt I was becoming too easily distracted at my old one, which was along the way most people traveled when entering the newsroom. I had stopped by the Toys "R" Us store in Times Square and purchased three Care Bear miniatures to place on the top of my computer. They were a little personal reminder, even if juvenile, to keep my composure. Inside, I was cracking. I came up with the idea at Emmett's, where I was regularly going for lunch, and had built up a friendship with the daytime bartender, Maria, who would not have poured me a drink if I handed her $1,000 in cash. Maria and I had been talking about childhood, and I noticed that the mammoth Toys "R" Us store in Times Square had Care Bears in their windows. I told Maria that I needed something to remind me of the important emotions in life and to keep my cool with my editor. My inner child, in part, was speaking. The fourth bear I wanted to get was Lucky, the one with the Irish shamrock on his chest.

I got one for Maria, who had supported me tirelessly and lovingly in my struggle to stay clean and sober, and one for my desk. I was arranging the Care Bears on the top of my computer monitor when a colleague walked by and asked, "Jayson, oh my God, did you hear what happened?"

Everyone was nervous about a possible terrorist attack. It was only weeks from the first anniversary of the September 11 attacks. I braced myself for news of the latest strike.

My colleague told me he had been walking in a stairwell on the far western side of the building when he watched a body come falling out of the sky. The worker said the body looked like that of Allen Myerson, a forty-seven-year-old editor on the business desk. In most work environments, when a colleague jumps off the side of a building, the immediate reaction is to mourn. In a newsroom, the mourning is mixed with a lot of reporting in an attempt to piece together the details of what happened. As a journalist, you always want to know "The Why." In our newsroom, there was a lot of blaming, a lot of sharp and serious comments that the business desk had come under such serious assault by Howell that Allen's suicide must have had some connection.

There was truth to all of it, we would later find. Allen's career had been sidelined when Joe Lelyveld and the business editor, Glenn Kramon, ordered his return from Dallas, where he had been the business correspondent. I knew from my conversations with him that Allen loved writing, and was not as comfortable as an editor. I knew he gave it a go, and was trying to move up the power structure, and had been rejected for the metro business editor job.

I was unaware of his intense personal problems, including a messy divorce that I found out about after a little reporting. Putting together the last few weeks of Allen's life, there were no obvious signs in the workplace that he was about to commit suicide. Detectives would later conclude that the divorce, work, and other matters drove Allen to suicide, but no factor was more important than the mental illness that all these stress factors were pushing to new heights.

Agis Salpukas, a sixty-year-old business writer for *The Times,* had pulled off what could only be described as a brilliant-to-the-last-moment suicide nine months after I arrived at *The Times.* Born in Lithuania in 1939, Agis's mother was killed in World War II. Agis was able to escape to Germany with his father, where he lived until he was nine. After the war, Agis and his father came to the United States, settling in the Bronx and then Queens. Agis graduated from New York City public schools, received an undergraduate degree from Long Island University and a master's in history from Columbia University.

In 1963, Agis got a job at *The Times,* and by 1970 he had become a national correspondent. He became the bureau chief in Detroit in 1973, and was given awards for his coverage of Watergate and the troubled Vice President Spiro Agnew. It seemed the perfect life of the rags-to-riches *Times* man. What was not known to his colleagues, though, was that Agis was struggling with depression, and it was beginning to affect his career. Agis was brought back to the newsroom in New York, where he took on less high-profile jobs. Agis also began getting outpatient treatment at the New York Psychiatric Institute, and started painting as a part of the therapeutic process.

Agis's friends would later tell me that he had been in the psychiatric institute in the days prior to his death, and had received a pass two days before to spend time with a friend and his wife. Agis, they said, returned to the institute in good spirits, and again received another pass. They now believe that his demeanor was a ruse, an attempt to get space so he could commit suicide. On January 4, 2000, his body was pulled out of the Hudson River. Detectives believed he jumped from the George Washington Bridge.

Allen's death stuck in my craw, particularly because there was not a person I could find that knew he was struggling with mental illness. His struggle was detailed in diary notes he kept that were later published by *New York* magazine. It reminded me of Monte's struggle with mental illness and her death. For Lynette, though, all of them reminded her of me.

"I worry about you, Jayson," she said, from the position of having seen me both in the office and drunk at the bar crying, babbling through tears about being sexually abused as a child. "You seem to take the death of Monte a little too hard, and now you are taking the death of Allen so hard and you did not even know him outside of the office. It seems like it is hitting a little too close to home."

Perhaps it was.

Seven days after Allen's death, I wrote a curious e-mail. Something inside me was triggering the part of me that knew there were things so much more important in life than work. Several weeks before, I had received a telephone call from a young woman who was a news assistant. I had met her months before at Jenny Holland's going-away party at Robert Emmett's. The young woman, named Zuza Glowacka, offered me a chance to come along with her snarky friends to the Russian Samovar, a well-known bar on West Fifty-second Street.

I was in one of my over-the-top moods (whether it was buying six pairs of the same pants and shirts or hundreds of dollars of flowers for someone, this type of mania was not uncommon) and I offered to buy so many drinks that I had accumulated a $1,000 personal bill by the end of the night. I was paying a hefty price for someone who was not drinking.

I was intrigued by the young woman's openness and personality, but declined her invitation. I was not in the mood to explain my stance on not drinking, and the Russian Samovar is one of those places you go not to drink, but get drunk, and really drunk at that. I wish I had gone. Instead, I spent my night trying to score coke and weed for some of the *Times*'s reporters and editors who had stayed to the end of the party. It was impulsive, the drive to do the deal that put me back on the streets thinking I could get it for them without using. I ended up in a housing project on Manhattan's West Side buying coke from a dealer, and supplying it to the assorted group.

My night ended in the cramped Lower East Side apartment of one *Times* reporter, who showed me the nipple rings on her breasts and snorted what was left of the coke. The story was not well received the next week in group therapy. I had made it a long way since then, and was intrigued further when Zuza called and invited me to hear friends of hers who were in a rap group perform live at a downtown club. I dashed off an e-mail and we made plans to hang out some time after the week I was taking off. In February, I had asked for vacation days during the week of the September 11 anniversary. The assignment editor tried to talk me out of it and asked me to cover an event at ground zero. This time, I forcefully declined. One week after taking Zuza to a Pan Asian restaurant overlooking downtown, I was ready to declare my love. At the restaurant, she recited Ralph Waldo Emerson off the top of her head, talked about how she volunteered in prisons and opined on the connections she saw between her background as an immigrant who had come to the United States at age three and the black American experience of isolation.

We next went to a birthday party in the lobby of the TriBeCa Grand Hotel, and then met up with a bunch of her friends at a bar, and then walked across the Brooklyn Bridge on our way home. Over the next few weeks, we had hung out several times, including several walks across the Manhattan Bridge and explorations of the city. I was ready to profess my love in the cab ride home after going into a playground and playing on a jungle gym in Riverside Park.

Zuza brought something innocent and special to life.

She also helped unlock something else. Something very unexpected.

CHAPTER TWENTY-THREE
ON THE BEACH

A colleague who was banished to the night rewrite desk for several years for defying Jon Landman's attempts to send him to become the paper's correspondent in Hartford, Connecticut, once said that when presented with the choice of choosing "life" or *The Times,* he chose life.

The colleague suffered dearly for his choice, but said that he suffered much less than he would have had he not defied the order to go to Hartford. For the first time in my career at *The Times,* I was choosing life. For the first time in many years, I felt I was making a healthy work-related decision. By the early fall, my friendship with Zuza was bringing a new energy and focus to me, an opportunity to recapture my youthful dreams and do something good with them.

We would spend late nights reading Emerson and Dostoyevsky, and talking about race relations and the immigrant experience. One night she read me a moving short story about her childhood and dreams that seemed to rekindle my childhood idealism. I had a good fall. I had also decided to make a move, to transfer from the metro desk and take a job writing news stories for the Sports Department.

The job was a step down in terms of the prestige of the department, but it was a way to get away from the metro desk and start a new career in a more nurturing department where the editor asks questions in his interview like, "If you were a fruit, what would you be?" (Kiwi was my answer.) My corrections had dropped dramatically, and I knew Jon and my editor could take credit for that, even though a chart could be mapped that showed how my corrections went up the more pressure they placed on me, and down when they loosened the reins ever so slightly. I was in no mood to argue. I was going to let them have that victory. Everyone could walk away happy. I would not have believed it if someone had told me that within a few months, I would be a raving psychotic.

Gerald had resisted my move to sports. Howell had approved the move, which was being pulled off by Bill Schmidt, who I knew wanted to see me succeed despite all the difficult moments.

The sports job was going to give me some time to focus on therapy and seeing where my friendship with Zuza was going. We were spending a lot of time in cafés, lying in Prospect Park reading on the grassy fields and talking about things we could do in the future. Zuza is one of those people who dreams big. I was one of those people who could make things happen. We spent hours together hanging out in the Starbucks on Seventh Avenue in Park Slope, Brooklyn, talking about places we could go and things we could do in the future.

My mind had not been on the job for the last few months, and it was ever so softly creeping into my stories. They were becoming peppered with my own inside jokes. I had told anyone who would listen that I was "going to the beach," my euphemism for taking it easy and only putting in the requisite hours. I was just punching the clock, but, as always, I was making my writing interesting.

My editor asked me in early August to write about whether the terrorist attacks were having an impact on the local entertainment industry, so I went to Kevin St. James, a bar on Eighth Avenue where Lorraine was now working, and spent a night and day with her writing about her tips. I interviewed the bartenders and waitresses from the B.B. King's Blues Club on Forty-second Street at the bar as they were drinking in Emmett's. A friend in public relations needed a boost for a client, so I wrote a piece that I pushed onto the front of The Metro Section by repeating some trend about banks that had been dryly said in the paper over and over in much more boring ways over the last eight months.

I went to the normal parties that *Times* reporters get invited to as perks, and turned them into items for Boldface Names, the gossip column in the paper that the editors swore wasn't gossip. During the annual MTV Music awards, a news assistant and I went to a *Stuff* magazine party featuring Pink, hung out, partied and got paid for the little item. It was more of the same at the *Men's Health* party, where editor-in-chief David Zinczenko told me how he was falling for the actress Rose McGowan and I told him how I was falling for some woman he had never heard of named Zuza Glowacka.

My obsession with her was obvious to me by the fact that we constantly sent each other text messages over our cell phones several times each hour, and the fact that we spent almost every waking moment outside of work, and many at work, together, talking, planning, thinking and learning about each other. What was less obvious, though, was how easy it was to send subtle messages to her through feature stories. Jacques Torres, the host of *Watch Chocolate*, made it into the lead of my October 9, 2002, story on heating oil because of her obsession with chocolate. Hudson Valley Oil Supply in Lake Katrine, N.Y., got a nod because its proximity to where she went to college. Steve Hiscox got a mention because of how close his home was to the house in Morris, N.Y., where she had fond memories of staying as a child.

During this period I began to self-examine, and take a look at why I entered journalism and how far off course my vessel had traveled. I had gotten into the business to help people, to inform them, to educate them, and now I was writing stories about the fashion industry. Soon, I would be writing about athletes.

All the energy I had poured into journalism, I thought, would have been better spent educating prisoners or creating a house somewhere in upstate New York that would be open to anyone, regardless of their ethnicity, race, gender, sexual orientation, class or economic background. Perhaps it would have been better spent tutoring or taking on causes.

What I had wanted from journalism's truthfulness and objectivity tenets, it was obvious to me, was not something it could give me, at least not at *The New York Times,* particularly not at a time when celebrity culture was driving the decisions.

Jon sent me an e-mail message on my last day in Metro wishing me well, saying I should be careful and avoid mistakes and that my former editors would be "rooting" for me from the sidelines. I could not tell whether it was a joke, since I knew Jon hated Howell's constant sports metaphors. I decided to take it for what it seemed to be, and that was good wishes. My objections to staying in the profession were somewhat removed from the turmoil I had been through in the newsroom, save Gerald's most recent slight in opposing my begging for a demotion.

That is why I was all the more surprised one morning when I received an e-mail message from Jim Roberts, the national editor, telling me that Gerald had drafted me to join the team that had been covering the Washington area sniper shootings.

I had recently moved into a new apartment, only days before, just off Seventh Avenue in Park Slope, Brooklyn.

Zuza and I went there and packed my bags.

Most reporters would have been dying at this opportunity. Before I left, I told Zuza that I was falling in love with her, and she recited a line from T. S. Eliot's *The Love Song of J. Alfred Prufrock,* a poem she knew off the top of her head:

"Would it have been worthwhile," she quoted, "If one, settling a pillow or throwing off a shawl, and turning toward the window should say: 'That is not it at all, that's not what I meant, at all.'"

I would have much rather stayed home, settled into my new job, and stayed close to Zuza. We talked about chasing our dreams together. There was little time for talk of the future. Duty called, and I did not know how to get out of it.

I was on my way to Washington to chase snipers.

CHAPTER TWENTY-FOUR
CHASING SNIPERS

I arrived in Washington on the Amtrak Acela Express bullet train early in the morning and, after calling Zuza to let her know that I had arrived safely, grabbed a cab and had them take me to the Ramada Inn in Rockville, Maryland.

As the driver made his way west down Constitution Avenue, it felt eerily familiar as we passed the United States Capitol and the White House, two buildings I had reported from, and the museums of the Smithsonian Institution, where my father worked, and the exit on Route 66 that leads to my parents' home in Northern Virginia. The streets were empty as we drove south on Rockville Parkway, down a slope and into the driveway at the entrance of the Ramada. At the front desk, I tried to use my debit card to hold my room, but there was not enough available cash for the days I was planning on staying there, which in itself was up in the air because of the nature of the snipers terrorizing the Washington area.

So, I called my parents to get their credit card number, went upstairs to my room and the newspaper clippings from the *Los Angeles Times*, *The Washington Post* and other newspapers that I had collected on my way out of the door of the newsroom in New York. I was having lunch in Emmett's one day in early October when Maria turned up the volume on the television set and we saw the second-day CNN broadcasts about someone taking a high-powered rifle and shooting at least five people in a seemingly indiscriminate way in Washington, D.C., and Montgomery County, Maryland.

"If they don't find a connection between the victims, and this truly is random, then this is either an intelligent and efficient insane person or some kind of terrorism," I said while still in New York, just after finishing cream of broccoli and blue cheese soup a little after three o'clock at Emmett's.

As I was walking out the door, I heard Maria yelling my name.

"Wait, Jayson, wait," she said. "It looks like there is another one."

I walked back into the bar. CNN was reporting that another woman had been hit, in a similar manner to the other shootings, a little bit before two-thirty. The killer had moved out of their target zone, firing on a woman who was loading items into her car. This time, though, the shooter had moved out of Washington and Montgomery County, Maryland, and had struck in Fredericksburg, Virginia.

I dialed my parents' house in Centreville, Virginia, which is between the locations of the Maryland and Virginia shootings. They were now within the kill zone. Several days later, there was a shooting of a thirteen-year-old boy outside Benjamin Tasker Middle School in Bowie, Maryland, not far from where I had gone to college at the University of Maryland. I watched from the bar as CNN played videotape of the Montgomery County police chief, Charles Moose, crying at the news conference where they announced that the school shooting had occurred.

I panicked on October 9, when a man was killed at a gas station I used to go to all the time in Manassas, Virginia, which borders Centreville. It was only seven days after the shootings began. I did not receive the call to arms until after the October 14 shooting of a woman named Linda Franklin, a forty-seven-year-old mother and F.B.I. analyst, inside a parking lot in Falls Church, Virginia, a quarter mile from the house where my brother Todd lived.

The Times was getting smoked on the story, despite the enormous resources we had in place, including sending several reporters in from New York, Atlanta, and other locations. Our major disadvantage was the fact that the local police were running much of the investigation, while officials from the Federal Bureau of Investigation and the Bureau of Alcohol, Tobacco and Firearms were standing mostly in the background until the thirteen-year-old boy was shot at the middle school. *The Washington Post* was dominating the exclusive elements of the news about the shootings, although their coverage was spotty, and the *Sun* in Baltimore clearly had the best handle on the story.

News of things like the Death tarot card left at the scene of the middle school shooting caught our reporters by surprise. They only learned about it when they read of the card in the *Post* and the other papers. We had been unable to confirm the existence of the card or the words written on it. One of the things Jim Roberts asked me to do was to focus on law enforcement sources in Maryland and Virginia, and luckily I had a Rolodex still filled with names of people who worked in local police departments in most of the area.

I had met many of the officers and commanders while working for Capital News Service in Annapolis, Maryland, writing for *The Washington Post*, stringing for the *Sun* in Baltimore, freelancing in the region for *The Boston Globe*, as well as working as an intern for *The Fairfax Journal* and the *Centreville Times* in Virginia. My Rolodex was born for this story. Still, I was surprised I was getting sent to cover it after listening to Gerald's trepidation about me going to the sports section, and I was even more confused once I found out it was Gerald who had recommended me. One thing that was clear to me was that the pressure was on.

Once in Rockville, I began going through my sources, calling them early in the morning and leaving messages. Because there was a region-wide task force to catch the snipers, I knew that even the smallest departments in independent cities like Greenbelt and Laurel, Maryland would have morsels of information. By the end of my first full day there, I was able to confirm through one of those local police contacts the existence of the tarot card and the words that were written on it.

Mr. Police
Call me God
Do not release to the Press.

I found it odd that any detective would tell me that much information, particularly on a card from killers who specifically said not to release the information to the news media, but it was already out there, and I knew that the motive for many detectives in cooperating with the news media was simply to be able to tell their buddies and grandkids that they were a part of the story.

"Look, that came from me," they would say, holding the tattered newspaper clipping.

A reporter could easily exploit that desire, and that opportunity to be a part of the story would sometimes override the best judgment of even the most hardened detectives when the story got big. That is clearly what happened with the tarot card left by the mysterious snipers. By the time I made it outside on my first day in Rockville, people were doing what I took to calling the Maryland Shuffle, zig-zagging on the way to their cars and asking people to escort them when they were in parking lots at night. The sound of a car backfiring would send people into sprints. This familiar region, where I had gone to movies as a kid and in college, was consumed by an obsessive paranoia.

A colleague who was reporting on the hunt for the snipers met me at a Brazilian restaurant next to the Ramada a little after eight o'clock one night. I had just finished writing a long letter to Zuza, and I was tired. I had spent most of the day on the "Call me God" card and was looking forward to a relaxing dinner. We were at the bar when we heard the sirens. A white van, which was the color and make of the vehicle the snipers were believed to be in, came screeching to a halt in the restaurant's parking lot.

My colleague ran outside to find out what was going on, and I ran to a window to get a view close to the action. Montgomery County, Maryland police officers with shotguns drawn were ordering the driver of the van out of the car and onto the ground in the parking lot. They swarmed in, hovering over his body. At the same time, one officer turned his shotgun toward the front door of the restaurant and pointed it at my colleague. The officer was yelling something at her, but I could not make out what it was. I was going to stay on this side of the glass.

Two officers were lifting the man up by handcuffs that they had attached to his wrists while the other officer was still pointing his shotgun in our direction and yelling. I called the desk to let them know that something was going down, but later would find out that this was a scene that was repeated all over the region during the three weeks in October when the snipers terrorized the Washington area.

Once it became clear that the man was not the sniper, the colleague and I returned to the bar, where she was drinking and recounting the incident with the officer, who apparently had yelled profanities at her, when I noticed a news flash screaming across the screen. CNN was reporting that law enforcement agents in Tacoma were digging up a backyard in connection with the sniper investigation. We thought, at first, that they were referring to Takoma Park, Maryland, but there was a live feed of the scene coming from a video camera in a helicopter. The clue that it was not Takoma Park was that it was light outside, and in Maryland at the moment it was pitch-black dark.

Soon after calling the desk, my colleague and I were given orders to split up. I was supposed to head to the sniper task force headquarters in Rockville while she was supposed to await more information on her assignment. The command center was just off Route 28, the same road I would take to go pick pumpkins around each Halloween when I was in college. I parked my rental car in a lot beside the command center and made my way through the fence that had been put up to protect police commanders and the media from being shot at if the sniper decided to make such a bold attack.

Inside the media area, there were tents and groups of reporters and cameramen chatting about how the chief was supposed to be out any minute now. Chief Charles Moose had received a lot of praise in the days immediately following the beginning of the sniper attacks, and had quickly become the most prominent black official in American law enforcement. That praise was quickly turning into criticism, most particularly because of what appeared at the time to be missteps in the investigation. The criticism had less to do with any missteps than a natural cycle. Whenever the media makes you into a hero, you better deliver results fast, because no one gets it worse from the press than someone who does not live up to the status of the pedestal they have been placed upon.

Chief Moose had risen up through the ranks of the Portland, Oregon police force, where he eventually became its first black chief. I had remembered reading about him years before, when he first came to Montgomery County, Maryland. I used to joke when I was in college at the University of Maryland that I would make the quick dash across the Prince George's County line into Montgomery if I was being chased by the police, because of the reputation of Prince George's officers for treating suspects, particularly black ones, with brutal force.

The chief became the first black police leader in a county that was overwhelmingly suburban and white, and I understood, at least on some levels, the position he must have found himself in while trying to prove himself. I imagined him getting into law enforcement because he thought law was more important than race. I imagined what pressure he must be under. I imagined what weight he must be carrying. I imagined what it must have been like to be second-guessed. I wondered whether in the back of his mind the chief was hoping, like I was, that the suspects were not black. "It's all we needed," I thought to myself. Just then, he came out, flanked by men I recognized from television as federal investigators working on the case.

The major news of the day had been about Chief Moose and federal authorities working out an agreement to give blanket immunity to any illegal immigrants who came forward with information on the sniper attacks. The day before I came down, investigators thought they had the snipers at a gas station in Virginia, but when they rolled onto the scene, they ended up arresting two illegal immigrants from Mexico who were promptly ordered deported. The move had sent the wrong message to immigrants who might have information, and the chief had set out that day to promise safe haven to anyone who came forward.

The look on his face, though, seemed more serious. Perhaps it was because I was seeing him in person, or perhaps it was because of what he was going to talk about. I could not tell. It was about five minutes after midnight when the chief started talking. I noticed how carefully he was speaking in comparison to the news conferences I had seen before on television.

Moose began by describing two men—John Muhammad and a juvenile—who he said were wanted to answer questions connected to the sniper investigation. Moose did not say they were suspects, but all the winks and the nods from the police spokesmen who were out of camera range made it amply clear that they were. I knew that somewhere on West Forty-third Street in New York a late editor was watching television, taking down the information and directing news researchers and others to look up addresses and telephone numbers for anyone connected to them. This was big news. They seemed to know who the sniper was. I wondered whether he had taken the juvenile hostage.

I felt a twinge in my stomach. The suspect was black. Whether upper-class and middle-class black people will admit it or not, we all cringe each time a black person is arrested for a major crime or caught in an embarrassing scandal, knowing full well that it is just going to play into the stereotypes that some whites and others find so easy to believe. I had hoped that the sniper was not black, but now that it became clear that he was, it made me wonder what type of overall implications it would have for issues like the death penalty and race relations.

I would not be at all surprised.

As Moose continued with his message, members of the media began turning to each other with raised eyebrows.

"We understand that you communicated with us by calling several different locations. Our inability to talk has been a concern for us, as it has been for you. You have indicated that you want us to do and say certain things. You have asked us to say, 'We have caught the sniper like a duck in a noose.' We understand that hearing us say this is important to you. However we want you to know how difficult it has been to understand what you want, because you have chosen to use only notes, indirect messages, and calls to other jurisdictions. The solution remains to call us and get a private toll-free number established just for you. We still ask you to call or write us at P.O. Box 7875, Gaithersburg, Maryland, 20898-7875. If you are reluctant to contact us, be assured that we remain ready to talk directly with you. Our word is our bond. If we can establish communications with you, we can offer other means of addressing what you have asked for. Let's talk directly. We have an answer for you about your option. We are waiting for you to contact us."

It was the first moment we knew for sure that the person or people behind the sniper attacks were communicating directly with the police by some means other than the tarot card and a note that had been found tacked to a tree at the scene of one of the Virginia shootings. The news conference told us that there had been calls and possibly other communications, but we were all puzzled by one element.

"Duck in a noose?" I asked, a puzzled expression on my face, as I turned to a television reporter by my side.

This seemed as if it was rapidly turning into a bad comedy.

I asked a police official I knew from other work for *The Times* about the juvenile, and he said that he was also a suspect in the shootings. That solved that mystery. I called my notes into the desk and then was asked to head back to the Ramada where I would meet up with the colleague I had left there and drive to the Clinton, Maryland, address of the woman who we believed was Muhammad's ex-wife. There was some concern on the desk that Muhammad could be there, but I knew that if he was, the police would have already found him and arrested him. They had known about him for at least several hours.

After a brief stop to get coffee and cigarettes, my colleague and I drove our two separate cars around the Beltway to Clinton and then pulled up into the row of nice suburban townhouses. A camera crew from some station was already there, but other than that, things seemed all quiet.

"Shit, TV is here," I said.

I knew that when television crews arrived at a scene one of two things happened, and sometimes both: people clammed up and stopped talking because of all the lights in their eyes, or people who wanted to be on TV started blabbing even though they did not know what they were talking about. On a breaking news story it is often hard to trust anything you hear once the cameras arrive.

After spending about half an hour outside the house waiting for something to happen, we left for a nearby hotel, where my colleague reserved a room for me with her credit card. I was willing to bet that my financial problems rivaled those of the snipers. I still had a $3,000 American Express bill to pay off from the days when I used credit cards to pay for living and money from my bank account for drugs. I had been slowly whittling my debt down with money I had saved from not drinking or buying cocaine.

Our game plan for the night was to work together on a story out of Clinton, trying to find out if the suspect had been there and about the ex-wife. In the worst-case scenario, we would write a story about the neighborhood and the schools where we believed his children were enrolled.

Each night, much as I had done after the September 11 attacks, I did not sleep. I stayed up with the television tuned to CNN, looking for little nuggets of news, clues, anything to go on. Just as I got comfortable in my bed, though, I received a telephone call from a Maryland State trooper I had reached out to on my first day in town.

"Where are you right now?" he asked, whispering into his telephone.

"I'm in Clinton," I said. "Why?"

"Just get into a car, get onto 270 and drive north until you get to Myersville," he said. "There has been an arrest."

I bolted out of bed and called Chris Drew, who was coordinating the coverage from the Washington bureau. Chris was not picking up his phone, so I left him a message to call me. I left on the answering machine that I was headed out on the road and driving north to Myersville. I knocked on my colleague's door, told her I was off, checked out of the hotel and slammed the rental car in reverse, knocking a coffee cup I had left on top of it onto the ground. The car jerked when I hit the brakes, and then I slammed the accelerator and headed out of the parking lot and onto the highway.

Chris called me on my cell phone and I filled him in on what I knew as I drove on Interstate 270. I told him I was headed to the scene of the alleged arrests, and that I would check in once everyone got up in the morning. I drove and drove with my foot on the pedal until I hit Frederick, Maryland, and then headed west into the Catoctin Mountains, uphill toward Myersville. I was flying. I pulled off onto Exit 42 and stopped at an Exxon on Main Street and bought five packs of Camel Dark Mint cigarettes and asked where all the police were.

The attendant seemed startled by my appearance. I thought it was just my New York speed being contrasted with Maryland time. I was tapping my feet, spinning in circles and talking to myself about what the game plan was to catch a view of the arrest site. Once the attendant told me the snipers had been caught at the next exit up, a truck stop, I hit the accelerator again and drove the car out of the parking lot toward the location. The exit itself was blocked by a large truck, so I decided to pass it and circle back on Interstate 70.

I thought the mountains in this area, outside the kill zone, would have been such a perfect place—close to the highways, remote, plenty of forests and parks to hide in—to decamp in order to prepare for another attack. I was restless and kept driving around the site to try to find a way to park and get a closer glimpse of the action, but the amount of police activity was making it impossible.

I called the newspaper's website and got Jade Walker, the fantastic overnight producer who used to be a reporter in Florida. In what was turning into full-on manic delirium, I dictated about six hundred words that could be placed on top of the previous day's report and told her to update the story's dateline to reflect that the news was now happening in Myersville, Maryland. I kept reporting whatever details I could get from the scene and my source in the state police until I got a call from Nick Fox, the national assignment editor who had come into work at six in the morning, who asked if I could drive back down to Montgomery County to cover a news conference.

I hit the gas and headed back down Interstate 70 as fast as I could. The sun was not shining, and I had to beat the morning traffic that was going to build up any moment now. I slammed the pedal as hard as I could, also because I felt myself fading in and out.

To say that I was tired would be the wrong expression. I was psychotic. Some people see stars. I was seeing electric butterflies. I stopped in Gaithersburg, Maryland, to get my head together and fill the car's tank with gas. I also grabbed a cup of coffee and then headed back down the highway. I pulled into the parking lot near the sniper task force headquarters soaked in sweat, physically tired, but mentally wide awake. My body was about to give, but my mind was racing. I thought about the consequences of both sniper suspects being black.

I had made it down to Rockville in an amazing amount of time, actually beating the morning news conference that Chief Moose was supposed to hold about the case. I decided to lie down in the backseat of my car in my ratty clothes, and take a nap. I had no idea how much I was mimicking, albeit unintentionally, the snipers themselves. They had been sleeping in a Chevy Caprice. I was sleeping in a Grand Prix.

I soon found out that the news conference would not be held until later in the day, and I went to my room in the Ramada. I picked up *The*

Times at Starbucks and started. That's when I noticed the datelines. There were bylines on stories with datelines that suggested certain reporters had been to places that they had never been. I knew that for a fact, because I had been talking to them all day from their homes, hotel rooms, and offices.

It would not be the last time such fakery occurred during the sniper shooting coverage. One reporter wrote a story datelined Prince George's County when, while they had been there two days before, they were actually back in their apartment in New York. Another person wrote a story datelined Baltimore, when I knew that stringers had been making phone calls for him all day while he jogged around the Washington Mall.

Quibbles about datelines were not the most pressing matter of the day. The most pressing matter was getting my next assignment. And it did not take long for that to come down. I was to profile Chief Moose at the night's news conference. I began frantically researching each detail I could find out about him, learning about his background, and wondering about his juxtaposition to Muhammad, particularly when it came to the role race played in their lives.

CHAPTER TWENTY-FIVE
BLACK CHIEF, BAD PROSECUTORS

I logged into a database that gave me the ability to retrieve all the major profiles of Chief Moose that had been written prior to the sniper shootings. I did not have a printer, so I saved them in a folder on my harddrive.

Then I pulled up all the major profiles that had been done in the sniper shootings and opened the two files on a split screen on my laptop. I began using the electronic highlighting tool in my word-processing program to mark the words that had been used to describe him before and then after the shootings began.

I honed in on the differences and then began to look for background information about where he had gone to school, what jobs he had held, what his dreams had been, information about his wife and children, and clues about who I should call for the profile of him that I was writing.

I started making phone calls to people who had worked with Moose, like Kathleen Kennedy Townsend, the lieutenant governor of Maryland, and Representative Earl Blumenauer, an Oregon Democrat. Moose was raised in a middle-class family in the final years of the Jim Crow era in Lexington, North Carolina, where his mother worked as a night nurse and his father worked in the public school system. As a student at the University of North Carolina in the 1970s, Moose studied politics and decided to become a lawyer. He enrolled in graduate school in Oregon with the intention of eventually obtaining his law degree.

According to the clips, Moose had said he joined the Police Department in Portland, Oregon in an attempt to learn more about law enforcement practices so he could better defend his clients. While in the Police

Department, though, Moose did not uncover the level of corruption that he was expecting, and instead found himself increasingly interested in doing good works through the department. I found a couple of references to his temper, but outside of that there were few blemishes on his record.

When he arrived in Maryland, he almost immediately came under fire from *The Washington Post* as he attempted to clean up a mess over racial profiling left by the previous police chief, but in time, it seemed, he settled the situation and was able to win the trust of his officers and the county chapter of the NAACP.

There were not many black men in power in my work life who exhibited such qualities of selfless determination while continuing to display some measure of gentleness, with the exception of Jerry Gray. The media had labeled Moose as bitter and moody during the sniper shootings, and I was surprised that he was not even more so, given the uphill battles he had to climb in order to make it to where he was. During the sniper shootings, Moose had become a daily presence in news conferences outside the sniper task force headquarters.

There were some questions about whether he was simply the public face of the investigation, but there was too much evidence from those in local law enforcement in Maryland and Virginia that he was indeed running the show, with a tremendous amount of cooperation from Michael Bouchard, the special agent in charge of the Baltimore field office of the federal Bureau of Alcohol, Tobacco and Firearms, and Gary Bald, the special agent in charge of the Federal Bureau of Investigation office in Maryland, as well as lawyers working for Douglas Gansler, chief prosecutor in Montgomery County.

The lawyers were necessary primarily to set up the rules of engagement with the snipers. Just because the snipers were brazen did not mean that the police could operate outside of the framework of the law to catch them—all it would take to send the prosecution haywire would be to make an illegal arrest; one, for example, based on racial profiling or without probable cause to make a search. The teams were working around the clock, and to give any one man all the credit would be an unfair analysis, but I could not help but feel a twinge of pride, African American solidarity, in Moose's accomplishments.

John Muhammad's race troubled me, enough that I brought it up in a conversation with Zuza. I mentioned that all it takes is one incident like this to give people an excuse to jump after the first stereotype that comes to mind. Luckily, on this news story, Moose was the racial counterbalance. So I took to profiling him in some detail and vigor, cutting him no slack for his mood swings and questionable decisions, but trying to present the full mosaic instead of just one sliver of the canvas, as is often the approach taken by the media.

After doing my research and talking to Representative Blumenauer, Lieutenant Governor Townsend and several others to gain a broader picture of the man, I rushed off to the afternoon news conference just before deadline. It was the big one. The parking lot was packed, and so was the media tent. It was the first official announcement since the arrests of Muhammad and his juvenile companion, a seventeen-year-old boy named Lee Malvo.

Moose started the news conference asking everyone gathered to take a moment to remember a Virginia state trooper who had died in an accident on his motorcycle the previous afternoon while responding to a call about shots being fired on Interstate 95. He then turned the mike over to Special Agent Bald, who said the words that everyone knew, based on interviews with sources speaking on the condition of anonymity, but had not yet been put on the record.

"At approximately 1:00 a.m. today a motorist called 911 to report seeing a 1990 Chevy Caprice bearing the New Jersey license plate NDA 21Z, associated with John Allen Muhammad, parked in the parking lot of the rest stop located at I-70 at mile marker 42, approximately four miles from the Washington County line, 11 miles west of Frederick City, Maryland. Maryland State Police responded, verified the tag and kept the vehicle under surveillance. Task force members responded to the location, approached the vehicle, and found two males sleeping inside. They took both men into custody without incident. The individuals were transported to an undisclosed location in Montgomery County, Maryland. The vehicle was secured and transported to a Montgomery County facility and a search warrant was secured and executed on the vehicle."

Special Agent Bald continued in the same calm and measured tone he used before the cameras regardless of defeat or victory.

"One of the individuals in the vehicle has been identified as John Allen Muhammad, also known as John Allen Williams. He is a black male with a date of birth of 12/31/60. The other individual is a seventeen-year-old male who will remain unnamed at this time because of his age."

The failure of law enforcement officials to name Lee Malvo was a lark, simply a matter of paying lip-service to the rules protecting juveniles before the cameras, because Bald, Moose, and the others knew we knew all about Malvo, because it was their people who were feeding us the details. Bald moved away from the podium, and Moose stepped up to the cameras.

Moose described the investigation as complex and praised the cooperation of the different investigators who were involved in the operation, and then proceeded with a long list of law enforcement agencies involved in the investigation. His list was exhaustive, but it did not even come close to encompassing all the prosecutorial, law enforcement and even military might that had been put into the investigation.

"There are no words that I can think of for all the men and women in law enforcement who again have shown the desire to go to the danger in order to keep other community members safe," Moose said, offering no surprises.

"I know that this has also been a trying time for the law enforcement community and the media," Moose continued.

The chief had repeatedly berated the news media for its irresponsibility in releasing certain details to the public, most passionately for releasing the contents of notes that the snipers had left at two crime scenes. This, though, was a time to make peace.

"I would be remiss," he said, "if I don't acknowledge the cooperation that we received from the media in conveying the many messages that we've needed in order to bring this case to where it is tonight. Although there remains competition among all of the various people in the media, we've also made great note of the restraint, the cooperation, the willingness on your part to withhold information for fear that it would somehow jeopardize this investigation."

Reporters were floored. Was he being sarcastic? No. He was being genuine. Wow, he must have been in a good mood.

The main reason to attend a news conference, as opposed to covering it live on television, is that you pick up little details, like a tear in someone's eye, and you get all the off-the-record information that sources like to give to the media once the cameras are turned off. The main question of the day, other than motive, was focused on the relationship between Muhammad and Malvo.

After the news conference ended, the same officials who dutifully declined to comment on certain matters in front of television cameras began providing details about Malvo's background: his mother's name and whereabouts, his life in Jamaica, a brief stay in Florida, and other details that were corresponding with accounts made by those being interviewed in Washington State, the pair's last fixed address before the sniper shootings commenced.

* * *

I went back to my hotel room at the Ramada and began hammering a 300-word lead to put on top of the 600 words of background I had already written about Moose. I started with an anecdote about Moose strolling into the sniper task force's command center that morning, noting that he was wearing a smile, an expression that was not on his face much during the twenty-one-day manhunt for the snipers. That night, I crashed for the first time in more than forty-eight hours, but woke ready to work, at about four in the morning.

The next day, I worked with colleagues to re-trace the trail of the snipers and the Chevy Caprice that they were driving, writing a story with another reporter about how Muhammad and Malvo were stopped and the police checked their license plate several times. Then I traveled to Baltimore at the request of my editors, simply to drive through the town and get a dateline for a story that we were writing. As I was about to drive into the city's Fort McHenry tunnel on the forty-three-mile drive back to Rockville, I received a phone call from Ed Norris, the Baltimore police commissioner. I pulled over to the side of the highway, imagining having to explain to police officers that I pulled over because I was on the phone with the commissioner.

I was lucky that Norris did not remember me from his days as the deputy commissioner for operations in the New York Police Department. In that position, Norris had been in charge of a widely successful program called Compstat that allowed police commanders to be held accountable and combat crime through technology that allowed them to map individual crimes and trends using complicated mapping software.

The program was so widely successful that George Tenet, the director of the Central Intelligence Agency, came to police headquarters in the fall of 1999 to observe how police commanders were able to track block-by-block crime statistics and make strong conclusions about everything from the way gangs operated in certain areas and the impact arrests had on disrupting them to how commanders were using their resources and where crime was moving.

For days before his arrival, I followed Marilyn Mode, the deputy commissioner for public information, around police headquarters, hounding

her to confirm that Tenet was making an appearance to review the Compstat program, and to try to find out whether it was something that could
be used to track terrorist groups and other threats to America overseas.
Marilyn would not confirm a thing, but also did not tell my competitors at
other papers, so I was able to score an exclusive on the story. The visit was
just one example of how everyone, from the police in China to the C.I.A.,
were modeling themselves after the Police Department put together by
Rudy Giuliani and Howard Safir.

Ed Norris, who also advised Safir on anti-crime strategies, was in
charge of the Compstat program they were modeling. One day Joe
Lelyveld received a telephone call from Lenny Levitt, the *Newsday* columnist who covers the Police Department. Lenny was asking about comments that Norris made in a private gathering at John Jay College of
Criminal Justice that were hard on *The Times* for its coverage of crime in
the city. Norris said that the media was distorting the facts, making it
seem as if crime was much higher than it really was, and that stories like
a *Times* exposé on a hammer-wielding man shot by police in Brooklyn
made officers fear coming under fire and more reluctant to do what was
best for the community.

An editor dialed me at police headquarters after Lenny made the call to
Joe. He ordered up a hit job, basically maligning Norris for making the comments about the media and *The Times* even before the public was aware of his
statements. It essentially became news because he was criticizing us, and we
were using the news pages of the paper to put him on the defensive. If he
remembered me, I knew I would be in trouble. Norris had made clear his dis-
pleasure with the article, and I knew that the "just following orders" defense
had not worked for Adolf Eichmann and was not going to work for me either.

I started off with a normal reporter suck-up move that began with a
speech about the great respect I had for him and his work in New York, and
how it seemed that success was being translated in his endeavor here in
Baltimore. Buttered up, Norris gave me all the details I needed about the
police officer who had stopped John Muhammad in a parking lot in the
city in the middle of the shootings.

I spent a rainy Saturday morning with bus drivers who had gathered
on a Silver Spring, Maryland, road to honor Conrad E. Johnson, a bus
driver from Montgomery County, Maryland and the last victim in the
sniper shootings. I wrote a story for the early editions on his funeral. On
Sunday, I got to see my brother at his house in Arlington, Virginia. On my

way out, I stopped by the Home Depot where Linda Franklin had been shot. A few minutes after pulling out of the parking lot, I received a telephone call from a prosecutor I had become friendly with who tipped me off to the fact that investigators believed they had their first piece of evidence that suggested Lee Malvo fired the shot that killed Linda Franklin.

I drove like a maniac to get back to the Ramada, where I called the desk to inform them of what I had heard, and told them that I would try to get some kind of confirmation from a prosecutor. I knew that Robert Horan, a cantankerous old man, was the prosecutor in Fairfax County, Virginia, and would be the best source of information about the Franklin shooting. I knew that Horan had a tendency to be imprudent and that he lived with his wife somewhere near the high school I attended in Clifton, Virginia.

I found his home telephone number in a deep search of a database full of public records, and started leaving messages for him to call me. Late in the afternoon, I was able to get Horan's wife, who was willing to put him on the telephone with me. In the conversation, Horan said that there was no clear evidence one way or the other that Malvo was the one who fired the shot that killed Linda Franklin, but that there was some solid evidence that Muhammad was in the driver's seat of the Caprice immediately after the shooting.

"A security camera videotape?" I asked.

"Perhaps," he said. "There are a lot of security cameras out here that are being re-evaluated; instead of looking for a white van, they are looking for a Caprice. They keep coming up with more examples every day."

"From the Home Depot?" I asked.

"Perhaps," he replied again.

I asked about those who believed that Muhammad was the shooter and Malvo was simply his sidekick.

"There will be evidence that the juvenile was the shooter," he said.

I ended up writing a front-page story, my first in some time, chronicling the news of the day and the possibility that Malvo had fired one of the fatal shots. While reporting on the story, it became clear to me that the police were looking into other shootings that could have been connected to the pair.

"We are looking into other incidents around the country and certainly in the Washington area," Douglas Duncan, the Montgomery County executive, told a colleague who fed the quote to me for the main story.

Attorney General John Ashcroft and his deputy, Larry Thompson, were now getting involved in deciding which jurisdictions would get the first stab at prosecuting Muhammad and Malvo. Even though Montgomery County was the location where most of the shootings occurred and their police had been the only local officers involved in the arrests in Myersville, prosecutors there were seen as unlikely candidates to take the lead because Maryland's death penalty laws were nowhere near as strong as Virginia's and had no provision for executing minors.

Federal prosecutors could take up the case, but the interstate commerce laws that would have allowed them to prosecute Muhammad and Malvo would have been tenuous at best. That meant that the Virginia jurisdictions, even though the fewest number of shootings occurred in those counties, were the most likely candidates to lead the first prosecutions. The Washington bureau of *The Times* had, oddly, been viewing the sniper shootings very much as a second-rate, unimportant story. That changed as soon as the Attorney General and the Justice Department got involved in the decision-making. They wanted to be all over the story, but the National Desk was providing spiteful resistance.

Many people ask why it takes *The Times* so long to get to certain stories. Part of the problem is that so much emotional energy and time are devoted to intramural squabbles, battles over sources, stories, and other elements that are driven by the careerism of many of the people involved. These battles cannot be entirely labeled as negatives, because internal competition at times prompts people to move more quickly, but most of the time speed is lost by these battles. If a reporter spends half a day angling to undercut his internal competitor, he is often going to be behind the other papers. The saving grace at *The Times* is that it is *The New York Times,* and sources will often give the paper a head start or help its reporters catch up because it is considered such an important paper.

Collaboration on the sniper story seemed to be going fairly well, though. Eric Lichtblau had been not-so-coincidentally recently hired from the *Los Angeles Times,* which was continuing to raid the paper. His job was to cover the Justice Department, so when they became involved we co-wrote the main story on Ashcroft's decision to send Muhammad and Malvo to face trial in Virginia, where Justice Department aides said there was the best chance of the two men receiving death sentences and swift executions.

It was not charming to listen to senior aides to the top law enforcement official in the country talk about making a legal decision on the best place to kill two people, a juvenile included, who had not yet been convicted of anything. It was not that I thought Muhammad and Malvo were innocent, it was simply my firm belief that our system of laws exists for a reason and that due process and legal decisions should not be colored by the politics of whichever administration was in power. All persons should be treated equally, no matter how heinous their alleged indiscretions.

Along with the main story, Eric and I wrote another one about a laptop that had been found in the Caprice that included information that linked Muhammad and Malvo to some of the killings. The same source who helped me get that piece of information would come back the next day and tip me off to a potential mishandling of the initial interrogation of Muhammad. The official tipped me to the fact that while Malvo had refused to speak to investigators, Muhammad was engaging in conversation. The source claimed that the United States Attorney for Maryland interrupted the interrogation in an attempt to take the case away from local authorities. The story ran on the front page and was hyped up both by my editors and myself.

If the United States Attorney for Maryland, Thomas DiBiagio, had returned one of several calls he would have had the chance to get us to temper the story, but the callback did not come until two in the morning, when Barbara Comstock, Ashscroft's shrill spokeswoman, reached me through the National Desk in my hotel room. It was a little too late by then.

A little less than a year later in the massive story on my misdeeds, *The Times* would correct the story by saying that the conclusions that Muhammad was on the verge of confessing were not justified by the reporting, even though a prosecutor was quoted in the story as saying so, and testimony in Virginia would later reveal that he had indeed engaged with the investigators over how he came into possession of the Bushmaster rifle that was used in the shootings. The correction that ran in *The Times* said that investigators were just building up a rapport with him (even though that would later be contradicted by the Virginia testimony).

The other complaint was that two assistant United States attorneys were not involved in the discussions about the custody of the two men. *The Washington Post* book *Sniper*, written by Sari Horwitz and Michael E. Ruane, two veteran reporters who covered the case, came to virtually the same conclusion in recounting the interrogation. The book recounts an angry conversation between DiBiagio and Gary Bald, the F.B.I. special agent, where DiBiagio demands that the two be brought to a hearing in Baltimore. *Sniper* recounts how Bald told DiBiagio that the two were "being interviewed at the moment and he didn't want to interrupt," and then claims DiBiagio responded by saying, "I order you to immediately bring the two defendants for their initial appearance."

Neither of the claims contradicts the crux of the story: investigators had Muhammad talking, and DiBiagio's actions prematurely ended the interrogation. The end result was that any chance DiBiagio had of being involved in the investigation was blown into smithereens.

To this day, I am still proud of that exclusive.

After that front-page story, though, is when certain reporters in the Washington bureau, including Eric, stopped assisting me. I was caught in some New York-Washington drama not of my own making.

CHAPTER TWENTY-SIX
YOUNG SNIPER

I was sitting in my room at the Jefferson Hotel, two blocks away from *The New York Times* newsroom in Washington and five blocks from the White House. The second floor of the Jefferson Hotel is where Dick Morris, the political pollster and advisor to President Clinton, allegedly met with a $200-an-hour prostitute while on visits to Washington.

I had been in Chicago attending the Democratic National Convention for *The Boston Globe* when word came down that Morris had been accused of seeing the prostitute and letting her listen in on conversations with Clinton. The five-star hotel was once the home to a Central Intelligence Agency director who spent his entire tenure there, and a base of operations for many *Times* reporters visiting Washington.

I was standing in my one-bedroom suite, dressed in an orange raincoat Zuza had let me borrow as I was leaving New York. A woman had just come by from the housekeeping staff to turn down the sheets, and I was staring at the hotel mini-bar, the door ajar after I had just pulled out a soda. There were rows and rows of liquor and I could neither take my eyes off them nor get my mind off of the fact that I wanted to have one drink. No one would notice, I thought. It would be no big deal.

I had been in Washington and out of therapy for several weeks and was already beginning to feel the effects, though I would not say them out loud to anyone, other than Zuza, whom I would text-message or e-mail during the day while working and talk to until three each morning. I wanted to get back to New York to see her and begin my new life in the Sports section, but I saw one clear advantage to being in Washington for the aftermath of the sniper shootings. My hope was that a good performance in Washington would ensure that I would be left alone once I returned to New York. I would be free from the harassment of my editors by earning back their respect.

I queried an editor who was working with the team of people who were covering the story about returning to New York, and was told that it would only be a matter of days before I would be released from sniper duty. Whatever comfort came from that notion was forgotten as I sat on the edge of my bed, listening to Eminem blaring from the CD player in the multimedia console.

I spent the entire "The Eminem Show" album walking back and forth between the edge of the bed, where I stared into the mini-bar, and my computer, where I was waiting for e-mails to land from sources. By the time I was halfway through Pink's "Missundaztood," I felt a force telling me that it was do or die, that I needed to get out of Washington. I pulled a small bottle of vodka out of the mini-bar and threw it up into the air, letting it land back in my hand. I went outside that night, literally spinning around in circles in the rain, talking to myself, telling myself that I needed to get control, just trying hard to get the edge off, to suppress the urge to pick up a drink. Inside, I felt as if there were steel butterflies in my stomach, that my mind and body were coming unglued and that it would take all the strength inside me to pull myself back together.

It is hard to say what triggered this moment. I had received a call from a reporter at the *Washington City Paper* who was writing about complaints reporters at *The Washington Post* and at least one person in *The Times* Washington bureau had about the Muhammad interrogation story.

I had not been getting much sleep, usually about three hours a night. The pressure on the sniper stories had been intense, the deadlines and word counts grueling. Most of my days were spent on the road, traveling to places like the federal courthouse in Greenbelt, Maryland, to report on the latest happenings. As I was coming unglued, I did not reach out to my family for refuge. I had long found them too decent to be drawn into my internal drama, thoughts, ideas and feelings that I knew, even drug-free, were of an unusual order. I had never really been too proud, regardless of my accomplishments, because I knew there was this beast inside me, and getting to *The New York Times* in my early twenties was not going to kill it.

That week had been a busy one.

The way the case was being handled never sat well with me, because, at times, it seemed as if Malvo was being railroaded without much thought to the culpability of others, like his parents and guardians. Separately, I could not help but wonder what kind of fierce rage would lead a seventeen-year-old boy to gun down innocent people. I wondered whether it had something to do with the cumulative effects of abuse, abandonment and race. We in the media tend to focus on the exceptions: the poor kid who rises above his family's poverty and becomes the billionaire; the black man who rises above racism to do something exceptional. There are too many sad stories where people get lost and head the other way.

My research in college on family history and demographics told me that many people benefited from their forebears, the knowledge that was passed on, the ideas that were handed down from generation to generation. Mistakes that a great-grandfather may have made were embedded into his own psyche and became a prophylactic that guarded against trouble for generations forward. On the same hand, those born into broken family lines—which almost all descendants of slaves were—suffered great consequences, none more than the lack of depth and knowledge that otherwise would have been passed on from lost generations.

In my worldview, it was often difficult to disassociate a person's hopes and dreams, and their failings and judgments, from their backgrounds. I also believed strongly that it was impossible to divorce the impact of oppressors' actions on the oppressed. Fox Butterfield, a *New York Times* correspondent, wrote a book called *All God's Children* about a man named Willie Bosket, that traced violence in his family all the way back to the tactics of the slave owners who once owned his family and then the Scotch-Irish who had taught them those methods. It was probably no coincidence, I thought, that the Israelis were building what amounted to enclosed ghettos for the Palestinians, or that many South African blacks continued with the murderous tactics of their oppressors even after defeating apartheid, or that the people who came over on the Mayflower oppressed the Native Americans with the same tactics that had been used against them in England.

We all learn from our forefathers, and we also learn from those who oppressed them. It is hard, in a world with such realities, to assign culpability, particularly when it came to a boy who was only seventeen. People can break free, but, in many ways, we are all products of our backgrounds.

After getting back from my walk, drenched in rain, I called Zuza, who was working on the photo desk, and let her talk me down from my heightened panic and agitation. I shut the door to the mini-bar and made it through the night without drinking.

Malvo was quickly moving from a potential victim of Muhammad to a cold-blooded killer in the minds of the news media. It had been a good week for exclusive scoops and a bad week for the two suspects. On Wednesday,

Virginia prosecutors filed murder charges against the men, and the police in Maryland confirmed for me that they were "strong suspects" in a robbery outside a pizzeria before the sniper shootings officially began, because a laptop that was missing in that attack matched the one that was found in the Caprice in Myersville. I followed the laptop the next day as others were distracted by the Attorney General's announcement.

The same source I used to weave together the piece about the United States Attorney in Maryland screwing up the Muhammad interrogation tipped me off that the Sony Viao laptop taken from a fifty-five-year-old man who was shot in front of the pizzeria included a "virtual diary" of their travels. The source said, "You could basically press the print button on that laptop and close a pretty strong case," and then added that "at the very least, it puts them at the scenes of places where they have been accused of shootings."

Eric was able to get the nugget confirmed by one other official who was at the news conference where Ashcroft announced that he was going to put Muhammad and Malvo on the Execution Express and send them to face trial in Virginia.

The success was exhilarating on one level, but holding my head together was becoming my key preoccupation. The day after my dance with the mini-bar, I was back in the saddle, on the search for a motive behind the attacks. I went out to Manassas, Virginia, where hearings in Muhammad's case were being held while Chris Maddaloni, a stringer who lived in Washington and was close with a friend from New York, went to the courthouse near where Malvo was being held in Fairfax, Virginia. Both were making separate appearances that day.

The big news came from the prosecutor in Fairfax, Robert Horan, who said Malvo had been spotted by witnesses at three of the shooting scenes, and that his fingerprints were the only ones found on the murder weapon, lending credence to the notion that the young man was heavily involved in the attacks, and perhaps had fired some of the fatal shots.

At almost any other newspaper, Chris would have received a byline for his contribution since it involved the major news of the day, but *The Times* had a vested interest in obscuring the contributions of its stringers. That story included contributions from stringers in Antigua, Atlanta, Arizona, Maryland, and Virginia. There was only one byline, though. Mine.

At the time, I certainly was not thinking about such matters. I was much more focused on getting out of Washington and returning to the apartment I had just moved into on Seventh Avenue in Brooklyn. In Union Station in Washington, as I was waiting for the next Amtrak train to arrive, I walked by a jewelry shop, where I noticed a bracelet made of silver metal and precious stones that were dark green, maroon, and other deep colors. The bracelet instantly symbolized strength to me. I slapped down my credit card impulsively and charged $200 to give it to Zuza as a gift for all her support.

I took calls on the story from the National copy desk as I was on the train heading back to New York. When I arrived in the city, I immediately went to my apartment, where I found a cactus and a pineapple and a monkey-shaped lollipop all left on my coffee table by Zuza and her roommate, Alexandra. I headed over to her apartment, where I spent the night.

The next evening Zuza and I were walking around the edges of Prospect Park, remarking on how each side of the large green space gave a window into the different elements of New York. The rich people lived along the grand edges of Prospect Park West, near my apartment, and middle-class residents lived along the north and eastern side where she lived. There was much more poverty along the south side, where we were walking. They seemed so close together, sharing the same park, but so utterly far apart in their daily existence.

That's when I received a telephone call from the National Desk. It was late, but *The Washington Post* had placed a story on their website that claimed Lee Malvo had confessed to several of the shootings. They wanted me to write a story and then get back to Washington to get the dateline. I separated from Zuza in mid-conversation about the impact the arrests of Muhammad and Malvo would have on the death penalty debate and race relations. I ran along Flatbush Avenue, where it separates the park and the Brooklyn Botanical Garden. On the way, I booked a train ticket to Washington to pick up the dateline.

Given the deadline, I knew this was going to be a toe-touch. A toe-touch was a popular and sanctioned way at the newspaper to get a dateline on a story by reporting and writing it in one location, and then flying in simply so you could put the name of the city where the news was happening at the top of the story. It is hard to imagine how many thousands of dollars are spent on "toe-touch datelines" each month at *The Times*. During the shootings, one correspondent left his office in Atlanta late in the afternoon as editors and stringers put together his story. He landed in Baton Rouge, Louisiana where the news was happening right around the final deadline. He did not write a word of the story. His only mission was to get to the location so a staff byline and dateline could make it onto the story.

I was going to have to write the entire story from New York and then get on a train and make it to Washington before the newspaper closed, a little before three in the morning. I began working my sources, and my best one once again delivered. I sat in my cramped apartment overlooking Second Street and Seventh Avenue, taking notes on what he was saying.

Malvo had virtually admitted to the killings in conversations with four investigators in the Fairfax County police headquarters. Investigators had found his DNA, the source said, on a grape stem recovered from the ground at one of the scenes of the shootings (this turned out to be false, they had recovered a print from a bag of dried raisin candies). I was able to cobble together a six-hundred word story, and then dash off to Pennsylvania Station in a cab. I arrived well past midnight in Washington. At Union Station, I promptly turned around and headed back to New York on the next train.

Toe-touches were not acceptable under the newsroom policy on datelines, but they were widely sanctioned and often ordered by editors on the National Desk. My trip to Washington and immediate return killed two birds with one stone, allowing me to put a dateline on the confession story. The one stop in Baltimore along the way also allowed me to put that city's dateline on the next day's story, which was reported entirely from New York.

Datelines, under Howell's "flood the zone" philosophy, were almost more important to National Desk editors than the content of the stories. Howell wanted the paper to read as if the The Times had been everywhere imaginable on any given day. National stories without datelines were frowned upon. The push took the normal dateline deceptions at The Times to new heights. The cognitive logic of my belief that I could get away with not visiting a city I was supposed to be writing from can easily be understood, though not excused, by the things I had done and witnessed so far during the sniper shootings. I had seen correspondents perform toe-touch and no-touch datelines, and watched some write stories from hundreds of miles away from where they were supposed to have been. I had partaken in some element of these deceptions, ones that were wholeheartedly sanctioned by the newsroom in an effort to make The Times seem omnipresent.

Over the next two months I traveled back and forth from New York and Washington, writing about the sniper trials, and focusing on trying to put together some semblance of a real life, devoting an enormous amount of attention to my relationship with Zuza. The topics related to the upcoming trials of Malvo and Muhammad interested me, particularly the impact that they would have on the death penalty at a moment when then Illinois Governor George Ryan was considering pardoning all death row inmates. And there were questions about whether juvenile executions were constitutional.

My deepest writings on the subject matter, though, were not at *The Times* at all. Instead, they came in the form of long letters to Zuza. The first of these essays came on a visit to Columbia, Maryland, during a break in the stories on the shootings, where I visited my birthplace and wrote about the sociological differences between the world outside of James Rouse's new town and the world within it. I was in Fell's Point in Baltimore to dig up a little more information on the sniper's stop in that city when I scribbled the essay into a notebook. After meeting with a friend of Zuza's who was staying with his mother in Baltimore, I headed back to Washington and finished the essay, which was meant to explain a little about the shattered dreams of my childhood.

The second one came after a November 23, 2002 trip that Zuza and I made to see a play being given by inmates at Sing Sing, the notorious New York State prison in Ossining, New York. I was in New York for one of my stops, and the sports section was preparing to run the one story I had been working on before leaving for Washington to cover the sniper shootings. I talked with editors on the phone about the details of a new NCAA attendance requirement for college football games, and then hung up and turned back to Zuza to talk about my views on the prison system.

Zuza had volunteered in a program that allowed students at her college to go and teach at the Eastern New York Correctional Facility in Napanoch. She had become involved in the program after a young woman who was a friend had been arrested on drug distribution charges, and was nearly sentenced to twenty years in prison. Her experiences with the men at Eastern shifted her views on prisoners, leaving her with a broader understanding of the criminal justice system, a sadness at some of the great minds lost behind the walls of prisons, and a stance on retribution not dissimilar to my own.

This was the first moment when I felt work becoming a distraction to more important thoughts, something that had not happened to me in my years at *The Times*. The job was beginning to feel more and more like an obligation, as opposed to the fire that kept me going. Zuza's thoughts and ideas were quickly taking its place. There was something else going on that I remember clearly, though I cannot be sure it had happened before. Voices outside of hers began to feel like someone scratching their fingernails against the chalkboard of my brain.

I answered the questions of the editors in the sports section without even thinking twice, leading to a long list of errors in the story, though they would not be uncovered until months later. One thing I could see clearly was that I was detaching even more from the job for the promise of something greater, something I was finding only in my relationship with her.

There was one exception, though: I could not help gravitating toward stories about Lee Malvo, the young sniper. It became more important to me to be near Zuza and by her side, particularly as the noises in my head were growing louder, the images coming more clearly into focus. It became clearer each day that Malvo had been abandoned by his mother as she traveled from island to island looking for work in the Caribbean, and that Muhammad had become the first person to show the young man any parental affection. Trying to gain some insight and understanding of Malvo was twisting my head completely.

At Sing Sing, we drove around the grounds, glancing at the guard towers atop the stone walled complex that looked like a fortress. Inside the visiting room, we handed over our cell phones and wallets, and had an invisible stamp placed on our hands that could only be seen under a certain light. We waited for a while in a large visiting room that, with its orange, green and brown hues, resembled a high school cafeteria built in the 1970s. When it was time to be transported to the prison's auditorium, we were all led outside to a courtyard where we waited in the rain for a bus to come pick us up.

Inside the bus, there was a cage that could be shut to separate the passengers from the driver. It was open today. As we drove around the grounds of the prison, we could see people walking through lighted above-ground tunnels that made it seem like I was glancing inside a slice of an ant farm. As if it were designed for torture, the Amtrak train lines ran right through the middle of the grounds, surrounded by tall barbed wire fences.

I could not help but notice the similarities between the grounds within Sing Sing and the campus of the University of Maryland. I imagined a day when New York State could close down Sing Sing because fewer people were going to prison, and its rededication as a campus of the State University of New York. The high-rise cell blocks could be turned into dorm rooms, while other facilities could be turned into academic and administrative buildings. There was already a cafeteria, a chapel and medical offices. The auditorium could be used for campus lectures and plays. I imagined how different our society would be if those thousands of inmates were in college instead of prison.

By Thanksgiving, I was unraveling. In one particularly obvious moment of questionable sanity, I bought Zuza and her roommates six dozen roses on the spur of the moment and arranged them in vases all across the apartment. A few days later, I spent the day with Alexandra cooking a full Thanksgiving meal for her, Steve Berman, the night photo editor, and others at *The Times* who were working on that holiday.

If that was perhaps sweet, the next move was a little more curious. Zuza took pictures of me prancing around the newsroom wearing a Persian head wrap that covered my face, Kermit the frog on my shoulders and a giant fake fur coat. I did a full tour de newsroom in this peculiar uniform. It is hard to know what I was feeling, other than it was exhilarating to shock everyone. Perhaps I was crying out for attention.

As there are few to this day at *The Times* who would not agree that I was talented, there are few who would argue that I was not a bit eccentric. How were they to know, since even I didn't, that my mind was unraveling on a whole new order. That night, *The Times* was publishing an account by me and David Halbfinger that concluded that the sniper shootings could have been prevented if they had put the pieces together from previous murders in four states that the pair was alleged to have committed.

In one shooting, a fingerprint from Malvo was recovered from a gun magazine dropped by one of the suspects, and it could have been matched to the young man's fingerprints on file with the Immigration and Naturalization Service.

The match was not made because the Alabama police are not connected to the same database as federal officials. The story got me thinking about Malvo's motives. Muhammad's seemed more clear to me, linked to some mixture of anger, disappointment, and insanity. Malvo was much more of a puzzle, and I told myself that I would look deeper into that mystery.

The claim is often made that members of the news media are biased in their coverage. The counter argument is that the news media simply reflects the opinions of society and the issues that people care about. Still, it is too tempting from the high and powerful perch not to interject your opinions about topics into the stories that you cover. This reality angers many careful readers, but goes undetected by most because it is usually very subtle—

giving an extra quote to the side you support, dismissing counter arguments offhand by sandwiching them in between the opposite side.

Anyone who suggests that the media is unbiased is being intellectually dishonest. We all bring our biases to the table in the form of what we consider important. The bias, though, is less pronounced in terms of conservative or liberal bias, but illustrated more powerfully by what we find interesting, that we somehow care about Mariah Carey and Britney Spears more than we care about kids starving in East New York, Brooklyn.

Perhaps there were saints who could take the power of journalism and act entirely objectively. I am simply not one of them. My biases in this particular case were that I identified with Malvo's apparent detachment and disillusionment, not excusing his actions, but fueling a desire to understand him more. My other biases were that I identified with his anger and questioned the ethical notion of executing juveniles. Still, one of the beauties of journalism was that the greatest bias was for the big story, and the power of that overrides the deepest desires for a particular outcome.

In late December, one of those stories came my way in the form of a tip that the investigation had uncovered little concrete evidence that Muhammad had fired any of the fatal shots in the Washington area. The revelation would make it difficult for prosecutors to convince a jury that Muhammad had fired fatal shots, as required under Virginia's traditional death penalty statutes. This story would mark the last of my toe-touch and the beginning of the no-touch datelines. I took the train into Washington, drove out to my parent's hometown of Centreville, Virginia, and did not even stop by to say hello before I headed back to New York.

The idea that Malvo may have been the primary shooter only further piqued my interest in him. I started making a round of calls to sources I had developed while covering the aftermath of the shootings. One of the knocks on me by Jon was that I could not pull off the writing of complicated front-page stories and make it sound good—I neglected thoroughness in reporting out the details. The same source who delivered on the respective Muhammad and Malvo stories came through with information on the lack of evidence against Muhammad, a notion that was supported by others I interviewed. The only problem was that my source had some bad information about evidentiary details.

It was true that the comments Malvo made to investigators seemed to suggest that he was the primary shooter. It was also true that hair linked to Malvo was found in the Caprice. It was true that there was a videotape showing Muhammad that suggested he was not the shooter in a particular killing, but it was from a Big Lots store just north of the Ashland, Virginia shooting, not the Home Depot in Falls Church. I also repeated the mistake about Malvo's DNA on a grape stem. The mistakes caused Horan to call a news conference to declare the story "dead wrong," without mentioning the fact that the broad conclusion of the story—that all the evidence was pointing to Malvo—still stood solid.

"I don't think that anybody in the investigation is responsible for the leak, because so much of it was dead wrong," Horan said, according to an Associated Press account of the news conference.

Horan added that sixty percent of the evidence reported in the article was incorrect, but offered no specifics. It was clear he was referring to the bullet points about evidence, but as soon as the news conference ended, Horan closed his office and went away for the holiday weekend, making it impossible for the editors in New York to come up with a correction. The story caused quite a stir, but after Horan's initial refusal to return phone calls from Jim Roberts, the national editor, I paid it little attention, because my sources were calling back to reaffirm and confirm many of its core conclusions.

I still was not any closer to finding answers about Malvo, but the new revelations were piquing my interest.

First, though, I had to make my plans for Christmas.

CHAPTER TWENTY-SEVEN
SETTING THE FIRE

I woke up to the sound of Zuza yelling at me to get up. I had fallen asleep on the old greenish-yellow couch that was in the living room of the apartment she shared with Alexandra and two other roommates, Toni and Chris.

"Get up, Jayson, get up," she said. "It's time to go. I am sorry I kept you up so late, but if we don't hurry up we are not going to make it on time."

It was a little before six in the morning on Christmas day. I had spent Christmas eve with Zuza in the home of one of her mother's closest friends, a university professor who was well-known in Polish and intellectual circles. I survived celebrating my first Polish Christmas, a sordid affair that involves hay and wafers and vodka, without a drink, but without much sleep either. We took Zuza's aunt from the apartment in Greenwich Village to her home in the northern Bronx, and then back down to Zuza's apartment in Brooklyn. We made it in around three in the morning.

The night before I was on the balcony overlooking Houston Street, I smoked and stared out into the darkness, occasionally engaging in small talk about the sniper shootings anytime someone asked me what I did for a living. I spent a lot of time thinking on that balcony, wondering about Lee Malvo and prison. I had considered going to the Washington suburbs to visit family on Christmas day. Zuza had thought about going with her mother to the apartment of family friends. Instead, we decided to spend Christmas making a surprise visit to a man named Daniel, a friend of Zuza's who is serving a twenty-two-year sentence for a 1990 double homicide he had committed when he was seventeen years old.

We jumped in a car and I drove toward Manhattan, making our way north on the Henry Hudson Parkway, crossing the George Washington Bridge into New Jersey and then taking the Palisades Parkway, surrounded by beautiful scenery, north toward upstate New York and the Eastern Correctional Facility.

Napanoch, New York is a rural, postcard-perfect looking town wedged between two state parks just south of the Catskill Mountains. For more than one hundred years, many of the jobs in the area were at the state prison or in businesses that provided the prison with goods and services. Eastern was opened in 1900 as the second New York State reformatory that rejected 19th century penology and its emphasis on obedience, silence, and labor.

Planners designed the prison to focus on psychological conversion of prisoners, encouraging them with rewards for good behavior, and focusing primarily on the convicts' reintegration into society. Eastern was to be the second prison in New York where sentences were not fixed and could be adjusted based on the behavior of prisoners while incarcerated. It did not work that way, though. Eastern needed construction work, so prisoners from the first reformatory in Elmira, New York, were sent over to finish the buildings. A precedent was set, with the older prisoners and parole violators going to Eastern and the youngest and most promising candidates for reform ending up in Elmira. The prison became like the rest in the state once the efforts at reform were abandoned in favor of more traditional punishment.

Soon after her friend was arrested for carrying enough cocaine to be charged with distribution under New York's tough Rockefeller anti-drug laws, Zuza started volunteering at Eastern, where she met Daniel, who was now in his early 30s after serving a little less than half of his minimum sentence. New York State bars volunteers from communicating directly with prisoners through letters and personal visits. The personal friendships Zuza began to develop with several prisoners led her to stop volunteering and begin corresponding with several inmates, including Daniel, who goes by the name Hakim.

As a seventeen-year-old in 1990, according to an account found in the archives of *Newsday,* Daniel and his nineteen-year-old brother had been indicted on several counts of murder, attempted murder and other crimes connected to fatal shootings inside the J.R. Minimart near Woodlawn Cemetery in the northern Bronx. The reason Hakim's crimes made news in a year when New York City recorded more than 2,000 murders was that, according to the *Newsday* account, he had said he was committing the robbery in an attempt to pay for college.

I did not know much more about Daniel other than the fact that Zuza was smitten with his intellect. She read me passages from his letters about

a variety of issues that would have forced many to confront their stereotypes about prisoners. Our trip was designed to give Hakim some surprise
company for Christmas, and as a part of an idea we had to start a writing
class in a local jail. By November, we had already begun talking to jail officials about the endeavor.

My father had written to inmates and researched Christian prison
ministries while I was a teenager. He was motivated, in part, by a family
friend's incarceration, but also by other relatives who were in prison. Just
before heading to Eastern with Zuza, I did an informal count and came to
the conclusion that at least fifteen of my close relatives were in prison on
everything from federal drug distribution convictions to capital murder.
Outside of my family friend, who was released by the time I was in college,
my father was most involved in the case of my cousin, Willie Thompkins,
Jr., who was on death row in Illinois.

Two days before Christmas in 1980, the bullet-ridden bodies of Gerald
Holton and Arthur Sheppard were found in a field in southwest suburban
Cook County, Illinois. Soon, the trail led back to Willie and his sister-in-
law, Pamela Thompkins. The state brought forward a case arguing that
four days before Christmas, Pamela arranged to buy cocaine from the two
men who were found dead in the Cook County field. The men were said to
have brought the cocaine to Pamela's home and placed it on a table where
two other people were seated.

The state then argued that Willie showed up with a gun and bound
the dealers with telephone cords. Prosecutors argued that hours later
gunfire erupted in the basement and Holton was killed. The state believed
that Sheppard was killed sometime later. Willie did not have a clean
record before the shootings. He had been convicted of attempted murder
and aggravated battery of a fellow member of a Chicago street gang who
was believed to be a police informant. In that case, prosecutors said Willie
kissed the victim on both cheeks before shooting him three times and
leaving him for dead. There was a strong case that Willie suffered from
serious mental illness, but none of that evidence was brought forward
during the trial or sentencing. After his conviction, his defense lawyers
presented no mitigating circumstances that could have helped him avoid
a death sentence. And there was a fairly strong case, based on witness
accounts, that another man was the shooter in the killings of both men.
The witnesses who testified against Willie received leniency on criminal
charges that were in some cases connected, and other instances not

linked, to the two murders. On top of those factors, two of the Cook County sheriff's officers involved in the investigation of the crime were later implicated in covering up a murder and fabricating a confession.

Willie had been on my mind a lot since I had been working the Malvo angle of the sniper case, and preparing for the visit to Hakim.

It was snowing outside when Zuza and I arrived in the parking lot in front of Eastern. We left our cell phones and wallets, except photos for our identification, in the car as we made our way up the slippery ramp that led to the visitor's entrance of the prison. Inside the room, Zuza tried to make small talk with the corrections officers as I absorbed my surroundings.

After being cleared, Zuza and I went into the visiting room, a much smaller version of the one at Sing Sing, with the same air of a high school cafeteria. There was a sentry posted at an elevated desk in the center of the room and several guards stationed at one side. There were rest rooms marked for inmates, and others marked for visitors, and lines that ran across the floor to prevent the inmates from approaching the doors or the vending machines. If an inmate wanted something from a vending machine, it had to be bought and brought to the table by a visitor.

When Hakim showed up, we quickly dispensed with all the pleasantries and his questioning the sanity of two people who decided to spend their Christmas making a surprise visit to a prison. After talking about life in general and his hopes and dreams, Hakim opened up about how he ended up in Eastern, recounting the fall day when he shot a man in cold blood during the hold-up.

"My brother and I needed, or I should say, wanted the money," Hakim explained. "I was holding my gun on the person behind the register when I heard gunshots coming from the back of the store, where my brother was. I just flinched and fired and hit him. I still can't get the faces out of my head."

Police detectives showed up that afternoon to question Hakim and his brother, saying that they just wanted their help in trying to solve the killing.

"That's when I put on my other side, my Bronx Science side," Hakim said, referring to the New York City public academy that is considered one of the top magnet schools in the country.

In the police cruiser, officers placed handcuffs on Hakim and took him to a jail in the Bronx, where he was thrown into a cell with other inmates. It was the last time, Hakim said, that he would see his brother, who had been arrested several hours after him. After spending most of the day in the prison, Zuza and I left, taking a Polaroid picture of the three of us before leaving to return to the city.

"Is something wrong?" Zuza asked, as I stared blankly into the snow covered trees after pulling into a gas station in Napanoch.

"I don't really know," I said.

After Christmas, I was supposed to return to Washington and write about developments in the sniper cases and find out more about Malvo and the recovery of the victims of the shootings. That, however, did not happen. I was tired from traveling back and forth from New York to Washington, the attempts to balance my new relationship with my job, and the trips with Zuza, which in December included our visit to Eastern, a trip to a home in Morris, New York, where she spent weekends as a child, and a journey to New Orleans, where we both spent a day teaching in an inner-city school system where one of her friends was a teacher. In addition to being tired, something in my mind had snapped out of place after the visit to Hakim. I could not stop thinking about the relatives I had in prison, the great mind lost by Hakim's incarceration, and unanswered questions about what drove two black seventeen-year-olds, Hakim and Malvo, to become killers.

I was supposed to return to Washington right after Christmas, but I didn't. I missed the first train I had scheduled to take because I was busy researching Malvo's background. I missed the second train I booked because I was researching the juvenile death penalty. I had come across a man named Roger Groot, a professor at Washington and Lee University in Lexington, Virginia. I wanted to interview him about related legal matters. I booked a train to go down there, but missed it too as I researched Malvo's confession. My personal life interests and my professional life were melding together, and I had reached the point of obsession.

I had promised to deliver a story on Professor Groot so it could run the day after New Year's, but missing the train made it impossible to get the dateline. Instead, I stayed in my apartment, conducted a long interview with him over the telephone and used descriptions from the professor and Washington and Lee's website to cobble together details about the scenes of the campus. It was not a far stretch from the sanctioned deceptions—toe-touch datelines and so on—that were rampant. I just was not going to go at all, but I was determined to get all the details correct. Though I did not witness things in person, at first the dateline on the top of the stories was the only falsehood. It was almost as if I wanted the stories to simply get out of the way, so I could get to the bottom of the issues I had begun to obsess about.

I began swatting stories down like they were flies that were distracting me, trying to knock them out of my way so the things my mind found more important, the things that I was fixated on, could take top priority.

It was not until December 31 that it sunk in how bizarre my existence had become. I had not left the apartment in three days. I had all I needed in the ample supply of coffee that was helping me stay up. I only spent several hours each night sleeping. I was supposed to be in Lexington, Virginia, but I had isolated myself entirely. Even Zuza and her roommates believed that I was on the road. I even missed out on New Year's Eve celebrations, when I theoretically could have been back, because I was cooped up in my apartment. I was beginning, once again, though this time without drugs, to have a secret life of my own, one that involved being locked up in a Brooklyn apartment, an obsessive and isolated world I was keeping secret from Zuza.

My mind was again racing, wild thoughts speeding through, and for the first time came the sounds, the noises, that would wake me up at night only to disappear soon after. My heart would pound almost as fast as my mind, fear of what might happen outside, away from my computer, consuming me each time I reached for the door knob. In late December and early January I did not make it out of my apartment, save a trip to a restaurant around the corner on Second Street and a nearby grocery store. By the second week of January, I made it out to Zuza's apartment several times, and several days later I dared to venture to the newsroom, but only late at night, under the cover of darkness, when no one could see me.

There were few voices I could stand hearing other than Zuza's and the subjects of my stories. My isolation increased as I stopped taking calls from friends and members of my family. When I was caught, I would only spend mere seconds on the telephone with them. My singular focus was getting to the bottom of Malvo's involvement in the sniper shootings. One of those few voices I could bear listening to was that of my friend and *Times* stringer Daryl Khan.

Daryl did not know it at the time, but part of the reason I asked him to join me on a trip to Virginia to cover preliminary hearings in the Malvo case was because I feared traveling alone. What I did not tell him was that the main reason that I was asking him to come help me write about the shootings was I felt paralyzed in the outside world without someone close beside me. I had tried a few times to get Zuza to come down to Washington with me, not telling her the reasons either, but her work schedule kept conflicting with my planned visits. When I did not have someone to accompany me or was too obsessive or manic, I simply did not go.

Instead I used my cell phone, laptop, television and other means to create the impression that I was there, to re-create scenes, to cobble together stories.

My concern for Malvo was evident in the January 19, 2003, story I wrote about him.

Who speaks for Lee Malvo now?

Not his father, Leslie Malvo. He has been absent from his son's life since the boy was 11.

Not his mother, Una James. Investigators say she abandoned him two years ago, handing him over to John Muhammad as collateral until she could pay for forged immigration papers, and last month she was deported to Jamaica.

Certainly not Mr. Muhammad. He is in prison, facing murder charges and possible execution. Prosecutors say that Mr. Muhammad and Mr. Malvo, pseudo-father and pseudo-son, roamed the country together for months in a homicidal rampage that left 10 dead.

"You want to speak for him," Zuza said, with pride and concern in her voice.

We began talking about the possibility of me writing a book about Lee Malvo, tracing his family history and examining how it contributed to his most recent violent actions.

By the time I came back from the hearings, where prosecutors presented evidence and Malvo was ordered to be tried as an adult, it was clear to anyone with any proximity that I was unraveling. Alexandra thought it was because of Zuza's unwillingness to commit earnestly to a relationship. Daryl kept his concerns to himself. Zuza thought it was the Malvo case, and after I returned from the hearings begged me to get off the story and cover something different. I tried to get help from an assistant sports editor in a roundabout way, but was told that it would be better for my career to stay on the national desk and continue reporting on the sniper shootings. I concocted a lie about a dying relative to try to convince Jim Roberts to let me off the story, but was rebuffed in that endeavor. I was a star now who could not even beg his way off a story. My mother, Fran, brought it up in the context of believing that I was working too hard.

"Why don't you just leave *The Times*?" she asked, after I explained that I was simply tired.

"Where else would I go?" I asked.

My hope was that I could pull myself back together.

My hope was that the much-needed vacation Zuza and I had planned would relieve some of my tension. My hope was that I would be able to recapture my focus and my thoughts. My hope was that my mind would return to me intact, instead of broken up into these million different little racing pieces.

CHAPTER TWENTY-EIGHT
AT WAR

As America was preparing for war, I was arriving in Castries, St. Lucia, on an American Airlines jet that had taken off from San Juan, Puerto Rico.

I had left New York with Zuza early that morning for a three-week vacation that we had planned to spend in St. Lucia and Spain, and perhaps the French colonial island of Martinique, where she studied during her junior year in college. Ice covered the ground in New York, but St. Lucia, which is located between St. Vincent and Martinique, was nothing but sunny.

Beauty is truly in the eyes of those who are looking at an object. Where others saw beautiful rows of bananas and cheap markets, it was easy for me to see hundreds of years of forced labor through slavery and people who were barely eking out an existence. Taking me on a vacation can be a bit of a danger, but Zuza was more than up for the challenge. She was an explorer at heart and had little interest in tourist traps and much more interest in real people.

Our first day was spent driving around the slums of Castries and then off to the banana fields, followed by an exploration of the ragged and elevated coastline where enormous waves crashed against the shore. As we drove past giant beer stands on the side of the road, the St. Lucian equivalent of McDonald's, I thought about how Malvo's mother, Una James, sold alcohol on the side of the street to make ends meet when she was living on the island of Antigua.

As we made our way across the country and down the western coastline of St. Lucia, we stopped and explored small towns, debating whether we should stay there. We kept on traveling until we arrived in Vieux Fort in the darkness of the night. I was the thinker, constantly analyzing, making observations, deducing things from what we had seen, while Zuza was the explorer, reaching out to locals and learning new things. That night, she fell asleep in the car during the most treacherous part of our journey, along the crumbling roads east of Vieux Fort around the western, mountainous edge of the country where the highway had literally been ripped to pieces. More than once we slid to the edge of embankments so narrow that only one full tire was on solid ground.

Near a town called Choiseul, I received a telephone call on my cell phone from an editor on the National copy desk who had called to ask several questions about a story I had written that was running on the front page about the victims of the sniper shootings. It was a toe-touch story, as opposed to a no-touch story, because I traveled to Washington to write the story and the paper was running an old date on the dateline. I had done most of the writing, though, late at night in the *Times* newsroom on West Forty-third Street and at other times in my apartment on Seventh Avenue in Brooklyn.

My moods and nightmares had hardly changed. It was good to have Zuza with me. It was good to be traveling. When I was not slamming a story into the paper or talking with her, my thoughts would fill with dark images as they did along the trip from Choiseul to the west coast city of Soufriere. I woke Zuza to tell her that I was tired and that I intended to stop at the next available hotel. What was really happening was that images of brutal beatings during slave times, planes crashing, and bloody accidents were flashing through my head for no apparent reason. Along the road I saw a familiar blue sign for a Hilton and headed straight for it, knowing it would be an affordable and comfortable option. I needed to be at a hotel so Zuza would be awake, and we could talk, and the images would go away.

We climbed a sharply sloped hill up a mountain to get to a gate where I told the sentries that we were weary travelers looking for a place to rest our heads for the evening. The guard made a quick telephone call, raised the gate and then gave us directions to the front desk. As I pulled up and parked the car, I knew something was different when a man approached the car, opened the door and handed me a large glass with a pink drink that he declared included some of St. Lucia's finest rum.

I handed it to Zuza, who looked at me bewildered, and then told the man that I would pass on alcohol. Soon we were being driven up another sharp hill to the $600-a-night bungalow that we had just unwittingly accepted. We took pictures of the flower petals attached to the toilet paper and sprinkled all over the bed, and laughed ourselves silly about how the two of us somehow ended up at the Jalousie Hilton Resort and Spa between the twin Piton Mountains, just south of Soufriere.

St. Lucia was an English colonial island with French names, in part, because of the battles between the two nations attempting to control its slave occupants, its fields of sugar cane and banana plantations. This particular location had been the subject of an island-wide controversy in 1991 when the luxury hotel was built on the site of the Jalousie Plantation, which symbolized both the intensive tourism development on the island and its checkered history.

Derek Walcott, the St. Lucian born Nobel Prize laureate, condemned the hotel as the equivalent of "opening a take-away concession in Stonehenge." The plantation was the home to thousands over the years when it was owned by French and British farmers, but construction went on with such strong support from the financially strapped government that opponents could not even stop tennis courts from being built atop an Amerindian burial site. The place had poltergeist potential, both from the Indians buried there and the slaves who had toiled in the fields.

On one of our late night strolls on the private beach that curved into the side of one of the Pitons, Zuza stopped to introduce herself to a worker who was driving one of the vans that shuttled people from the bungalows to different parts of the resort. Within minutes we had a deal for the man to give us a tour of parts of the island. We had already been to the run-down town of Soufriere, where we ate in a restaurant as children begged us for food through the window and a man named Kingsley climbed a coconut tree and then asked for $10 for the privilege of letting us take a picture of him.

The next day our driver, whose name was Glenn, took us into Castries, where we ate coconuts chopped open on the side of the road and where a woman in the market who sold me a dress for Zuza fought with us jovially over our marital status, as we strenuously insisted that we were brother and sister. The days may have been filled with colorful moments, but my nights and daydreams were less charming as the images I was hiding under my ear-to-ear smile grew increasingly disturbing. Even with Zuza beside me, I could barely sleep.

Sitting in a café in northwestern St. Lucia, sipping on espressos, my drug of choice, Zuza and I decided to get in a boat and travel to Martinique. Since the normal boat service between the two islands had gone out of business, we begged German and English visitors who docked in Rodney Bay to give us a ride to the island. Our attempts were unsuccessful, so we spent the night in a seedy hotel until we were able to find a flight out of St. Lucia that was landing in Fort-de-France, the capital of Martinique.

I could tell things were different the moment we landed at the slick new airport in Fort-de-France, along the western coast of Martinique. Instead of the ready-for-a-bribe-looking St. Lucian immigration agents, the customs officials in Martinique's capital were well-dressed men who spoke in formal French accents. At the car rental location they had options, as opposed to St. Lucia. Over the next few days, the nightmares faded as we spent twenty-hour days traveling across the country, visiting its cities, ravines, lakes, deep forests, and beachfront cafés.

The sugar cane fields and banana plantations were there, but where there were beer stands in St. Lucia, there were French cafés with croissants and espresso in Martinique. The half-empty cities with beggars were substituted by teeming cities with shopping malls like those found in American suburbs. The public beaches of Martinique were cleaner and better populated, mostly with tourists who had come to the island from France, and better kept than the private ones in St. Lucia. We searched almost desperately for signs of poverty. It was almost as hard to find people from Martinique who did not look down on their St. Lucian neighbors as it was to find a person who had been to the island only several miles to the south. Black Martiniquians, who made up more than ninety percent of the population generally considered themselves French. Zuza wondered whether those in France considered them French.

"Do you think St. Lucia would look like this if it had remained a colony of Great Britain?" I asked Zuza as we drove on a nicely paved highway. "I mean, St. Lucians would die to have just one road like this, and they are everywhere in Martinique. The cafés, the university, the houses, everything is as nice as it is in France. It really puts the benefits and the costs of independence in a whole new light."

Despite their freedom from colonial overseers, many of the people we had talked to about independence in St. Lucia did not couch matters in terms we had expected. Some talked of St. Lucians being tricked into fighting for independence by local political leaders who were interested in little more than the trappings of power and control that would come for them by separating from Great Britain. Others talked about how the only countries in the Caribbean that were doing well were Puerto Rico, a territory of the United States, and the countries that remained territories of the European powers that once dominated these islands.

Martinique versus St. Lucia, remaining a colony versus freedom, the cafés versus beer stands, the shopping malls versus the poverty, the dependence versus self-reliance—became constant refrains in our conversations with everyone from a graduate student who taught at the University of the West Indies, a public school teacher, to a random encounter with a man in a bookstore. The two books I had brought along for the trip were Howell's oral history of the civil rights movement and a detailed history of the Caribbean. Before leaving for the islands I had met with a New York literary agent to discuss whether there was a book in the life of Lee Malvo, and from that meeting and reporting, I came to the conclusion that his life was not dissimilar to Willie Bosket, who Fox Butterfield wrote about in *All God's Children.*

After we left Martinique, we flew back to St. Lucia for a day, then to New York for a connecting flight to Spain, where Zuza was supposed to join her mother for the wedding of a family friend. The three of us spent our first day together in Spain visiting the Prado and talking in the cafés that had been found by Zuza's mother, who treated me like an adopted son. I brushed off her comments of concern about me, explaining that my pained face was merely a toothache that had been plaguing me for some time.

By the time Zuza and her mother had left for a town near Barcelona to attend the wedding, the toothache was the least of my worries. My head was again filled with rapid thoughts, moving so fast that they could only adequately be described as a low pitched ringing. My thoughts were racing, though they would slow down enough at times for a cogent idea, so I tried to focus, tooth in pain, head moving too quickly, on the task at hand. I began writing the "Concept" section of my book proposal on Malvo:

"It became hard to sleep once I noticed all the similarities.

Three months into covering the trials of John Muhammad and Lee Malvo, the man and the juvenile arrested in the Washington, D.C.-area sniper shootings, I was sitting across from the man and woman who inspired this book idea. Neither of them had anything to do with the case. One was Zuza Glowacka, a Polish-American woman from New York who had taken an interest in prisons after teaching in the state corrections system. The other was a young black man, Daniel Kelly, who had been convicted of two murders when he was only seventeen. I had accompanied Zuza to visit Daniel at a prison about two hours north of New York City.

After the meeting in the visiting room at Eastern Correctional Facility in rural Napanoch, New York, my mind drifted to how much Daniel reminded me of so many of my own family members—young, intelligent, charming black men who somehow found themselves in prison. Several weeks later, I was back in Virginia watching Lee Malvo in the courtroom, talking to detectives and lawyers who had spoken with the young man accused of twenty-one shootings.

They all said he displayed intelligence, wit, charm and gentleness that made him the last person they would have imagined—excusing the overwhelming evidence, of course—being involved in such senseless shootings. It was hard to ignore the remarkable similarities among Malvo, Daniel, and the fifteen or so relatives of my own who were incarcerated, for charges ranging from drug possession to capital murder. Zuza encouraged me to look for answers about the history of violence in my own family and that of Lee Malvo, suggesting the search would not be in vain 'if it at the least ended my restless angst.'"

I might as well have been writing my diary. Months later it would become much clearer how much I had internalized the process of covering the trials. I kept on writing, borrowing some of Fox's parallel ideas about Willie Bosket:

> On my search for answers about Lee Malvo, race reared its head again—but this time in a much less immediate and much more historical measure.
>
> The evidence suggested that Lee Malvo was a brutal killer, potentially responsible for many of the shootings. But it also became clear that he was, unfortunately, no aberration in his family. He was the latest in a long line of intelligent malefactors—victims of racism, circumstance and shattered dreams, and perpetrators of crime. I wondered whether there was a connection, whether the roots of how it had ended for all of them could be found in the unique history of American slavery.

I proposed starting the book with an anecdote from Todd Petit, the young Virginia lawyer who was appointed Malvo's legal guardian. Petit rushed to the Fairfax County police headquarters on the November afternoon Attorney General John Ashcroft ordered Malvo sent to Fairfax for his first trial. Malvo had not been appointed counsel yet, but a juvenile court judge had already asked Petit to serve as one of his lawyers and his legal guardian. Without lawyers to advise him, Fairfax County police detectives took Malvo to an office in the headquarters building and began questioning him about the shootings.

Petit immediately went over to police headquarters, where a police commander unceremoniously threw him out of the building. Thinking that the prosecutors would see the danger in questioning a juvenile before he had the chance to meet with his counsel, Petit ran over to Horan's office where he was again told to leave. In a last-ditch effort, Petit went to the night officer at the juvenile court building and was told that there was no way to reach the judge in the case—the curious part being that the judge was on the phone with prosecutors later that same evening. Malvo confessed to some of the shootings, and some of the evidence from those conversations made its way into the January hearing, where a judge ordered that he should be tried as an adult for capital murder.

The questioning, if not illegal, was certainly of questionable ethics, but there was little doubt among observers—reporters, lawyers and detectives included—that it would sail right into trial. I never heard anyone voice any doubt that they thought Malvo was involved in the shootings, but many speculated that he had confessed to ones he did not commit in order to protect Muhammad. It did not matter, though, because under Virginia law the prosecutors in the two different courtrooms where the men were being tried presented totally different, if not contradictory, theories, and there was nothing in the law to stop them.

From that moment, I wanted to take readers to Petit's first meeting with Malvo, who had turned business cards into a homemade checkerboard in the Fairfax County Adult Detention Center. They had stripped most of the amenities out of the cell and isolated Malvo so he could not communicate with the other inmates. Petit recounted how they talked about the Los Angeles Lakers, NBA basketball in general and his family, and other things that hardly seemed like the obsessions of a ruthless killer. It all raised one elusive question: How did he get this way?

I hoped to answer that question by traveling to the Caribbean and tracing his roots back to slavery in Jamaica, where a brutal form of slavery developed that could find its roots in other British colonies. The most noted enhancement upon previous versions of slavery was the addition of a component designed to break apart families, to weaken the spirits of slaves who would have little to fight for if they were isolated from their loved ones. Not only were the family values of much of the Caribbean shaped by these methods, I believed, but the brutal history of Jamaica was little more than an appropriation by the descendants of slaves of the tactics of the slave masters who lorded over their relatives with ruthless tactics and little mercy.

Tracing Lee Malvo's family history on either side could show key elements of both of these influences. Lee was born to Leslie Malvo and Una James on February 18, 1985, at Victoria Jubilee Hospital in Kingston, Jamaica. Leslie Malvo abandoned Lee and his mother for another woman while Lee was still a young child. Lee was abandoned by his mother not too long afterwards when she left him to live with relatives as she traveled to Antigua and other islands, spending her money as quickly as it was made. Mother and son reunited several years later when Una allowed Lee to move in with her in Antigua. That is where they met John Muhammad. Those who knew Lee said John treated him like the father, or perhaps like the parent he never had in Leslie or Una.

John Muhammad was a father looking for a son after his children were taken away from him in Washington State in 2000, and Lee Malvo was a son looking for a parent when he traveled there to join Muhammad. The preliminary research I had done suggested that on both sides of Lee Malvo's family tree, for generations, fathers had left their children to be raised by mothers as they moved on to other women. On both sides of Lee Malvo's family tree, there was crime and violence. My plan was to spend four to five months researching Lee Malvo's history, and deliver a manuscript some time in 2004.

I was hoping that once I returned to New York from our trip to St. Lucia, Martinique and Spain, I would have conquered whatever phobia I had of traveling to cover the story. If it was because I did not want to be outside of the presence of Zuza, for sure, three weeks in her presence, twenty-four hours a day would cure me of that problem. If it was because I was afraid of traveling alone, I would just stiffen up and find a way to do it. At the least, I had until the trials began in November before my lack of presence in Virginia would truly be noticed.

CHAPTER TWENTY-NINE
BURNING DOWN THE HOUSE

I had a term for stories that explored "different" cultures as "safari pieces," where the word "community" could easily be replaced with "jungle" or "reserve," and the people could have just as easily been giraffes or cheetahs. They were stories designed for the same demographic that lived in Manhattan, below Ninety-sixth Street, and they could be written from anywhere in the world, from the jungles of southeastern Africa to the outer boroughs of New York City.

The subjects did not have to be black. They could be Asian, they could be Native American, and they could be white too, and all you needed to see for proof of that was a *Times* story written from Staten Island, the borough that might as well not have been a part of the city.

"Jayson, you just need to get ahold of yourself, and focus on what you want to get out of this," Lynette said as we stood in the stairwell of the Times Building.

I had just told her that I was trying to get off the sniper story and come back to the city.

"I want a break, about four years of my life back and ten years off," I said. "I don't know what I am doing."

"Listen, you just have to make it through this and not sabotage yourself," she continued.

Later that cold March evening I was walking with Zuza along Seventh Avenue in Brooklyn. We were on our way to an Italian restaurant near the Starbucks coffee house at Garfield Place. The restaurant had already been the site of several phantom dinners that were expensed, which told me one important thing. No one was looking at the receipts on Forty-third Street. I also knew that things were so chaotic among the line people who handled finances and expenses in the newsroom that I could have bought my tickets to Spain on the company dime and no one would have noticed, let alone said anything if they did. Planning for coverage of the war in Iraq—buying biochemical moon suits and other equipment for reporters—was only taking more attention from the routine.

I had spent the weekend looking at clips from Africa, pondering the idea of whether I had any interest in working overseas as a foreign correspondent. Zuza and I had been throwing around the idea of going to Africa, where she could do humanitarian work and I could write about more salient issues than Fashion Week. All the painful lessons, though, that I had learned as a cub reporter, the ones about all lives not being equal proved themselves true in my cursory examination of the *Times*'s clips from Africa.

It was not that the correspondents did not hustle, and it was not that they did not know what the most important stories were; it was simply that the pieces landed on the back pages of the main section. It was simply that life or death on that continent was not a major news story. The one thing that was clear was that it took a lot of dead Africans for anyone to notice on West Forty-third Street.

What was the point in going to cover something that I cared about, something that might be inspiring, if it had no chance of doing any good because it was going to find itself on a page where it would be easy for Americans to ignore, where no one was going to read it?

I continued looking into this idea to give Zuza a chance to do some of the things she wanted to do out of a hope that it would provide me some inspiration. After all, she was a smart liberal arts college graduate wasting her time sitting behind a cubicle carrying photographs to editors and answering phone calls. She was going to spend the month working on the foreign desk, though, which would give us both a little more insight on how decisions about the importance of stories were made.

I asked her to keep her ears tuned in and her eyes open. Mine were always. As enamored as I was with Zuza and the prospect of spending some large portion of my life with her, I was having a hard time finding pleasure in anything. I, like most people, attempt to put my angst in one easy to recognize, simple to understand box, the words I could pull up to explain what was troubling me. There was no simple explanation, no simple reason. I was unfulfilled, and I was, again, hurting.

The physical pain that had manifested itself in the form of toothaches was back, and I was increasingly struggling with my head spinning. One dizzy night, after more than forty-eight hours with no sleep, I woke up on the cold, wet floor of my bathroom. I had no idea how I had gotten there. All I remembered was falling asleep while typing on the couch and watching something on television. The incident caught my attention, but I thought very little of it other than to go see a doctor if it happened again.

Several days later, I had picked up two bouquets of flowers, some light bulbs and chocolate for Zuza and her roommates. I knew Toni was in the throes of writing the end of her more than 100-page thesis, and Alexandra and Zuza were always game for chocolate and roses. As I reached for the door to open their apartment, I felt a sharp twinge in my chest that spread straight to my head. Upstairs, in the kitchen of the apartment, I nearly fainted as I was cutting flowers, and Alexandra began asking what was wrong. It seemed I lost consciousness for a brief moment.

The two of them demanded I go to an emergency room, and they came along for the four-hour wait at Methodist Hospital in Park Slope, where doctors and nurses ran a battery of tests, including an electrocardiogram. The tests came out inconclusive, but I was referred to a specialist. After x-rays and other tests, the specialists decided that they wanted to do a biopsy of something odd that they noticed on a lung.

I had tried to quit smoking recently, but threw that idea out the window because of the nervousness it caused and was back to over a pack a day by the time the doctors got to me. I was nervous about a lot of things during these days, including my mortality. I took that time, waiting for results from the tests, to reflect on my life over the last few years.

I had given up drugs and alcohol, and moved on to a better way of living. One of the fruits of this better way of living had been meeting Zuza. I knew that if I had still been using drugs or drinking, even though I might have made plans with her, I would have never followed through, at least not past the first meeting. I enjoyed meeting with Maria at Emmett's around lunchtime, but was none too thrilled to find myself hanging out there, sipping on cranberry seltzers and knocking back shots of espresso, late in the evenings. It was one step in the wrong direction.

I had always been able to disassociate a bit from my surroundings. It is a beautiful defense mechanism for those who have been sexually assaulted or otherwise traumatized. It allowed me, the real me, to go off into the corner and not emotionally feel a given moment, whether I was being praised, having sex, being yelled at, or being granted something I did not want. It was almost like a switch that I could flip on and off, but as of late I had little control of the thing.

I was clearly in love, and cautious emotional detachment had been tossed to the wind. As a drunk or a drug addict, being in a relationship always took second fiddle to the substance, something that could regulate the ups and downs of life and eliminate the natural emotions.

My heart felt unguarded and Zuza, as well-meaning as she might have been, was not one who could be considered the most gentle on the heart. She was always moving too fast, on to the next thing. There was never a moment to slow down and define things, to gain the comfort I was seeking.

I had neither mental clarity nor emotional stability. I had been warned that in the first few years of recovery from a drug or alcohol problem not to make any major changes in my life because of the emotional frailty that comes with trying to focus on not relapsing and coping with life without the substances that had been my sword and my shield.

But I could hardly use that to explain to my bosses why they should not send me to the sniper shootings. I could hardly say to Zuza, yes, I am in love with you, but it is probably a bad idea to become friends with you now because I need to not make any big changes in my first few years of sobriety. I liked change anyway. Change is what kept me safe, kept me feeling as if I was moving forward, as if I was living. Restlessness was my psychological enemy.

What I did not know, though, was what poor shape I was really in. I could talk my way through the best therapy session sounding removed and detached from my previous emotional outpourings. I could sit in a conversation and give a friend solid advice on living, without hinting in any respect that I was ailing. There were, perhaps, only a handful of people to whom I was truly willing to open myself up—my friend Liz; and a young cub reporter at *The Times,* who had seen his share of tough times, named Jacob Fries—to them, I could share that I was in great pain, or at least hint at it. I was used to having the answers, so even in those conversations I was reluctant to hint at some psychological ailment that I had not yet solved.

Jacob was leaving *The Times* after coming to the paper more than a year before. He had been jerked around, and those of us who had been watching from afar knew that the ending to his movie was not going to be too easy. It started when Jacob, as an intern, stood on principle and refused to file a story that he felt was bogus. It got worse when he fought an editor as she tried to turn a story he was writing about people demonstrating at the World Economic Forum into a *New York Times* readers' safari.

Jacob also had timing working against him. He arrived at the paper as an intern only several months before the September 11 attacks, significantly reducing the likelihood that he would land on the front page or the front of The Metro Section, as would be required for him to get promoted. At *The Times,* there are those who fill the paper, and those who come swinging in only on the big stories. The heavy hitters were coming in from all corners, reducing the chances of all the Jacobs of the paper.

"You're doing a good job, just keep your head together," Jacob said to me in the stairwell where we smoked in the Times Building. "While everyone in the world is focused on your success, you just need to focus on your recovery."

Jacob made the comments only a few weeks before leaving *The Times* in August 2002. I wish I had taken his advice. What I could not know, of course, was that I was dealing with something more complicated while learning the skills necessary to live life, to cope, without drugs and alcohol. I did not know at the time that drugs and alcohol were not only my tools to cope, but that they were medicating a mental illness that comes in waves, and that I had just been going through a dormant period.

The waking up on the bathroom floor, the blackouts, the boundless energy, the restlessness, the angst, the dizziness, the images in my head, the sounds, all should have been signs. I thought I was just under a lot of stress.

In early March, soon after arriving back from Spain, I received a call on my cell phone.

"Where are you?" asked the voice coming through my cell phone.

It was Jim Roberts, the national editor, on the other line, and this time, I answered truthfully. I was in New York, which was convenient, because he wanted me to come in for a meeting.

"Jayson, I was wondering what plans you have for the future," Jim asked in the meeting in his office only a few doors down from Jon Landman.

"I don't know," I said, giving up on an attempt to get out of the current situation. "I don't mind staying just where I am, in between sections, waiting. It buys me some time to figure out what I want to do."

By buying some time, I meant that it gave me a chance for an exit strategy. I was increasingly daydreaming about not doing journalism, but had yet to start daydreaming about what else it was I would be doing. It was as if, in moments, an enormous fatigue had overtaken me and in others not so long afterwards, a startling madness. Jim would later describe me as a bit detached in the meeting, disconnected from the conversation, as if it were not happening.

I guess I was supposed to get up and jump for joy at the chance that Jim had offered me in the meeting to cover more of the region, but nothing these days was making me happy. There was something about the process of hunting and seeking, searching and finding answers, and writing them that I loved, but after four years at *The Times,* it was eating me.

One might contend that I simply did not have what it took to do the job, and here is where the contrasting explanations come into play. When I was on top of my game, when the right levels of chemicals were pushing through my brain at the right hypomanic pace, I was on. When things were moving too fast, or the world felt too depressing, I was a mess of a grand extreme.

Work had become a secondary priority to pulling myself together. I had not been eating or sleeping much, and felt like my moods were on a yo-yo string, rapidly pulling up and down, literally going within minutes from laughing to crying, to laughing to crying. It was an emotional rollercoaster that had emerged for no apparent reason, and I was loath to travel far from the confines of my apartment. I wished someone like the nun from the movie *Airplane* would walk in and slap me and tell me to get ahold of myself. I had this feeling, though, that that was not going to work either.

I should have been thrilled with the chance that Jim was giving me to cover the Middle Atlantic region, and I went through all the motions, telling myself and anyone else who would listen that I was, hoping that if I said it enough times I would begin to believe, and if I began to believe it would then come true. But true excitement never did come, and the strange happenings at home were worsening.

Sometimes, I wondered, whether psychological suffering was not linked to artistic creativity.

Just before leaving for Martinique, I moved into a new apartment on President Street in Park Slope. The apartment made up an entire floor of a brownstone and it was found in just one day as Zuza and I went shopping. We had no intention of living together, but she forcefully believed that one of the things ailing me was that I had no home, no center of gravity. I had lived for a long time on the Upper West Side and in the brownstone in Clinton Hill, but she was right in the sense that I hardly ever planted my roots. I was always preparing for the next big thing. This was finally supposed to be a home.

The nights were still cold from the lingering winter, and my most vivid memories of that apartment are staying up shivering on my couch, watching late night television and popping Advil after Advil to take the pain away from the toothache that was still ailing me. After our trip overseas, Zuza was spending more time hanging out at places like our Greenwich Village nightspot, the Groove, and I had taken to more isolating.

I had an apartment I liked, but few close friends left to share it with. I had a job I would have killed for years before, but hardly wanted. I had a woman in my life who fulfilled my dreams of what a partner should be, but one who was unwilling to take our relationship where I wanted it to go. Nothing seemed to make me happy, and my mind simply could not translate what was going on as mental illness, as some type of a disease.

One morning, I woke up unable to get out of bed. My tooth was hurting, in wrenching pain, and my back was aching. I had not felt this poorly since the days that I did coke, and instead of getting up, I just lay there. It was winter. There were no birds chirping. I reached from my bed to the windowsill that overlooked President Street, and grabbed a copy of *Lenin's Tomb,* a powerful book about the fall of the Soviet Union.

The next thing I remember was waking up to darkness. It was late in the evening, and I had missed nine calls on my cell phone, including one from the dreaded "111-111-1111," the number that appears when someone is calling from *The Times* office on Forty-third Street. Luckily it was just Zuza, checking in on me.

I got up out of bed and walked toward the doorway. I felt a little dizzy. I reached for something to get my footing, and there was nothing. My head banged against the doorway. I retreated back to my bedroom. Several nights later, I woke up in the middle of the night with my mind racing, and virtually repeated the same scene, except that this time I again walked right into the double doors between the living room and the library.

I knocked over a copy of *Did I Ever Tell You How Lucky You Are?,* the Dr. Seuss book that Zuza and Alexandra had given me after moving into the apartment, and the get-well card they gave me after getting out of the hospital.

After getting up, I made my way to the kitchen, where I had set up my company laptop next to an ashtray. I had tried to quit smoking, but felt it had been driving me crazy, but found that two packs a day were not doing the job of calming me or bringing me into focus. I had not seen Zuza in days. She had either been working or I was supposed to be traveling. I had not left the six rooms of my apartment.

I did not have to look at my watch to know. The darkness told me that I had missed the train to Richmond that I was supposed to be on earlier that afternoon.

The war in Iraq had begun, and the assignment, which I had come up with on my own, was to write about the workers behind the scenes at the place where American soldiers' bodies were being taken. The logic was that this was the one place in America where the killing in Iraq could not be ignored, where the death and destruction did not look like some video game on TV.

I had promised to turn the story in on Monday, and had made some telephone calls to prepare myself. It was the first story that was not about the sniper shootings where I found myself choosing to use my no-touch dateline deception. I had done much of the reporting for the story already, contacting the military command for the Atlantic Fleet to get in touch with the people who notified families that their loved ones had been killed in action.

I had talked with a spokeswoman for the Navy who was based in Norfolk, and she had given me the details of how these death notifications were performed and the services that were provided afterwards, including help with death benefits and counseling. My notebook was full of enough details that it would only take a quick phone call or two to complete the story even though I had missed the train.

I slapped a dateline on top of it and sent it in. Then I began working on my second story of the day. I wrote a piece—without a dateline—about the sniper shootings which focused on written motions that had been filed in court in Virginia in the Malvo case. In the motion, the prosecutor was charging that Malvo was responsible for the October deaths of the woman he was charged with shooting, Linda Franklin, and of Dean Harold Myers, the man who John Muhammad had been charged with killing. It was looking increasingly likely that the two prosecutors would argue Malvo and Muhammad both killed the same man.

A few minutes later, my cell phone was ringing. It was a national assignment editor.

"Where are you?" the editor asked.

"Norfolk," I said, lying, sitting and shivering, in the kitchen of my apartment with a blanket around me.

"Can you get to Gaithersburg, Maryland before midnight?" he asked. "We want to run the Moose story."

The Moose story was my profile of chief of police Charles Moose, who had helped capture the snipers. I had written most of the story in my Brooklyn apartment, and now the editor was asking me to drive from Norfolk to Gaithersburg, Maryland, a two-hundred-and-thirty-mile drive and an unreasonable request, even if I had not been sitting in my apartment in Brooklyn.

"Sure," I said. "I will call you when I get there."

I never got there, because I never left. I just called the desk a little bit before deadline and told a copy editor that they could slap a Gaithersburg dateline onto the interview with Moose. I was able to interview him because of Liz's friend, David Vigliano, who was Moose's literary agent. The chief was upset with the way *The Washington Post* had been treating him. It was one of those classic media messes.

The Post had been working on a book about the sniper shootings and had approached Moose to see if he would cooperate with their endeavor. When the chief said no, *The Post* started writing stories raising questions about whether it was ethical for Moose to profit from the sniper shootings.

Since it was the *Post*'s daily business as a newspaper to profit off of the misery of others, they did not really stop to think about what it looked like to launch their own book project about the shootings on one hand, and then criticize Moose on the other for doing the same thing.

So Moose had arranged to talk with me about the aftermath of his life since the shootings. The story was supposed to sit in the queues for a couple of days, so I knew I would have time to swing through Maryland and pick up the toe-touch dateline, but the Montgomery County Ethics Commission came back with an unexpectedly early ruling that barred Moose from profiting from his book and movie deals about the shootings.

In the telephone interview, before the ethics commission decision, Moose said that he would consider leaving his job as police chief if they came down with a ruling that was not favorable.

"I don't know why I am under attack," Moose told me. "I feel that my job here is not finished, but the thought has crossed my mind, 'What if you do really have to leave? Do you have to walk away from being the police chief in Montgomery County?' The desire is to do both, to find a balance."

The only lie in the story was that Moose was speaking "in an interview here in an apartment he shares with his wife, Sandy." Half of the interview was conducted in his apartment in Gaithersburg. He was there. I was on a phone line hundreds of miles away.

The story had been filed days before, and the assignment editor was just asking me to drive through the town to do the toe-touch dateline. I was more than willing to say, "yes," since I had no plans to go anywhere.

By that weekend, I had decided that I was in no shape to go anywhere. I had awakened one morning late in the week to the sound of banging on my door. I opened the door to the sound of my landlord yelling and screaming my name. I turned around, and the bathtub was running, and I turned back and his wife was coming up the stairs with towels in her hands.

We worked hard to clean up the mess. I could not even estimate how long the bathtub had been running, and I tried to jog my memory to get some sense of when I turned it on, but I could not remember that either. I explained to my landlord that I had been a bit stressed out lately and that I had been waiting for some medical tests that had left me a little out of sorts.

"What is it for, a brain tumor?" he asked.

I was supposed to be in Maryland. Well, that was if I had any intention of going anywhere. Instead, I was coming up with a way to do virtually all my reporting from my apartment, with occasional after-midnight stops to the newsroom to drop off or pick up something. This time, I was supposed to have already been to Baltimore, and then I was supposed to rent a car and head off to Hunt Valley, Maryland.

Jim had asked me to find an average American family with a son or daughter in Iraq, sitting at home, watching, waiting, wondering what was going on with their loved one. I found the Gardner family through a database search of recent news clippings from my desk over the weekend in the sleepy sports section, where I had written most of the story and then e-mailed it to myself so I could access it at home from my laptop computer. I did not even bother trying to go to Baltimore on this one, and reported out most of the story over the weekend in conversations with Martha Gardner, whose son, Corporal Michael P. Gardner II, was stationed in the Iraqi desert.

I was at the apex of some strange mind-racing high when I wrote the lead.

HUNT VALLEY, Md., March 24—Martha Gardner finds herself lost in thoughts these days, her mind wandering as she stands out on the back deck of her home here. She has been misplacing things, like her earrings and the book reports she must grade.

She finds herself jolted out of the numbness at moments, realizing that she has been staring blankly at a framed photograph of her eldest son, Cpl. Michael P. Gardner II, a Marine scout in southern Iraq. During breaks at the school where she teaches, she rushes out of her classroom to catch a glimpse of the 24-hour news coverage—a blessing and a paralyzing curse, she says—hoping for signs of a quick end to the war, but dreading an image of her 33-year-old son dead or wounded.

Ms. Gardner says she is trying to be strong for her husband and three other children. When she needs to get away from the calls, the e-mail messages, the Web sites and television images of war, Ms. Gardner tends to the red, white and blue pansies potted on the front porch of her home here in this rural suburb north of Baltimore. But sometimes, the worries, the knots in her stomach, the telephone calls from friends and other mothers and television images provoke tears she cannot stop.

The story was, indeed, a fabrication, but it was so in the sense that I had not actually traveled to Hunt Valley, Maryland. I had cobbled together all of the details from my telephone conversations with Martha Gardner, and double-checked the descriptions with the photos that were filed by the photographer who had actually visited the house.

Martha Gardner appealed to me in more ways than one. There was a Godly air about her, despite her motherly worry; a notion that it was all in God's hands and that He had a purpose for everything. It reminded me of a peace that I had once known during childhood, even if just briefly. I carefully went through the database of photographs that I had access to.

Reporters would often use images to reconstruct scenes. Usually they would ask an editor on the photo desk to either e-mail them or have someone like Zuza bring them the pictures. The difference for me was two-fold. One was the matter of honesty. Typically, when a reporter had not been to a scene they would not run a dateline atop the story, or one would run identifying their real location and laying out how the scenes were re-created. It is often done in stories that retell a major event—that the reporter did not witness—in dramatic detail months or years after the event.

It was not an acceptable method of reporting on a feature story. The editor, since the time was there to do it, would say to go to the location and do it. That was not going to be an issue, since I was not going anywhere. I used the recreation techniques to retell the scenes, and the pictures to note things like the red-white-and-blue pansies.

I received kudos from several senior editors, who probably want to remain nameless, for the writing of that story. In retrospect, it makes me wonder about something Edgar Allan Poe once wrote.

"Men have called me mad," Poe wrote, "but the question is not yet settled, whether madness is or is not the loftiest intelligence—whether much that is glorious—whether all that is profound—does not spring from disease of thought—from moods of mind exalted at the expense of general intellect."

I cannot speak for the broader population, people at large or even generalize about a group of people. I can answer the question for me, and it is simply that at this fully psychotic stage, I was performing some of my best, although most fraudulent, writing.

The best psychiatrists do not like to use the word psychotic to describe the moods of their patients at a general moment. The best ones ask questions like: What do you mean, psychotic? Was the patient delusional? Seeing hallucinations? Grandiose? What?

Most broadly, psychosis refers to a loss of contact with reality. When we use the word manic loosely, we generally refer to someone talking fast, jumping from idea to idea, full of boundless energy. Psychosis is the line where a manic becomes a maniac, the point where you cannot tell the difference between what is real and what is not.

I was frightened, confused, and distressed by my actions, by the places I was waking up, wondering whether I was dreaming or standing wide awake when I saw the fiery red Georgia O'Keeffe painting, which I do not own, hanging in my library. Researchers say that a person's first psychotic episode will appear in their late teens or early twenties -- that is if they are among the lucky, or not so lucky, three percent of the population to go through such an experience.

I had begun to smell, hear and see things that did not actually exist, but most profound were my sharp bursts of emotion, my rapidly cycling feelings that seemed impossible to express. I could not complete everyday tasks like taking a bath, without a crisis arising. And the thoughts of death, the thoughts of ending the noise, the thoughts of ending the pain were everywhere, virtually consuming me.

In the most hyper moments, my ideas and energy seemed boundless, until I reached the point of irritation and psychosis, which signaled the start anew of another cycle of powerful melancholy. In those moments of sadness, though counterintuitive it may seem, my hesitations and reservations allowed me to sculpt my words, helping me to harness those manic ideas.

It would have been perfect, had the powerful, rapid swings not been the closest I felt to the ferry ride in Dante's *Inferno*, with its "endless night, fierce fires and sharmming cold"; with its delusions, its grandiosity, the hallucinations and horrid images and thoughts, all seemingly conspiring, for me, and against me, intertwined, at the same time.

CHAPTER THIRTY
GOING DOWN IN THE FIRE

"**Z**uza, what are *you talking about?!*" I yelled. "You are wrong, just dead wrong!"

It was a Friday evening, and Alexandra had met Zuza and me in SoHo. She had gotten back from an appointment for a tooth extraction at the New York University College of Dentistry, where she was having work done on her teeth for a relatively low price. We had eaten at Penang, a restaurant in SoHo, and then walked across the Manhattan Bridge together.

I had reached a whole new level of irritability and it was now coming out into the open. I had bought flowers for Zuza and Alexandra, and when a man complimented them, I offered to come across the street and shove my foot and one of the roses up his rear end. I yelled at a man begging for change as he rolled toward us in his wheelchair. I was curt on the telephone when my mother called as we were reaching Atlantic Avenue.

"Jesus, Jayson, what the hell is wrong with you?" Zuza shot back. "You usually agree with me on this point."

She had just critiqued my last few stories for *The Times,* pointing out her objection to how much emphasis the paper was putting on every dead or missing American soldier without giving equal play to the thousands of Iraqis who were dying in the war.

"All I am saying is that it is the same story about the missing, the grieving, over and over again," she continued. "We put stories about people whose sons are not even dead yet on the front page, and we are putting stories about dead Iraqis in the back of the paper if we are putting them in the paper at all."

She had a point. We were standing on Flatbush Avenue, near its intersection with Seventh Avenue, in front of a store with a giant sign that read "Big Daddy's," when we agreed to disagree. It's not that she was not right.

I was just in no mood to hear any criticism of my work. I guess it was a sensitive issue at this point in time.

She was not off about the paper's coverage and overemphasis of the losses on the home front, but I had at least thought I had come up with some creative story-telling ideas. One involved teaming up with a reporter in Iraq, who provided me with the name of the wife of a young soldier. The reporter wrote about the young soldier and I wrote about his newlywed wife.

As much as I remained against the war in Iraq because I saw no solid reason to invade at the time, my sympathy for the soldiers, who were not given much of a choice in the matter, had grown over the past few months. Talking to families of the soldiers, like the Gardners and others I did speak with, helped me see the war in singular terms—the individual fear, the individual loss. It had, perhaps, even further strengthened my resolve against the war.

Whatever problems I was having, my nose for news, more precisely for what editors wanted, remained intact. That's part of the reason that I was first out of the blocks among the national news media in focusing on the Jessica Lynch saga.

It was not that Lynch had suffered any more than other captives in Iraq. It was simply that stories about her—because she fit a certain profile—would get good play in newspapers and on television stations. The fright caused by an All-American-looking woman in the hands of evil Iraqi captors who might harm her, even sexually assault her, played strongly into racial and gender stereotypes. I was beyond pretending that this was not what the media beast wanted. The beast wanted Jessica Lynch, not Shoshana Johnson, the black woman who was taken captive along with Lynch.

The story that the Pentagon built up around Lynch fit into those same stereotypes, and it was as fake as anything I had ever written.

It was the same sort of thinking that led me to Sarai Thompson, a twenty-one-year-old newlywed who was living alone with her dogs outside Camp Lejeune in North Carolina as her husband, Alan, fought in Iraq. The idea popped in my head that following a month in the life of a soldier in Iraq and then paralleling it with the life of their spouse would be an interesting endeavor.

A colleague who was reporting in Iraq came back with the suggestion of profiling Alan, a corporal and member of a Marine artillery battalion that was among the first to enter Iraq, and his wife, who was somewhere near Camp Lejeune. My colleague provided me with a telephone number and over the next few weeks, I stayed in constant contact with Alan's wife. The Thompsons seemed, like Lynch, the perfect, All-American couple.

They were both raised in West Virginia, and she had followed him to North Carolina after spending a brief amount of time in college. Soon, they were married. And soon, thereafter, he was off to fight in Iraq.

My colleague and I became conduits between the couple, separated by a war and 6,000 miles of land and ocean.

My colleague allowed Alan to use his satellite phone to call Sarai. I relayed messages back to Alan, and passed on pictures from the battlefield back to Sarai. Rich detail was accumulated and my editors knew that I was collecting most of it from New York, but planned to just fly in to get the dateline in North Carolina. There was just no flying in.

In the end, there was nothing wrong with the story other than the dateline. All the hours and hours of conversations with Sarai and Alan provided rich detail. Perhaps there was a reason I was not careless with this story. Perhaps on some subconscious level, I felt I owed it to them for all the time, all the tears, all the moments of total frustration that Sarai let me in on.

I started off writing the story to make sure my editors stayed off my back, and ending up, like it or not, writing it for Sarai—something that she and Alan could some day show their children. The story landed on the front page, along with others that had fabrications. It was the solid piece that slipped through the cracks of deception.

I was convinced after this story that I was getting better. I was asking all the right questions—even if I was not showing up on location. I knew the color of her sheets, because I asked her, and perhaps that attention to detail was a sign that I was pulling myself together. Just as I was beginning to feel that way, though, others were beginning to notice that something was off with me.

I came into the office for one of the first times in daylight in a while, and Lena Williams, the sports reporter and New York Newspaper Guild unit chairwoman, pulled me aside in the middle of a conversation with Charlotte Evans, the head of copy editors, to ask if everything was all right.

"Baby, you don't look so good," Lena said. "Are you all right?"

"I am fine," I replied. "Just tired. I need a little rest."

"You know," Charlotte started in. "You have been writing about a lot of death and sad things, you might want to consider going upstairs and seeing Pat Drew in the employee assistance program."

This was my way out. This was my chance to admit what had been going on. This was my chance to get some help. I hesitated. I did not even have to tell them. I could have just gone up to see Pat and let her know what was going on inside me, how I was feeling and what I was doing.

The closest I had come to reaching out for help was in a conversation I had in a stairwell with my reporter friend Lynette Holloway. In the stairwell in early March, I told Lynette that I wanted to get away from the sniper stories.

"I don't know why," I said. "I just want to get off this story. I just want to be home. I just want to be home, safe, around Zuza. I am tired of this."

"Wherever you go, there you are," she said, laughing.

The idea was planted in my head, but for reasons I have been unable to ascertain—perhaps that I had more time, perhaps that I was getting better—I did not go see Pat Drew. I moved on to the next story, a piece about wounded soldiers at the National Naval Medical Center in Bethesda, Maryland.

In that story, I cobbled together wire reports with a fresh interview with a corporal whose arm was in a sling to put together a front-page story on those who were wounded in battle. I also relied on White House pool reporters' notes from that day that President Bush went to the medical center to visit the wounded.

I tried to re-create scenes as I had done before, then actually considered for a moment heading to Bethesda, but thought otherwise when I found a lance corporal who was willing to talk with me from his home. He described for me his life and things that had gone on in the ward, and I did my best to re-create them without having to go to the medical center.

The story was supposed to be about those who were treated at Bethesda, so I specifically selected Lance Cpl. James Klingel, because he had been released, was back home in Ohio and would be able to speak freely without a Navy public relations person on the telephone watching over his every comment.

> Lance Cpl. James Klingel of the Marines finds himself lost in thought these days when he is not struggling with the physical pain, his mind wandering from images of his girlfriend back in Ohio to the sight of an exploding fireball to the sounds of twisting metal.

I embellished a bit with the line about the images of his girlfriend back home, although he did say he missed her and he did say that he had horrid images of exploding fireballs and twisting metal. The thoughts happened separately, but I brought them together for the lead.

Often, Corporal Klingel says, he is jolted from sleep at the National Naval Medical Center here, at times because of the aches and throbs in his right arm and right leg, and at other times because of the images of the Iraq war that the chaplains say will not likely go away soon.

More than two weeks after being seriously wounded by a rocket-pro-pelled grenade that hit his armored vehicle, Corporal Klingel says he is glad to begin walking again, but disheartened because he will most likely limp the rest of his life and need to use a cane.

In the worst moments, though, Corporal Klingel, a scout, said he questioned the legitimacy of his emotional pain as he considered the marine in the next bed, Staff Sgt. Eric Alva, a distance runner whose right leg was blown off by a land mine, or Seaman Brian Alaniz, a Navy medic down the hall who lost his right leg when a mine exploded under him as he rushed to aid Sergeant Alva.

"It's kind of hard to feel sorry for yourself when so many people were hurt worse or died," said Corporal Klingel, 21, who added that it was about time for another appointment with a chaplain.

All the details were from what Corporal Klingel told me. Corporal Klin-gel provided me more details about Staff Sergeant Alva and Corpsman Alaniz, and I cobbled together what they had said to news services, in the White House pool report on President Bush's visit and other interviews. The talk of private moments was pure speculation and complete fiction.

For people like Sergeant Alva, 32, a supply chief who says he felt a sense of responsibility for many of the younger marines under him, stepping on a mine and losing his leg has been not just a physical ordeal. When mili-tary officials had him appear on television to discuss his injuries and the war, Sergeant Alva, who promised to run again in the Marine Corps Marathon, appeared confident and sturdy.

But in more private moments last week in the hospital, Sergeant Alva acknowledged that he had anger that he directed inward and toward the news media that he said were too hard on soldiers and a public that he said that did not really understand the costs of war.

"There is no point in explaining how I feel," he said, "because no one really is going to be able to understand it."

For the 495 wounded service members, recovery will continue long after most other Americans have moved on other things, as they try to stitch back the pieces of their lives. For many, their time at Bethesda and other military medical centers is the last stop on the road home, a chance to learn how to live without an arm or a leg, to battle long-lasting pain, to cope with loss of independence and to heal emotional scars that can be as acute as physical damage.

I returned to Corporal Klingel, detailing how his unit came under fire while providing security for a convoy facing sniper fire. He told me in pained details, his voice choking up at times, about the twenty other Marines who were wounded in the fighting, and the one man he believed was killed in that firefight. He told me about how President Bush had made the rounds that week, and how it lifted his spirits.

I relied on details from the White House pool report, which only reporters can gain access to, in order to fill in the blanks of President Bush's trip. Many news events that involve the White House and are covered in great detail and with great authority in newspapers are not actually witnessed by the correspondents. They rely on pool reports from the one or two reporters who are allowed to follow the president closely. Those reporters write up a report that is shared with all the other correspondents, who are allowed to lift from it freely.

Some people who have reviewed my case in the news media will say that reporters are only supposed to write about what they witnessed. They choose to ignore that much of journalism does not operate that way.

Standing in front of a statue called "The Unspoken Bond," which shows a corpsman, as Navy medics are called, carrying an injured marine, Mr. Bush praised the heroism of the wounded and the work of the doctors here. But Corporal Klingel said that many here did not feel much like heroes. He said he went to visit a chaplain the next day because of the dreams he was wrestling with nightly.

It was so easy for me to write about what other people were struggling with, but impossible for me to more than intellectualize the battle raging in my head. I was in total denial. I thought I was through with struggling.

The next major story I was asked to look into came from an idea that the head of the *Times*'s research department had. Going over the Pentagon records on the Iraq war, he calculated that only two soldiers remained unaccounted for—one in Danville, Virginia, and one in Los Fresnos, Texas.

I had initially set out to write about both of them, and selected Danville as the scene of the story. It was not too far away from New York, and I could get there on a train or a plane fairly easily.

I was given a week to complete the story, so I did not fret over it so much. This time, I was actually going to try traveling. I even booked a ticket on Amtrak to get me halfway there, where I would rent a car and head down to Danville almost immediately. Just maybe, I thought, I was ready to hit the road again. I would never know, because things changed.

The Department of Defense news release landed in my e-mail inbox.

No. 267-03

IMMEDIATE RELEASE   April 23, 2003

DOD IDENTIFIES AIR FORCE CASUALTY

The Department of Defense announced today that Maj. William R. Watkins III, 37, of Danville, Va., was killed in action April 7 while supporting Operation Iraqi Freedom. Watkins was assigned to the 333rd Fighter Squadron, Seymour Johnson Air Force Base, N.C.

Watkins was the weapons system officer of an F-15E that went down April 7 during a combat mission in Iraq. The incident remains under investigation.

The pilot of the F-15E, Capt. Eric B. Das, was also killed when the aircraft went down.

http://www.defenselink.mil/releases/2003/b04232003_bt267-03.html

Major Watkins' death meant that there was only one missing serviceman in Iraq. It was Sergeant Eduardo Angiuano, of Los Fresnos, Texas.

* * *

"Could you bring me a cowboy back from Texas," read the text message Alexandra sent to my cell phone.

I was supposed to be in San Antonio, on my way to Los Fresnos, which is just north of Brownsville. I had talked to my parents that night while they were on vacation, telling them that I had landed at the airport and that I would be in touch soon. Piecing together those last few days at *The Times* has been a difficult endeavor, because I relapsed, not into drinking or doing drugs, but into psychosis, with its similar effects—the blurriness, the vague recollections, the lost time. All sorts of chemicals distort reality. I guess they are similar. Some chemicals you put into your body; some come from within your body.

What I have been able to piece together, though, is that somewhere in my final days of working at *The Times*, I came across an article written about the grief of the Angiuano family, whose son, Edward, a sergeant, was missing in Iraq.

Without the benefit of my notes and laptop computer, which are now at the *Times* headquarters on West Forty-third Street, it is hard to say when I picked up what from whom. I do know, though, that I was able to confirm that Sergeant Anguiano was the last of the missing, that there were remains yet to be identified at the mortuary in Dover, Delaware, and that I lifted liberally from an Associated Press story and another one published in the *San Antonio Express-News*.

What I do remember from those days, though, is not leaving my house save for an occasional trip every other day to go to Ozzie's to get a cup of coffee. I remember reading something in a book about Rwanda. I remember flooding the bathroom again. I remember coming out of it on the Friday the story was published and going out with Alexandra and Zuza, and walking across the bridge to get home that night.

There is a blank spot for that weekend. I cannot recall what happened until the next Tuesday when I was jolted by the telephone call from Jim Roberts. It was the fateful call saying that someone had complained that my story, with its descriptions of Martha Stewart patio furniture and the Anguiano house, was just too similar to the story Macarena wrote for the San Antonio paper.

I do remember one thing that happened between leaving Alexandra and Zuza that night, and the call from Jim the next Tuesday. Moments after leaving them, as I was walking down President Street between Seventh Avenue and Sixth Avenue, I dialed Zuza's cell phone number and it rang and rang until it went into voice mail. I called back and there was no answer, so I tried Alexandra's cell phone.

"Hey," she said, picking the phone up cheerily.

"I just wanted to apologize for being in such a bad mood and so irritable," I said.

"It's okay, honey," I recall her replying. "You seem to have been going through a lot lately, and had a brush with your own mortality, and I don't think you have given yourself enough time to really take care of yourself."

"Yeah, I know," I said. "I am just sorry. Could you also tell Zuza that I am sorry?"

"Maybe you want to call her and tell her yourself," she said.

"No," I said. "Just let her know for me."

But I tried Zuza again and she picked up the phone.

"Hey, can I give you a call back in a few?" she said. "I am on the last forty pages of *The Invisible Man*."

The irritation, the scratching on the chalkboard of my brain was back again. I did not want help. I just wanted to shut my eyes, and maybe rewind, and start it all over again—before all the heartache, before all the pain, before the visions, the noises, and the lost time.

I did not know where I wanted to be or what I felt. I just knew I did not want to be right there, right in that moment, in my own skin. I knew I wanted a new chance at life.

I would get my wish in the next few days.

Just not in the package that I or anyone else expected.

ACKNOWLEDGMENTS

A memoir is essentially viewed as a person's own story, but in reality it would have been impossible to tell my tale without the assistance of others who witnessed situations, reminded me of things I had forgotten, were observing me when I was in the worst moments of my illness and supporting me through the writing and research of this book.

No one was more important to the research and writing of this book than my friend, Zuza Glowacka. Zuza left her job at *The Times* and was thrown into difficult personal, emotional and financial situations because of my actions, yet her support was unwavering even as she struggled to understand my disease and deal with the consequences of my actions, many of which caused her great pain. Zuza took the time to learn about manic depression, and took the perspective that she would no more turn her back on me than she would have turned her back on someone suffering with cancer. She held my hand through the difficult process of finding medications that would temper my illness and provided excellent editorial advice in the construction of this manuscript. I am grateful for her support, and am looking forward to the publication of her first novel, which she is busy working on at this moment. Out of the two of us, she is the one with the real writing talent.

I am also grateful for the support of my family members, who tirelessly provided encouragement and advice. My parents, Thomas and Frances Blair, also worked hard to understand manic depression and to help put together the pieces of my life and our family history that were relevant to understanding my story. My brother Todd and his fiancée Rachel Mein were also wonderful supporters during the aftermath of my resignation and in the writing of this book. My family has my love and appreciation.

There are some friends that I would like to single out for thanks, and they by no means include everyone who was helpful in my life and the writing of this manuscript. Liz Kelly was a tireless supporter who read early drafts of my manuscript and was in constant contact every day. Without her, this book could not have been done. Heather Lloyd and her boyfriend, Rob Hinkal, provided great support and made several trips to New York where they helped me during the most difficult moments of treatment. Among others who have supported me wholeheartedly are Amie Parnes,

Olive Reid, Daryl Khan, Alexandra Von Ungren, Dean Vigliano, Chris Chadzynski, Toni Walker; Cristelle Champagne, Sunny Mindel, Ted Faraone, Kasia Urbaniak and Ashala Gabriel. I ask forgiveness from anyone I failed to mention.

I am indebted to David Vigliano, my friend and agent, and the wonderful staff of Vigliano Associates, as well as Michael Viner, Deborah Raffin, Mary Aarons, Robert Kent and the wonderful staff of my publisher, New Millennium Press and Audio. For legal advice and friendship, I am indebted to Barry Slotnik, Amaila Pena and New Millennium's general counsel, Ed Reilly.

My doctors and therapists, who helped me understand, survive and get control of my substance abuse problems and mental illness deserve mention. Included among them are:

Marilyn White, the founder and executive director of the Realization Center; Patricia Drew, the director of the employee assistance program at *The New York Times*; Dr. Scott Marder of Silver Hill Hospital; Dr. Alexander Kolevzon of the Mount Sinai Medical Center; Dr. William Sobel of New York-Presbyterian Hospital's department of psychiatry and the Weill Medical College, and Dr. Sharon Hird.

I would be remiss not to thank the many wonderful employees of *The New York Times*, some who have remained friends and others who have drifted away. It would probably not be appropriate to mention them by name, but I am sure those who left their fingerprints on me know who they are and understand that I am grateful for the friendship that they provided.

A special thanks goes to those who have helped me maintain my sobriety. This project would have been impossible if I had not been able to stay clean and sober. My friends, family, therapists, members of self-help groups and others all contributed, helping me learn how to take life and sobriety, one day at a time.